The ANCIENT STONES of WALES

by

CHRIS BARBER

and

JOHN GODFREY WILLIAMS

BLORENGE BOOKS
Abergavenny, Gwent
1989

First Published 1989

ISBN Hardback 0-9510444-6-X
ISBN Softback 0-9510444-7-8

3, Holywell Road, Abergavenny, Gwent
NP7 5LP. Tel: Abergavenny 3909.

Typeset by Able TypeSetters, Unit 27, Enterprise Way,
Newport, Gwent NP9 2AQ. Tel: (0633) 244534.

Printed by South Western Printers Ltd.
Caerphilly, Mid-Glamorgan, South Wales.

Front cover photograph: Arthur's Stone, West Glamorgan.   *Chris Barber*

Back cover photograph: Pentre Ifan Dolmen, Dyfed.   *Chris Barber*

The first triangulation or Trignometrical survey, on which our Ordnance Survey maps are founded, began in 1791, and was finished (England, Wales, Scotland, Ireland) by 1852. Since that time, there have been many editions.

We dedicate this book to the staff of the Ordnance Survey, whose expertise and endeavour in producing the finest maps in the world has made our task possible.

Standing stone near Werthyr, Anglesey, Gwynedd.   *Chris Barber*

CONTENTS

PREFACE

In recent years there has been an increasing interest in the mysteries of prehistoric stone monuments. Unfortunately, the genuine researcher seeking literary sources which describe these ancient stones, finds that there is a complete lack of readily available and concise information on the subject. In particular, up until now no book has been published which deals exclusively with all the known prehistoric stone monuments of Wales.

To remedy this omission the two authors of this book have jointly compiled from their many years of independent research a gazetteer of all the acknowledged prehistoric stone monuments in Wales. Classified into three main groups (standing stones, stone circles and dolmens), they are described in brief detail and map references of every site are included so that the monuments can be accurately located with the aid of an Ordnance Survey map.

Photographs of many of these ancient stones have been included to give the reader some idea of their appearance and to assist identification. These photographs comprise the best single collection of Welsh megaliths that can be found in any book.

Erected well over 2,000 years ago, these large stones have many legends and mysteries associated with them and mention is made of some of these. It is hoped that the information and views contained in this book will encourage the reader to make personal investigations which can be both fascinating and rewarding.

John Godfrey Williams
Abergavenny, November 1988.

ACKNOWLEDGEMENTS

We are grateful to a number of people who have given assistance in a variety of ways to make the publication of this book possible. In particular we thank Richard Williams for assistance with research and helpful suggestions for improvements to the manuscript. Steve Barber is thanked for preparing the index, and we are grateful to Steve Lawless and David Tilton of Able TypeSetters for their quick and efficient service. To Derek Lawton we are indebted for assistance with the design of the book and undertaking artwork for the cover. The staff of South Western Printers we thank for their quality printing. For permission to include various quotations in the book we thank John Mitchell, Paul Screeton and Tom Graves.

Finally we would like to give our appreciation to all landowners who have given us assistance in our field work.

INTRODUCTION

I first met John Williams whilst browsing in an Abergavenny bookshop and was introduced to him by the owner, Ken Lockyer. We had heard of each other and soon found that our mutual interest was in megalithic sites. However, it was ten years before we next made contact. John, having just read my books *Mysterious Wales* and *More Mysterious Wales* wrote to me putting forward the idea that we should work together on a book about the prehistoric stones of Wales. We met again the following week and before long the project was well under way.

Over the years there have been many books written about the mysteries of standing stones but never before has an in-depth study and a gazetteer to all the megalithic sites in Wales been compiled. The Principality is an ideal area for a special study, for it is a realistic size to be covered by one book.

Saeth Maen, Powys.   *Chris Barber*

During the last decade there has been a growing awareness of the importance of these ancient sites and their links with our ancestors from the past who undoubtedly possessed a now forgotten knowledge, often termed the "ancient wisdom", which it would seem gave them the ability to harness terrestial forces. Many people shake their heads in scorn and disbelief at such ideas while others with more open minds are eager to give them worthy and careful consideration.

The theories of Alfred Watkins and his term *Ley Lines* are now well known and his intriguing book *The Old Straight Track* has been re-published in paperback form and is widely read. His theories have been examined and derided in recent years on a number of television programmes, but Ley hunting has become a popular activity and there are thousands of enthusiasts who tramp the British countryside seeking and examining possible alignments.

However, it should be emphasised now, that this book does not deal with *Ley Lines* as such, but sets out to coin the term SCEMB Lines and presents a much more realistic approach to the whole matter. It is the result of an amalgamation of material gathered by John Williams and myself working separately over many years. John's knowledge of the subject is vast and his research has taken him thirty years. His notes are recorded in a set of folders compiled on a county-wide basis covering the whole of Britain. For my own part, I have spent just twelve years, mainly gathering material and photographs for my *Mysterious Wales* and *More Mysterious Wales* books and for a book that I previously had in mind on the standing stones of Wales. So it was very satisfying and desirable that we should pool our knowledge, resources and enthusiasm in a joint publication.

Many readers might think that we are dealing with a mystery that can only be found in Britain or the well-known site at Carnac in Brittany but, in actual fact, this form of prehistoric engineering exists on a world-wide scale. Megalithic monuments can be found in Asia, Japan, Korea, India, Iran, Syria, along the north coast of Africa, from Tripoli to Morocco, the Caucasus, the Crimea, Bulgaria, Sweden, Denmark, Britain and Europe.

Ytumcegid Dolmen, Gwynedd.   *Chris Barber*

These mighty stones and dolmens were erected for some long forgotten purpose and the answer may well lie in the mysteries of magnetism. The earth itself is like a giant magnet which is affected by the phases of the sun and the moon. Just as the sea is tidal, there is also an ebb and flow of the terrestial current. It can be surmised that magnetism is a source of energy that was once used by an ancient civilisation.

However, it must be emphasised that this book does not set out to solve the baffling mystery of the purpose of these ancient stones or discover anything really new, but hopefully it will make people think and perhaps point the way to important discoveries and explanations in the future. In addition, it will appeal to walkers traversing the lonely mountains and moors in search of these often remote stones and present challenges to the map reader endeavouring to locate these sites.

To obtain photographs for the book we had to visit locations that otherwise we would never have seen. Lonely, intriguing places where the spirit of the past lingers on. Windswept slopes, rocky hillsides where shadows of the enigmatic stones were cast by evening light as the sun sank dramatically beyond the horizon. It is difficult to describe the rewards and the atmosphere of such experiences, but those who follow our search for the truth will tramp the same paths and enjoy the same degree of excitement and satisfaction.

Chris Barber,
Llanfoist, November 1988

Chapter 1

STANDING STONES

"A standing stone, embedded in the earth, is in mute communion with the harsh inorganic world of its birth."

Don Robins

Stones are concreted masses of earthy or mineral matter found on or in the earth and they have an immense variety of ingredients which have been merged together by natural forces of heat and pressure into all kinds of shapes and sizes. The prehistoric stones featured in this book are those reasonably large masses of natural stone which weigh anything from a few hundredweights to over 25 tons and which have been taken by man in ancient times from their place of origin. They have been roughly carved into shapes which must have been considered convenient or perhaps necessary and placed in the surface of the ground in such a way that they are obviously different to the natural rocks and stones in the immediate vicinity. Although these stones are usually regarded as rough and unhewn, they must have been worked on by some kind of tools to separate them from their place of origin, which is often a considerable distance from the spot in which they have been erected.

Post y Wiber, Clwyd.   *Chris Barber*   *Carreg Lefn, Gwynedd.*   *Chris Barber*

There are three main basic types of prehistoric standing stones in Wales which can be classified under: single standing stones, stone circles and dolmens (generally described as burial chambers). The most numerous of these are the single standing stones which are usually found sticking out of the ground in isolation, although sometimes there are groups of two or three of the shorter stones and then it is very difficult to decide whether they are the remains of a stone circle or a dolmen. Nearly all of these single standing stones can be said to be of the pillar type in as much that their height above the level

9

ground is greater than the measurements of their breadth and width. Most of them have a roughly rectangular section at the point where they protrude out of the ground.

The Growing Stone, Powys.   *Chris Barber*

Standing Stone at Llanrhidian, Gower, West Glamorgan.   *Chris Barber*

The Fish Stone, Powys.   *Chris Barber*

These ancient stones are found in all shapes and sizes and vary in height above the level of the ground, in which they have been so carefully placed, from about 2 feet to over 18 feet for the tallest standing stone in Wales (the Fish Stone . . . see page 12). They often taper upwards to a cone or a point and it is possible that they may have had definite shapes when they were erected thousands of years ago, but constant wind and rain have obscured any real signs of this for the present-day viewer who usually regards them as shapeless lumps of erect rock.

It is estimated from the results of the excavations that have been undertaken at single standing stones that about one third of the total height of the stone is buried in the ground. If the proportion was less, then the megalith would be top-heavy and could be made to topple over without much effort. This means that if you look at a standing stone which is 6 feet above ground level, then there is likely to be at least 3 feet of the stone below the surface. This rough guide can be used to estimate the weight of a standing stone, for none have ever been known to have been taken out of the ground and physically weighed. When the weights of these huge stones are quoted it is often pure guess work, for the actual calculations of the volume are never shown and no weight densities of the particular kind of rock of the stone are ever mentioned. It is amazing to consider how many of our prehistoric standing stones are still very firmly embedded in the ground and it is a tribute to the builders who knew exactly what they were doing thousands of years ago.

Sometimes a close inspection of what appears to be a large piece of unhewn rock will reveal indications that at least part of the stone has been carved, perhaps by stone tools, before it was placed in its upright position some four-or-five-thousand years ago by people who have left us many mysteries and enigmas relating to their very effective and probably efficient handywork.

One notable exception to what may be termed as shapeless lumps of rock is the 18-feet-high Fish Stone at Penmyarth, Cwmdu near Crickhowell, Powys (SO 183199). From a distance it looks like a huge salmon jumping vertically with its tail touching the ground. This is the tallest standing stone in Wales and is unique due to its shape and size. It stands at the top of a steep bank about 25 yards from the River Usk and is embedded in rocky ground which would be about 20 feet above the normal level of the water in the river so that it is never likely to be affected by flooding. This huge megalith is supposed to have been taken from a quarry on the other side of the River Usk, as there are no rocks of a similar type on that east bank of the river. As yet, no one has attempted to explain the removal of such a very large stone (of about 27 feet in length) across the river. It was then taken up the steep bank and placed in its present position in a large hole which had been excavated to receive it.

The colours of these prehistoric stone monuments vary with the kind of stone used, but the predominant colour is grey and some of them are, called Maen Llwyd or Grey Stone. There are a lot with shades of green, blue and even red but many of these are partly covered with moss or lichen of a greyish-green or orange-yellow colour which tends to obscure the true colour of the upright monolith. Very little notice has been taken by writers of the colours of standing stones and in the St. David's area (Dyfed) there are a few which have not been recorded and this is probably because they now serve as gateposts. They are of the lovely purple stone which has been used to good effect in the walls at the west end of St. David's Cathedral.

During the summer months, the moss and lichen on some of the standing stones dry out so that the surfaces above ground level change colour to a dirty grey-black or brown, which then begins to peel away and reveal the true colour of the megalith so at times when the sun is shining one may see a flash of light caused by the sun's rays striking on the sparkling white or colourless quartz that will be found in all these stones in varying amounts.

Archaeological literature gives only a few mentions of the geological content of these stones but they must be of a very hard and durable nature and carefully chosen by the ancients, to have lasted such a very long time. Quite often these hard upright megaliths have been erected in an area where the stone in the immediate locality is so soft that it would weather away completely in a few hundred years. When one looks at some of the stone in the outer walls of our older buildings or the grave stones of local material in our churchyards and observes how badly they have weathered over the years, then it may be appreciated how well prehistoric man chose suitable stones to erect as standing stones which have withstood the battering of the elements for thousands of years.

Many people today think that the single standing stone marks the position of an important burial, perhaps of some local chief, but our archaeological excavation reports show very little evidence to support this view. Even when human remains have been found at the foot of these stone pillars, it is usually ashes of the burnt human bones and there is nothing to indicate that these were placed in the ground at the time of the erection of the large stone.

Maen Llia, Powys.   14   *Chris Barber*

Another view is that these megaliths were erected as boundary markers for the old manorial or county boundaries. One supposed example of this is a tall stone named Hirfaen, which is situated just below the summit of Bryn Hirfaen at Llanycrwys, Dyfed (SN 624464), on the boundary between the old counties of Carmarthen and Cardigan.

Hirfaen, Dyfed.   *Chris Barber*

According to *Illustrated Archaeologist* (1893), it is mentioned in *The Book of Llan Dav* in the foundation charter of Talley Abbey as being a well recognised landmark in the 12th century. However, it is unlikely that any Lord of the Manor would go to all the effort needed to transport such large hunks of stone (it is 16 feet high) just to mark his boundary on an isolated hilltop. It is more likely that this stone has stood silently in this position for thousands of years just like hundreds of other prehistoric standing stones in Wales. A few of the standing stones that have been used as markers for the manorial boundaries usually have the Lord of the Manor's name or initials cut on one side and those of the adjoining Lord of the Manor on the other side. These markings were usually made at the beginning of the last century and reference to them will be found in the written accounts of the perambulation of the manors.

Ancient stone bearing a 5th-century Latin inscription at Penbryn, Dyfed.   *Chris Barber*

Stones with incised crosses in Llangerniew Churchyard, Clwyd.

Prehistoric standing stones have also been used by the early Christian priests and they either cut them roughly in situ into the shape of a Latin cross or else a cross was incised on the face of the upright stone, such as the one in the churchyard at Bridell in Dyfed (SN 177421). At other times those prehistoric standing stones which were near churches were taken down and replaced with a more appropriate Christian cross, which in some cases became preaching crosses to which later there were added raised stone pedestals.

A revolutionary explanation relating to these enigmatic prehistoric standing stones is that they were used for the channelling along SCEMB lines (which are mentioned later in this book) of natural forces and powers. Although the evidence relating to this theory may not satisfy the dogmatic kind of scientist, the dowsing results and the photographs showing unexplained patches of light should be carefully considered in the hope that they might yield some clues towards solving the great mysteries that surround these ancient megaliths.

There are many different ways of looking at these prehistoric standing stones. Some people may regard them from a prosaic point of view as just ugly lumps of unhewn stone, while the more romantic type will see in their air of mystery a golden age of man, when he was nearer to nature and possessed a now-forgotten knowledge and ability to use and adjust the terrestial forces for his benefit.

Some of the secrets relating to our ancient pillar stones may have been known to the great Welsh mystical poet Henry Vaughan, who in his book of sacred poems published in 1650 and called *Silex Scintillions,* has written a strange poem called *Man.* It has four verses of seven lines. Each and every verse has a peculiar reference to standing stones. The last verse of this poem is as follows:

> *He knocks at all doors, strays and roams,*
> *nay hath not so much wit as some stones have*
> *which in the darkest nights point to their homes*
> *By some hid sense their makers gave;*
> *Man is the shuttle, to whose winding quest*
> *And passage through these looms*
> *God ordered motion, but Ordain'd no rest.*

Henry Vaughan lived most of his life at Newton Farm, Scethrog, near Brecon, which is about five miles south of the old county town. On the west side of the main road, about halfway between Scethrog and Brecon, is a greyish-green prehistoric standing stone which Henry Vaughan must have passed on many occasions on his journeys to

The Llanhamlach Stone, Powys.   *Chris Barber*

and from the county town. This megalith is in the Parish of Llanhamlach (SO 089267) and is about 5 feet high. Henry Vaughan may have put the palms of his hands on the upper part of this stone and experienced what is called the Spiral Powers or 5th Wave Band Power, which resulted in his puzzling reference in the above poem to the stones' winding quest.

It was at this prehistoric standing stone in October 1959 that John G. Williams first obtained photographic results which showed strange light effects possibly caused by a concentration of ultra-violet light. The odd happenings related to these photographs are mentioned later.

Henry Vaughan may also have been aware that dowsers had detected underground streams passing under these prehistoric stones and would not have been prepared to declare this publicly as he lived in a very disturbed period of civil wars and political oppression. Fortunately today, attitudes are more tolerant so that a genuine seeker of the truth has a better chance of making personal investigations which could open up a vast new field of exciting research with far-reaching and staggering implications.

"Despite our centuries of mocking and despising them, the pagans still have much to teach us about living with the reality of the forces of nature."

Tom Graves

Chapter 2

STONE CIRCLES

"Laugh not so lightly, king . . . For in these stones is a mystery and a healing virtue against many ailments."

Attributed to Merlin speaking to Aurelius
Geoffrey of Monmouth

The Druids' Circle (Meini Hirion), Gwynedd.   Chris Barber

Stone circles are a group of three or more prehistoric standing stones that have been erected in the form of a circle with the stones generally not more than about thirty yards apart. These stones vary from about 1 foot to 10 feet in height and are mostly of the pillar type. They are similar in many respects to the single prehistoric standing stones and consist of a very hard durable material which does not necessarily come from the rocks in the immediate vicinity of the stone circle. There is not much recorded about the geology and origin of these stones used in the Welsh stone circles and it appears that not one of them features the special blue stones peculiar to outcrops on the Preseli Mountain in Dyfed, which can be seen in one of the most famous stone monuments in Europe, namely the stone circle called Stonehenge.

The diameters of the stone circles in Wales are not usually more than 30 feet so they are much smaller than the better-known stone circles in England, but they are just as mysterious. The number of stones in a stone circle can vary from 3 to about 30, but one must take into account the fact that many of the smaller stones have been removed during the thousands of years that have passed since the stones were originally placed in a circle. A study of the extant literature covering the descriptions and reports of activities at these stone circles will show that it is not often that two different observers will record the same number of stones in any one particular circle. This means that any theory based on the numbers of stones in a stone circle is on very unsure foundations.

The stones positioned on the perimeters of Welsh stone circles do not seem to have been originally placed equidistant on the radius and there is no clear indication that any of these stones have been placed in a special position in relation to the circle. It is not usual to find any large stone that has been erected inside the circumference of the circle, although there are a few exceptions where a large stone will be found in the centre of a stone circle. However, it is possible that this stone may have been placed there at a much later date than the erection of the original circle of stones by local inhabitants who made use of this stone circle in some religious ceremony or Druidic service.

There are a large number of small stone circles in North Wales which are usually called round huts and are sometimes shown as part of an enclosed hut group. These have diameters of 15 to 25 feet and have an earth bank with stones a few feet high. None of these are listed in the Gazetteer because they could be the remains of an ancient hut or of a carn or mound. Such peculiar structures are no doubt of pre-Roman date and deserve careful investigation.

The purposes of stone circles is not known, although there are a few vague references to their use by the ancient Druids for their bardic ceremonies. The main contemporaneous record of the Druids was made by Julius Caesar and it is now believed that these stone circles were erected at least 2,000 years before his time. Although Julius Caesar mentioned the Druids, he does not seem to have written anything about the numerous prominent prehistoric stone monuments in Britain which one would expect to be noticed by him and his Roman leaders.

According to some dowsers there are no streams of underground water passing beneath the individual stones of a stone circle. They think that there is an underground spring below the surface of some part of the inside of the stone circle and that streams run underground from this spring between some of the standing stones on the perimeter of that circle. These underground streams do not run between every pair of stones on the outside of the circle so this is no help in ascertaining the exact number of original standing stones in any stone circle.

The Druids' Circle (Meini Hirion), Gwynedd.   *Chris Barber*

The stone circle with the largest individual erect stones in Wales is the Druid's Circle or Meini Hirion near Cefn Goch in the Parish of Dwygyfylch in Gwynedd (SH 722746). This is mentioned in some books as *A Stone Circle near Aber. The Scientific Journey Through England and Wales and Scotland*[1] contains a drawing of this stone circle, drawn in August 1801 by Mr. W. Alexander. It shows the tallest standing stone in the circle, which is said to be 9 feet high, and other large stones and numerous smaller stones. This is probably the earliest published drawing of a Welsh stone circle. Experience has shown that it is not always safe to rely on the details of prehistoric stone monuments in drawings made before 1870, for in this particular instance no other printed work mentions more than eleven large stones except *The Penguin Guide to Prehistoric England and Wales* by James Dyer (Allen Lane, Londo, 1981), p.347, which says there were thirty stones of which ten still remain standing, some as much as 1.8m high.

One of the large standing stones in this stone circle is called The Deity Stone and this was once held in considerable awe by the local folk. They claimed that if anyone used bad language near this large stone then it would bend its head and hit the offending person. Immediately opposite is another large standing stone which is called the Stone of Sacrifice and on its top is a cavity which is large enough to hold a small child. The local belief was that if a young child was placed in this hollow for a few minutes during the first month of its life, then it would be lucky for the rest of its days.

There are more legends relating to the Druid's Circle than to any stone circle in Wales. One such tale claims that horrible cries are sometimes heard from the Stone of Sacrifice and frequent moanings and sobbings sound above the wind on stormy nights. Another legend relates how a group of witches once held a meeting just outside this stone circle and, when their vile orgies were reaching a wild climax, stern warnings came from the Stone of Sacrifice which frightened the women so much that two of them suddenly died and one went raving mad.

A few of the Welsh stone circles have been badly damaged during the past few centuries and it is regretful that no official action was taken to preserve these monuments until it was too late. One such stone circle was Meini Gwyn or The White Stones, which had the local name of Buarth Arthur or Arthur's Cowyard and is near the crossroads and carn at Castell Garw in the Parish of Llandyssilio East, Dyfed (SN 142266). There are now only two stones out of an original seventeen standing stones which were from 4 to 7 feet high and were set in a circular encampment 30 yards in diameter surrounded by a rampart 3 feet high.

The great Welsh antiquary Edward Llwyd in the 1695 edition of *Gibson's Britannia* writes *"Buarth Arthur or Meiniu Gwyr, on a mountain near Kil y maen llwyd, is one of that kind of circular stone monuments our English historians ascribe to the Danes. The diameter of the circle is about 20 yards. The stones are as rude as may be, and pitch'd on end at uncertain distances from each other, some being 3 or 4 feet high and others 5 or 6. There are now standing here fifteen of them; but there seem to be seven or eight carried off. The entry into it, for about the space of 3 yards, is guarded on each side with stones much lower and less than those of the circle, pitch'd so close as to be contiguous, and over against this avenue, at the distance of about 200 paces, there stand on end three other large rude stones, which I therefore note particularly because there are also four or five stones erected at such a distance from that circular monument they call King's Stones near Little Rolricht in Oxfordshire. As for the name Buarth Arthur (sic) 'tis only a nickname of the vulgar whose humour it is, though not so much (as some have imagined) out of ignorance and credulity, as unaccountable monuments to the memory of that Hero, calling some stones of several tun weight his Coits, others his Tables, Chairs etc. But Meineu Gŵyr is so old a name, that it seems scarce intelligible. Meineu is indeed our common word for large stones, but gŵyr in the present British signifies only crooked, which is scarce applicable to these stones unless we should suppose them so denominated because some of them are not at present directly upright, but a little inclining. It may be, such as take these circular monuments for Druid Temples may imagine them so call'd from bowing, as having been places of worship."*

Meini Gwyn, Dyfed.   *Chris Barber*

When seen by John G. Williams in July 1962 there were only two standing stones 3 feet and 4 feet high and there appeared to be some prostrate stones in the long grass. Meini Gwyn or Buarth Arthur was thus unrecognisable with the description given by Edward Llwyd nearly three hundred years ago. However, there has been little change in the attitude of the average person towards these unique prehistoric stone circles. It is hoped that there will be a change towards a more logical and intelligent understanding and one of the objects of this book is to encourage and induce such a change of mind.

None of the Welsh stone circles are laid out in a precise circular form and this is one of the puzzling features of our prehistoric stone monuments. The most notable deviation from the true circle is Bedd Arthur, a stone enclosure on Mynydd Preseli, in the Parish of Meline in Dyfed (SN 131324). It is on a slight slope just below the brow of the hill and is an oval shaped formation of standing stones about 2 feet high. According to *Mynachlog-ddu, A guide to its Antiquities*[2], the longest diameter is about 70 feet and the twelve stones visible are placed rather irregularly, although *Arch. Cam*[3] (1984) has a plan which shows fifteen stones.

This Bedd Arthur is one of the many supposed graves of King Arthur and nearby are a number of other prehistoric stone monuments which have names connected with Arthur. These are:—

1. Cerrig Meibion Arthur or The Stones of the Sons of Arthur in the Parish of Mynachlog Ddu (SN 118310).
2. Coetan Arthur at Carn Meini on Mynydd Preseli also in Mynachlog Ddu (SN 142326).
3. Carn Arthur, a rocking stone on the southern slopes of Mynydd Preseli (SN 135324) which is also in Mynachlog Ddu and was known locally as Coitan Arthur.
4. Cerrig Marchogion (The Stones of Arthur's Knights) which are on the Parish boundary between Mynachlog Ddu and Meline (SN 102322).

It is also interesting to note that the Blues Stones used as standing stones at Stonehenge in Wiltshire originally came from Carn Meini mentioned above.

Carn Meini means "place of stones" and the rock of the Blue Stones is spotted dolerite, which is a dark blue in colour with fuzzy white spots.

Bedd Arthur, Dyfed. *Chris Barber*

Some of the stone circles which only have small standing stones and are in rough country can be difficult to identify even if they are marked on our Ordnance Survey maps. One of these is the stone circle near Tal-y-ffynonau in the Parish of Llanbedr in Clwyd (SH 610240), which has fourteen stones, none of which would be over 2 feet 6 inches high, and these are usually covered with growing bracken. It may be an important centre as it was here on a sunny afternoon in August 1976 that two dowsers carried out an unusual experiment. On separate occasions they mentally put themselves on what may be called loosely the Second Plane of Existence and walked towards the stone circle to find that when they each got to the outer edge of the circumference they came up against an unseen barrier which prevented them from going any further.

There is of course no explanation for this happening and such experiments are not generally mentioned to sceptical people who are always ready to scoff at experiences that are not accepted as authentic by science. Strange things can happen at prehistoric stone circles and sensitive people are advised not to try out any experiments when they are inside a stone circle on their own. There may be more than a grain of truth in some of the legends relating to these ancient, mysterious monoliths and stone circles.

"To this day there stand these mighty stones gathered together into circles — 'the old temples of the gods' they are called — and whoso sees them will assuredly marvel by what mechanical craft and by what bodily strength stones of such bulk have been collected to one spot."

Hector Boece

REFERENCES
1. *The Scientific Journey Through England and Wales and Scotland* by Thomas Walford (John Booth, London, 1818).
2. *Mynachlog-ddu, A Guide to its Antiquities* by E. J. Lewis (E. C. Jones and Sons, Cardigan, 1972), p.21.
3. *Archaeologia Cambrensis* (1984), p.62.

Chapter 3

DOLMENS

"Each type of megalith contains its own enigma, and each place where they are found poses a variation of their riddles."

Francis Hitching

The third classification of prehistoric stone monuments in Wales can be put under the heading of dolmens. They are sometimes referred to as cromlechs or burial barrows and there are more dolmens proportionately to prehistoric stone monuments in Wales than in any other part of the British Isles. They appear to be made up of larger stones and are more complex than single standing stones and stone circles with which they are regarded as being contemporaneous, so this may be important.

Pentre Ifan, Dyfed.   *Chris Barber*

The basic dolmen consists of a very large and heavy capstone which is always flat on the underside (nearest to the earth) when in its original position and sometimes flat on the top. These capstones are supported by three or more sturdy upright stones which rise to about 4 feet above ground level and rest just underneath the outer edges of the capstone. This often gives the dolmen an appearance of a stone chamber and usually one of the narrower sides of the dolmen is left open. The number of supporting stones under the capstone vary, but they do not seem to number more than ten even at one of the larger megalithic monuments which have been described as double dolmens because they have two large long capstones. In many cases the capstones are still delicately poised on top of the supporting stones, which usually taper towards their tops and it has been suggested that the capstones were meant to be rocked on top of their stone supports. In the last century there were in fact still a few dolmens where it was possible to move the huge capstone in a slight rocking motion.

An example of a delicately poised capstone.   *Chris Barber*

Twlc y Filiast Dolmen in a collapsed condition, near Llangynog, Dyfed.   *Chris Barber*

Excavation of Gwernvale Dolmen , Powys.   *Chris Barber*

There are rocking stones which are regarded by most people as natural geological features caused by long periods of weathering, but the possibility should also be considered that they were perhaps set up by people with special skills to act in a similar way to their massive dolmens.

The weight of the capstones of the larger dolmens is often over twenty-five tons and such massive stones would need very careful handling to place them so precisely on top of a number of upright stones.

The stones often needed to be quarried in places that were some distance from the site of the dolmen. They had to be hard and durable and some shaping was probably necessary before the supporting stones were fitted into place beneath the cumbersome capstone.

In addition, there are stone cists, which have smaller capstones and short supporting stones which are positioned at or just below ground level. At the other extreme are the large burial barrows, which are constructed mainly above the level of the surrounding ground and consist of stone-lined chambers covered by a huge mound of earth and stones. They sometimes have flat slab stones for walls and roofs and at least a few of them can be classified as dolmens. In practice it is difficult to lay down acceptable definitions for dolmens, burial chambers or stone cists.

The confusion is more evident when one considers the term cromlech. According to *A Welsh and English Dictionary[1]*, by Rev. Thomas Richards, *"Cromlechs are a sort of monument supposed to have been altars for sacrifice before Christianity whereof some account is given by Mr. E. Llwyd in his Annotations on Mr. Camden's Britannia in Pembrokeshire and Anglesey. From "crom" the feminine of crwn, crooked and llech, a flat stone."* In some cases the word cromlech is used to refer to a circle of standing stones enclosing a mound and it is often used to describe prehistoric stone monuments in France. They are particularly abundant in Brittany, where the Breton language is similar in many respects to Welsh.

Dolmens are found in country areas that are isolated and one puzzling feature about them is that their huge capstones and supporting stones are all above present-day ground levels whereas remains of Roman buildings erected at least 2,000 years later are found several feet beneath the ground. One would reasonably expect the dolmens to have been submerged by now if we have to dig up Roman remains. One possible explanation is that the earth around the base of the dolmens was not allowed to accumulate and hide the ancient stones because the dolmens had been used for some purpose of which there appears to be no written record available. This appears more likely when one considers that during the last one-hundred years photographs have been taken by different people at varying times and of numerous dolmens which, when printed, show patches or streaks of light alongside or in the sky above the dolmens. Further mention and examples of such phenomena will be given later.

An examination of the Gazetteer of Sites given in this book will clearly show that the most common name used in the descriptions of dolmens is Arthur. If dolmens are of pre-Christian origin, then the name Arthur cannot possibly have any connection with a fifth-century British hero king, neither can any of such sites realistically be said to have been constructed to mark the burial place of King Arthur.

Another name that is wrongly used to describe some of the Welsh dolmens is Samson. These can have no claim to have the slightest association with the Old Testament strong-man or with the Celtic saint of that name. It is possible that Samson is a corruption of the Welsh word simson which, according to *The New Welsh Dictionary[2]*, means *"unsteady"* and, according to *A Welsh and English Dictionary[3]*, it means *"tottering, ready to flutter."* This seems an appropriate description of the huge flat capstones of the Welsh dolmens, for a few of them such as Pentre Ifan or Coetan Arthur at Nevern, Dyfed (SN 099369), look as though they are ready to fly away.

An amusing corrupted Welsh name for several dolmens is Gwal-y-Filiast, which has been translated as *"The Greyhound's Kennel."* A lot of people glibly accept this as being true and only a few perhaps wonder why our ancestors built such large kennels for their dogs with flat stone roofs weighing sometimes as much as twenty tons, while there is no sign of any building in which the dog owner may have lived. Dolmens which have been called Gwal-y-Filiast are at Glyntaff House in the Parish of Llanboidy, Dyfed (SN 170256), on Mynydd Llangyndeirne, also in the Parish of Llangendeirne, Dyfed (SN 465177), near Tyddyn-ddu Caerhun, Gwynedd (SH 741718), Llanfair-Is-Gaer, Gwynedd (SH 513660), at St. Lythan's, South Glamorgan (ST 100723), and at Llangwm in Gwent near a crossroads (ST 445968).

Coetan Arthur, near Criccieth, Gwynedd.

A name which makes sense for these dolmens is Gwely yr Arth, which means the bed or resting place of the bear. This could infer that the dolmen was the collecting place of the Polar Forces coming from the Great Bear constellation region before they were channelled out along SCEMB lines by the movement of the unstable or rocking capstone. Perhaps gwely in Welsh became confused with bed in English and then with bedd in Welsh, meaning grave, which may help to account for some dolmens being called Beddau Arthur or Bwrdd Arthur, meaning Arthur's table. Gwal-y-Filiast at Llanboidy, Dyfed, mentioned previously, was called Bwrdd Arthur in 1695 by Edward Llwyd in Gibson's edition of Camden's Britannia.

It is difficult to say that there are any common basic forms of design for the Welsh dolmens, but it seems that the long axis of the large capstones are usually found to be north and south, and even today, after over 4,000 years in their positions, some can be said to be pointing upwards towards the Great Bear constellation.

Dolmens are similar to the huge blocks of stone which are called rocking stones, logan stones or maen sigl. Log means to rock in old English or French dialect, and the name logan stones is used for huge masses of rock that can still be moved in a few cases by a slight pressure from the human hand. Examples of these can be seen in Devon and Cornwall, while the name maen sigl is used for similar objects in Wales.

Lythans Dolmen, South Glamorgan. *Chris Barber*

The Buckstone, Gwent (before it was toppled over).   *Chris Barber*

Photograph of the Buckstone, Gwent (before it was toppled over in 1885).   *Unknown*

One maen sigl or shaking stone used to stand on the brow of a hill overlooking Whitesands Bay at St. David's in Dyfed (SM 730278). RCAM No. 939, p.321, has a description and a good photograph showing the large block of stone balanced on supporting stones. Edward Llwyd in about 1695 reported that this shaking stone was out of motion and he ascribed its displacement to the Commonwealth troops. According to *The British Tourists[4]*, it was mentioned as being immovable when visited by Henry Penruddock between 1774 and 1777. This all seems most puzzling when you read a book published much later in 1892 entitled *The Description of Pembrokeshire[5]*, where it is described as being so equally poised that with one finger a man may shake it.

The Pontypridd Rocking Stone, Mid Glamorgan.   *Chris Barber*

Another strange rocking stone is Carreg Siglo on the mountainside at Pentre Bach, Pontypridd, in Mid Glamorgan (ST 082902). This was called the far famed logan stone in *The Book of South Wales, The Wye and The Coast[6]*. It is calculated to weigh about fifteen tons and John Timbs, in *Abbeys, Castles and Ancient Halls of England and Wales[7]* (London 1890), p.475, writes that a moderate application of strength will give it considerable motion, which may be easily continued with one hand. In 1815 a bardic congress was held here and the last Archdruid, Morien O Morgan, writes about it in his book and has a photograph in *The Royal Winged Son of Stonehenge and Avebury[8]*.

This was republished by the Research Into Lost Knowledge Organisation in 1985 under the title *The Mabin of the Mabinogion*. A large political meeting was held at the site of this rocking stone in 1910 and in 1984 two students from The Polytechnic College of Wales at Pontypridd observed a strange object passing in the night sky over this fascinating prehistoric stone monument.

These dolmens deserve very careful examination to see if anything in the way of cement or mortar has been added to the stone surfaces in ancient times. At least two additions to the capstones and the supporting stones of dolmens have been noted. A very old and hard cement on the south of an upright stone about 3 feet above the ground was seen at Gwernvale Dolmen, which is on the side of the A40 just outside Crickhowell in Powys (SO 211192) when it was overgrown and covered in brambles in 1959. In later years, the main road was diverted and the dolmen carefully excavated by an archaeologist who gave a detailed report with plans in 1977.

Arthur's Stone, Herefordshire.   *Chris Barber*

Another dolmen with an unexplained kind of cement or mortar is Arthur's Stone on Merbach Hill in the Parish of Dorstone in the old county of Herefordshire (SO 318431), just across the Welsh border. A very small piece of this pale grey mortar with black or sepia spots was taken to the National Science Museum at Kensington, London in May 1957 for geological analysis without revealing the source of the matter. The subsequent report mentioned that it was found to contain granules of coal. This mortar was still in a small crevice on the west side of the south end of the huge capstone of the dolmen on 11th March 1988.

The presence of this small amount of mortar raises a number of interesting questions. There is no record of any restoration work on this capstone for at least the last 300 years. In addition, the place where the mortar can be found is not where one would expect any strengthening work to be necessary and the granules of coal must have come from at least 30 miles away, where coal would be found on the edge of the South Wales coalfield.

Dowsers have detected underground streams of water leading out from under the south ends of dolmens and sometimes other underground streams are thought to pass below the capstone. There are a few cases where holy or virtuous wells are found in the vicinity of these strange ancient stone monuments.

"Megalithic man understood a force which is present today and available to us."
Paul Screeton

REFERENCES
1. *A Welsh and English Dictionary* by Rev. Thomas Richards (Thomas Price, Merthyr Tydfil, 1820), p.139.
2. *The New Welsh Dictionary* (Llandebie, 1953).
3. *A Welsh and English Dictionary* by Rev. Thomas Richards (Merthyr Tydfil, 1839).
4. *The British Tourists* by William Mavor, 1798, Vol. III, p.235.
5. *The Description of Pembrokeshire* by Henry Owen.
6. *The Book of South Wales, The Wye and The Coast* by Mr. and Mrs. S. C. Hall (London, 186), p.223.
7. *Abbeys, Castles and Ancient Halls of England and Wales* (London, 1890), p.475.
8. *The Royal Winged Son of Stonehenge and Avebury* by Morien O Morgan (London, 1900).

Chapter 4

SCEMB LINES

"Many of the sites are situated in a definite pattern on the surface of the planet. They exhibit a surprising level of astronomical, mathematical and geophysical information."
David D. Zink

The term SCEMB lines is used in relationship to the alignments of prehistoric sites with one another, which are sometimes more than 10 miles long, to distinguish them from the Ley lines sought by the many misguided followers of Alfred Watkins. This Hereford man was a skilled photographer and, for many years, served as the secretary of the antiquarian society known as The Woolhope Field Club. He used this position to promote his ideas of the Ley system, in which he never defined or restricted the kind of sites to be included in the alignments and put forward no realistic ideas for the purpose of these alignments with the result that his critics called them fanciful and illogical.

Alfred Watkins observed that many ancient sites such as mounds, moats, churches and other holy places were often aligned in straight lines which he called leys. He suggested that they might represent ancient trackways. In actual fact, some years before Alfred Watkins made his 'discovery', Colonel Johnston, Director General of the Ordnance Survey, pointed out to two archaeologists in 1895 that it was possible to draw a straight line on the map between Stonehenge, Old Sarum, Salisbury Cathedral and Clearbury Ring.

SCEMB is a word made up of the initial letters of the types of prehistoric sites to which the alignments are restricted and these are all at least 2,000 years old or are situated at places where there are reasonable indications of the presence of a much earlier site which can be dated to prehistoric times. These prehistoric sites can be said to come within the general classification of standing stones, stone circles, camps, carns, earthworks, mounds, moats and burial barrows.

Standing stones are of a hard durable kind of stone and are usually found singularly in open country, moorland or mountain and are noted in books or shown on official maps. They vary in size and shape and only rarely have any recognisable markings been cut on them, apart from a few with Ogham alphabet incisions or Christian crosses or symbols which were cut after the date of their original erection.

Stone circles are those circles of stones fixed firmly in the ground with four or more stones 2 feet high and above, being within a circle of at least 20 feet in diameter. Remains of such stone circles can still be found on open land in Wales and the stones can vary in size and shape on the circumference of the circle, although there are no circles to compare with the size and complexity of Stonehenge.

Camps are the embanked enclosures of pre-Roman origin which are marked on Ordnance Survey maps as Camps, Enclosures or Forts. These are often quite large and take all kinds of shapes. Very often they are found in prominent positions on high ground so that they stand out against the background of a rural landscape.

Carns or tumuli nowadays are only found in the rural areas and are large rounded artificial heaps of earth and loose stones usually not more than 10 feet high and 30 yards across. During the course of urban development, very large numbers of them have been removed and obliterated. In mountainous areas, they are sometimes such noticeable features in the locality that they become landmarks, especially when they can be seen projecting on the brow of a hill from miles away.

Earthworks are large disturbed areas of land of prehistoric origin which might be the remains of pre-Roman camps, forts or settlements and take various forms, shapes and sizes. On Ordnance Survey maps, they can be marked as Earthworks, Settlements or Camps and comparison of the maps will show that they have been given different names over the years.

Large mounds which are marked on the Ordnance Survey maps are often similar to those substantial rounded heaps of earth and stones which are called carns or tumuli.

Moats are those artificial pools of water found in the flatter parts of the countryside and usually surround a small earthwork or mound. Excluded from this category are the moats that surround Norman or later castles.

Burial barrows or dolmens are those collections of large prehistoric stones which appear in some cases to be (or have been) covered with earth. Those called dolmens or cromlechs are usually found with most of their stones showing above ground level and have large, flat, long and wide capstones which occasionally give the appearance of being pivoted on some of the supporting stones so that they could be rocked. Rocking stones weighing many tons are included in this category, although some people regard them as natural features caused by the weathering of wind and rain over a very long period of time.

Investigations going back over thirty years have shown that every recorded prehistoric stone monument is positioned on at least one of these SCEMB lines. This applies to over 4,200 of these sites, which have been indexed under countries, counties and parishes with Ordnance Survey reference numbers for the whole of the British Isles. This means that each one of these prehistoric standing stone sites is placed where the original builders put them, in direct alignment with at least two or more of the pre-Christian sites mentioned above. This only applies to the stone monuments and may not apply to camps, carns, tumuli, earthworks, mounds or moats, although the majority of them are found on SCEMB lines.

These SCEMB lines can easily be checked by any person on the One Inch or larger scale Ordnance Survey Maps for any part of Wales, preferably those on which there are marked a good number of the prehistoric standing stone sites which are listed in the Gazetteer. The simple way to do this is first to go through the map carefully square by square and underline any of the prehistoric sites mentioned above. Most of these are shown in Gothic lettering on Ordnance Survey maps.

When this has been done, take a ruler and, using one of the prehistoric stone sites as a centre, slowly rotate the ruler until it is noted that there are two others of the marked prehistoric sites appearing along the edge of the ruler which indicates that they are in a direct alignment with the first site chosen as the centre. Draw a line along the edge of the ruler to join up these three sites, each of which may be as much as 5 miles apart on the ground and then continue rotating the ruler around the centre, stopping to mark any other alignment where two or more of the underlined sites show along the edge of the ruler at the same time indicating another three sites are in direct alignment, until a complete circle has been made about the original centre.

Now move the ruler to another point marked as a prehistoric site and repeat the process until a complete circle has been made around this centre point. This should be repeated until all the prehistoric stone sites that are marked on the map have been used. Care should be taken to ensure that the alignments drawn on the map should pass through the marked site, for otherwise it should not be treated as a SCEMB line.

When you have finished marking alignments on an Ordnance Survey map in this manner, which might take a few hours to do properly, then you should find that there are a number of SCEMB lines which often meet or cross at certain points. Where this happens, you should measure the angles between the lines which meet or cross. It will be found that the angle of $23\frac{1}{2}°$, which is the angle of the Earth's declination to the sun (which will be referred to as the Solar Angle), or its multiples of $47°$, $70\frac{1}{2}°$ and $94°$ occur more often than one would expect. The lines on the side of these angles should then be marked in red to their full length so that they stand out from the map and indicate any possible polar or solar connection of the alignments.

The angle of the earth's declination to the sun varies slightly over a long period of time by about ½° but 23½° is regarded as a good average. It is an awkward angle which cannot be obtained by the simple division of any normal angle found in the basic geometric figures such as 90° or 60°. It can be found approximately by using a right-angled triangle where one of the sides is 9 and one is 4. It is odd to notice that the number 9 is often associated with the Sun and the number 4 with the Earth.

Solar angles have been found in more than half the angles between the meeting points or crossing points of the SCEMB lines. This is much greater than one would expect according to the law of averages. According to this, if there were a large number of random angles used, all the different angles would work out to appear about the same number of times between these alignments.

Thus, taking ½° angles, there would be 360 different ones between 0° and 180° so that the angles of 23½°, 47°2, 70½° and 94° could be expected to turn up on average four times out of every 360 different angles mentioned, or once in ninety times. When they turn up on the SCEMB line system more than this average, in fact some maps aligned and marked show these angles occur more than fifty times the average numbers that could be expected, then it is reasonable to assume that these SCEMB lines meet or cross at these solar angles because the alignments were planned with that purpose. This conception is very difficult to grasp due to the present ideas about the abilities of ancient man, but when it is considered as a possibility, then a completely new view of our prehistoric stone monuments must be taken. At the end of the book are a few examples of the many SCEMB lines and these can be checked either by using the up-to-date Ordnance Survey maps or by plotting the positions of the sites on ordinary lined and squared graph paper.

It has been found that the average person does not have the mental capacity to appreciate the significance of the SCEMB line system. Generally the view is taken that unless it is acknowledged by experts then it is impossible. The curious reader will no doubt try out the SCEMB line system by drawing lines on Ordnance Survey maps as previously described. It is important that one keeps strictly to prehistoric sites and resists the temptation to include churches unless there is good sound evidence to show that a particular church was built on what is generally termed as a pagan site of pre-Christian origin. You will find that you are faced with the perplexing problem of explaining the presence of a very large and exact system of alignments made by people who were supposed to be unintelligent savages.

SCEMB lines can be considered as the possible paths or channels along which certain natural forces, such as polar or solar forces, can be directed or beamed to and from prehistoric standing stones. How these forces were used is yet another mystery of ancient man that has to be solved, but there may be some clues in the vitrification of some of the stones such as at Top o' north, a vitrified fort at Rhynie, Aberdeen, Scotland (NJ 485294) or that at Llwyn-y-fedwen, near Gliffaes Hotel, Cwmdu, Powys (SO 157204), where the lower part of the stone seems to have been molten in the place where it now stands. These stones were probably subject to temperatures of more than 1,000° Centigrade, which is not likely to have been obtained by a brush wood fire in the vicinity of the stones.

The strange photographic results which are sometimes obtained at these prehistoric standing stones may have been influenced by some kind of vibrations passing along these SCEMB lines and these should be borne in mind by those looking for a sensible explanation.

"And though recognition of the Earth force has been eclipsed for centuries, and its practical application fallen almost completely into abeyance, now surely is the time for a revival of interest, supplemented by all the resources of modern science."

Guy Underwood

Chapter 5

HAROLD'S STONES, TRELLECH, GWENT

Harold's Stones, Gwent.   *Chris Barber*

Three huge stones stand in a field close to the Monmouth to Chepstow road at the south end of Trellech (SO 498052). For some unknown reason they are locally referred to as Harold's Stones. They are 9, 12 and 15 feet high and stand in a line about 20 yards long.

The first reference to these stones appears to have been made in 1698 by Edward Llwyd in *Parochialia*[1] when he just mentions three stones pitched on end. Over a hundred years then pass by before any further literary reference is made. In 1802 William Coxe in *A Historical Tour Through Monmouthshire*[2] includes a poor illustration showing a man standing near the three stones which makes them appear to be over 40 feet high.

In *Kelly's Directory of Monmouthshire and South Wales*[3] we learn that according to tradition they were erected by Harold in commemoration of a victory over the Britons. Obviously this is wildly improbable, for King Harold, the last of the Saxon kings, was killed in 1066 at Hastings, at least 2,000 years before the date that is now generally accepted for the erection of these prehistoric stones. The tradition was again mentioned in *The Post Office Directory of Monmouthshire*[4] but seems to have passed out of favour after A. Morris in *Geography and History of Momouthshire*[5] wrote that he considers Harold's Stones were in existence many centuries before Harold's time.

There is a different version of this tradition in *An Archaeological Index to Remains of Antiquity of the Celtic Romano-British and Anglo-Saxon Periods*[6], which says that the three stones mark the spots on which three chieftains fell in battle with Harold, who defeated the Welsh in Gwent.

A Topographical and Statistical Description of the County of Monmouth[7] states Trellich or Treley is supposed to have derived its name from three Druidical stones, standing in a field adjoining the road, near the church. They appear to be formed of a concretion of sileceous pebbles in a calcareous bed, commonly called pudding stone and of which some neighbouring rocks consist. The Welsh for Three is Tri, while Llech means any broad flat stone, although it can be used to mean a covert or hiding place. Triley or Treley seems to be a corruption of the original Trillech, and in the Parish of Llantillio Pertholey in the county of Gwent there is a place called Great Triley (SO 314177), which was the site of three prehistoric standing stones. Arch. Cam. (Archaeologia Combrensis) (1855), p.122, after describing the stones at Trellech, mentions that there could be little doubt of the existence of a similar monument at Triley, consisting of three meini hirion although nothing of the sort now remains. *Arch. Cam.*[8] (1861) apparently refers again to these monoliths when mentioning a group of three stones said to exist near Abergavenny.

David Lloyd Isaac, in *Silurianna or Contributions Towards The History of Gwent and Glamorgan*[9], states that Harold's Stones are recorded in connection with a grant of land in the seventh century in the ancient book "Liber Landavensis" apparently as a boundary point but does not give any details. One writer in *Cymru Fu*[10] thinks that there was a fourth stone which stood on the common some distance away. It was stupidly destroyed about one hundred years before. However, no other books seems to give mention of this stone so it appears unlikely that it ever existed.

Illustration of Harold's Stones in 'A Historical Tour of Monmouthshire', 1802, by William Coxe.

The earliest depiction of the three stones is on the sundial base in Trellech Church which dates from 1689 and is thus curiously earlier than any known written description. There is a good photograph of this sundial in *A Guide to Ancient Sites in Britain*[11] by Janet and Colin Board. Published photographs of Harold's Stones are suprisingly few and one of the earliest seems to be in *The Official Handbook to Abergavenny, Crickhowell, Usk and Raglan*[12].

Sundial in Trellech Church, Gwent.

Harold's Stones are associated with the many long-distance throwing legends that are told about a number of prehistoric stones. Fred Hando in *The Pleasant Land of Gwent*[13] (R. H. Johns, Newport, Mon., 1944), p.59, writes . . . *"A legend told in Abergavenny connects these stones with the famous Jack O' Kent. In one of his many contests with the Devil, Jack O' Kent leaped from the Sugar Loaf Mountain to the summit of the Skirrid Mountain, where his heel mark may still be seen. The Devil pooh-poohed this feat whereupon Jack hurled three huge stones over a dozen miles of country to a little city which was ever afterwards called the City of the Stones."* In a later book, *Monmouthshire Sketch Book*[14], Fred J. Hando writes that the three great stones were flung from the Skirrid by Jack O' Kent along the line of midwinter sunset at Trellech.

One wonders if these legends of long-distance stone-throwing are the folk memory of an important happening in the remote past. There is a SCEMB line from Arthur's Stone in the Parish of Dorstone, just across the Welsh border in the old county of Hereford (SO 31884322), which goes south through a motte and bailey on the south-west side of the River Olchon between Clodock and Longtown (SO 327281) then on through a motte which rises at least 20 feet above field level at Trefedw near the railway line and the River Monnow in Llanfihangel Crucorney (SO 330217) to end at an ancient site called Carn Pwll, which is the boundary point of three parishes, namely: Llanfihangel Crucorney, Llanddewi Skirrid and Llangattock Lingoed (SO 335185). This carn site is on a sort of plateau 1,000 feet above sea level and towering another 700 feet above it is the peak of The Holy Mountain of the Skirrid Fawr, which is Welsh for The Big Shake. On the summit can be seen the remains of a chapel dedicated to St. Michael.

When you look at The Holy Mountain from the north it is an awesome sight, for you can clearly see that the mountain has been split in half with a deep cleft between two cliffs. This immense split was by tradition supposed to have been caused by an earthquake at the time of the crucifixion of Jesus Christ.

The Holy Mountain, Gwent.   *Chris Barber*

Carn Pwll is a peculiar name for a mound of stones as it means Carn Pool. At one time there was probably some distinct feature here, which may have been a prehistoric standing stone used as a boundary marker for three parishes. These are Llanfihangel Crucorney, which means The Church or Place of St. Michael the Archangel at a hillock or tump of fear or dread; Llanddewi Skirrid, The Church or place of St. David at the Shake, which shows that St. David was brought into the original name and Llangattock Lingoed, which changed its parish name for some unknown reason in the last century.

There does not seem to be a SCEMB line between Carn Pwll and Harold's Stones, but it is odd to find that there is one from Carn Pwll going WSW through the other Trellech or site of three stones at Triley, mentioned earlier (SO 314177). This goes on to Gaer or ancient fort near Pen y graig in the Parish of Llanelly, Gwent (SO 225154). The latter is also on another SCEMB line which goes north from Twyn Ffynhonnau Goerion, the mound of the Little Cold Spring on Coity Mountain above Blaenavon, Gwent (SO 232081), through to Great Oak Standing Stone, Crickhowell, Powys (SO 223185), which is later mentioned as one of the sites where strange photographs have been obtained.

On 28th December 1983, John G. Williams and his son, Richard, took Professor William Blackbird, of Regina University, Canada, a pure-blooded North American Indian, who is chief of his tribe, and his wife, Lizabeth, an educational consultant, to visit Harold's Stones at Trellech. John G. Williams recorded the occasion as follows:—

39

"Professor Blackbird found that when he used my copper swivel right-angled dowsing rods, the arms of the rods rotated as he held the sleeves in his hands in a clockwise direction, particularly when he stood about 5 feet to the east of the southern stone. When I tried and got the same results we discussed the situation and came to the conclusion that we might be using some form of energy that was coming up from the underground stream which could be associated with what I call the Solar Positive Force.

My son, Richard, and I returned to Harold's Stones on 18th July 1986 with fifteen members of the Bristol Dowsers' Society, who included Len Lockyer, a noted dowser. While I stood by the irongate at the entrance to the field where the three stones are positioned, Richard took each of the group individually to the tallest stone and showed them how to experience the Fifth Wave Band or Spiral Power. Each member of the party experienced the strange power of these tall prehistoric standing stones. I then showed them the effects that I experienced when contacting what I call the Seventh Wave Band or Ultra Violet Light Power and advised them to be very careful for it is a dangerous experiment."

The above has been vaguely referred to in *Unkown Gwent*[15], which mentions dowsers being thrown back as if by some invisible force field at Harold's Stones. This is the first published account of an unusual happening at these particular stones and could perhaps be the dawning of a wider interest in the three silent stone sentinels of Trellech, which can impart useful knowledge to the right kind of recipient.

"We cannot ignore the fact that so many people receive a 'tingling' feeling when they touch quartz-laden stones."

Michael Balfour

REFERENCES
1. *Parochialia* pt.III, p.9, by Edward Llwyd (1698).
2. *A Historical Tour Through Monmouthshire* by William Coxe, p.260.
3. *Kelly's Directory of Monmouthshire and South Wales* (London, 1814), p.229.
4. *The Post Office Directory of Monmouthshire* edited by E. R. Kelly (London, 1875), p.9.
5. *Geography and History of Monmouthshire* by A. Morris (Newport, 1905), p.95.
6. *An Archaeological Index to Remains of Antiquity of the Celtic Romano-British and Anglo-Saxon Periods* by John Yonge Akerman (London, 1847).
7. *A Topographical and Statistical Description of the County of Monmouth* by G. A. Cook (London, 1821), 2nd Ed., p.124.
8. *Archaeologia Cambrensis* (1861), p.59.
9. *Silurianna or Contributions Towards The History of Gwent and Glamorgan* by David Lloyd Isaac (Newport, 1859), p.261.
10. *Cymru Fu* (18th October, 1890), p.220.
11. *A Guide to Ancient Sites in Britain by Janet and Colin Bord* (Paladin, London, 1979), p.109.
12. *The Official Handbook to Abergavenny, Crickhowell, Usk and Raglan*, No. 18 of Burrows Royal Handbooks (Ed. Burrow, Publisher, Cheltenham, 1904).
13. *The Pleasant Land of Gwent* by F. J. Hando (R. H. Johns Ltd, Newport, Mon, 1944), p.59.
14. *Monmouthshire Sketchbook* by F. J. Hando (R. H. Johns Ltd, Newport, Mon., 1954), p.23.
15. *Unknown Gwent* by Alan Roderick (Village Publishing, Cwmbran, Gwent, 1986), p.64.

Chapter 6

GORS FAWR

". . . circles aligned into a sacred network, a web of energy whose secrets have been long forgotten, except in the clouded and confused remembrances of folklore."

Don Robins

The most important Welsh stone circle is Gors Fawr, which is in the centre of the most dense concentration of dolmens and standing stones in Wales. It is situated on rough moorland about 100 yards west of the main road at Llan in the Parish of Mynachlog Ddu in the old county of Pembroke (SN 135295) and in the same area are the special greenish-blue rocks from whence the noted Blue Stones of the inner circle at Stonehenge were quarried.

Gors Fawr Stone Circle, Dyfed.   *Chris Barber*

Gors Fawr is surrounded by gorse bushes whose yellow flowers brighten up the rugged landscape and tend to suggest that the name of this ancient stone circle might have some connection with gorse, but the name for gorse in Welsh is eithin or aith. On referring to *A Welsh and English Dictionary*[1], it was found that the word Gors was not listed. So it is likely to be a corruption of a Welsh word which phonetically is very similar. It could be gorsaf, which means a station or standing place; so that Gorsaf Fawr would mean the big standing place, which would be appropriate in this instance.

On the Ordnance Survey maps of 1919 and 1952, this large stone circle is marked 𝕲𝖔𝖗𝖘 𝕱𝖆𝖜𝖗 𝖘𝖙𝖔𝖓𝖊 𝖈𝖎𝖗𝖈𝖑𝖊 but on the first edition Ordnance Survey of 1843 its position was marked as just 𝖈𝖎𝖗𝖈𝖑𝖊. It seems odd that the site does not get a mention in *Archaeologia Cambrensis*[2] until 1911, while the earliest book reference seems to be *Collecta Archaeologia*[3], which is surprising when it was shown on an Ordnance Survey

41

map nearly thirty years before. Later writers giving details of this stone circle seem to agree that there are sixteen large stones in the circle, which has a diameter of about 72 feet, with the tallest stone only being 4 feet 4 inches high. It was noted in 1962 that one of the largest stones, which is about 3 feet 6 inches high, was in the form of an isosceles triangle at the south end of the line of the circle made by the upright stones.

There are two prominent standing stones at the gap or entrance on the east side of the stone circle and about 10 yards further out on the east side is another large stone embedded in the earth which may have been placed in position by the stone circle builders. About 40 yards from the west side of the stone circle is a long large maenhir lying prostrate which would have been about 6 feet high if it had been placed upright in the ground and thus it would have been higher than any of the stones now forming part of the stone circle. Neither of these two stones appear to have been mentioned in any previous reports which describe this important ancient monument.

About 150 yards north-east of the stone circle there are two even larger erect greyish-green monoliths about 7 feet high and 15 yards apart. These do not stand out against the background to the north of the stone circle due to the high gorse, the house and buildings and the high stone walls of the nearby farm. This farm is called Duffryn Dwndwr, which is an unusual Welsh name. Duffryn means valley and it is interesting to note that Dwndwr means Hurlers, which is the name given for one of Cornwall's largest and best-known stone circles in the Parish of St. Clear (SX 258714).

John G. Williams has always felt that there is something very special about the Gors Fawr stone circle, for he has experienced a peculiar warm welcoming feeling whenever he has gone there. In particular, he vividly remembers one occasion when, after a shower of rain, he saw the sun breaking through the low clouds to the west and the mist slowly clearing as the clouds moved over the Preseli mountains to reveal the colourful and rugged landscape that had barely changed during the previous five-thousand years. It was with a sense of awe that he felt the clouds were opened like curtains to show him some of the beauties and mysteries of this lonely moorland stone circle.

The Preseli Hills, Dyfed.   *Chris Barber*

When the clouds rose, he could see skyline to the north and prominently visible was a peculiar megalith which has been called The Warrior Stone. This is a strange pillar-like stone over 6 feet high and placed on top of a rock outcrop or carn of stones a few feet above the level of the brow of the hill, which is partly covered over with earth and grass. The stone is of a greyish-white rock and, from the east, its outline resembles a

The Warrior Stone, Dyfed.   *John G. Williams*

Greek warrior's head in a tall helmet, which explains why it is so named. This stone is not mentioned in any book or identified on any published map. It is at Bwlch Ungwr between Carn gwr and Carn Breseb in the Parish of Meline (SN 138330). A few hundred yards to the north-west is Carn Meinyn, which is the place where the famous Blue Stones of the inner circle of Stonehenge were quarried.

If you stand by the Warrior Stone and look south down the valley to Gors Fawr and beyond, you will see a landscape that has barely changed over thousands of years apart from a few whitewashed farm houses and buildings and a couple of narrow winding lanes. The Warrior Stone is not easy to reach from the south, for you have to ascend a steep hill which is so boggy and muddy that it is advisable to keep to the tracks made by the sheep that seem to thrive on this mountain.

Side View of the Warrior Stone.   *John G. Williams*

43

Coetan Arthur, Preseli Hills, Dyfed.   *Chris Barber*

Cerrig Meibion Arthur, Dyfed.   *Chris Barber*

The strangeness of the surroundings of Gors Fawr Stone Circle can be best felt and appreciated from the Warrior Stone. From there can be seen Bedd Arthur (Arthur's Grave), an oval shaped stone enclosure of twelve stones which is in the Parish of Meline (SN 131324), and a little further away in the Parish of Mynachlog Ddu is a huge boulder which looks like a rocking stone (SN 135324). Down in the valley on the boundary of the Parish of Meline and Mynachlog Ddu are Cerrig Marchogion or The Stones of Arthur's Knights (SN 102322), and not far away, also in the Parish of Mynachlog Ddu, are Cerrig Meibion Arthur or the Stones of Arthur's Sons near Cwm garw (SN 118310).

The presence of so many Arthurian sites so close to Gors Fawr must be significant. Those that believe that Arthur was a 5th-century king would expect to find plenty of legendary lore linking these ancient stone sites with their Arthurian names, but there seem to be no records of such tales. Alternatively, Arthur may be considered as Arth Fawr, The Great Bear and a representation of the Polar Force. There is in fact an important SCEMB line passing through the Gors Fawr Stone Circle. It starts at The Warrior Stone (SN 138330) and goes south through Gors Fawr Stone Circle (SN 135295) to a large prehistoric earthwork on the side of the railway at Clynderwen on the other side of the main road from the railway station and church, which is marked as Earthwork on the One Inch Ordnance Survey map (SN 123190).

This alignment can be checked by any reader who knows how to use graph paper. The position of each site can be pinpointed by reading off from left to right against the bottom or top scale the first three numbers of each site and by reading off from the bottom to the top against the left or right scale the last three numbers in the reference to the site. When these three sites are correctly plotted on the graph, they can be joined by a straight line like all SCEMB lines.

On 24th August 1983 John Williams and his son, Richard, visited Gors Fawr and carried out some dowsing experiments. They found, as expected, that if they placed the palms of both of their hands on the top of one of the stones in the stone circle they experienced the spiral power which pushed them away from the stone either to the right or the left. At about 2.00p.m. the sun was shining and the spiral power seemed to be very strong, and they wondered if this power would pass through one human body into another human body. Richard Williams took off his wellingtons and socks and stood barefooted on the almost flat surface of one of the larger stones in the south-east part of the stone circle, and felt nothing unusual. John G. Williams then held him by one hand to steady him on the stone and had a normal response but, when he caught hold of his son's other hand whilst he was still standing on the stone, the spiral power was experienced very strongly and Richard was pulled down from the standing stone.

These peculiar experiences at Gors Fawr gave plenty of food for thought, as nothing of a similar kind seems to have been previously recorded. The potential of the powers and forces utilised by the ancient builders of these monuments seem enormous and perhaps provide valid reasons for the existence of these megaliths. Perhaps the SCEMB lines were used to channel these powers and forces into and out from such strange stone circles as Gors Fawr. A great deal of work needs to be carried out through serious research into this prehistoric riddle by people with patience and open minds.

"There exists a striking network of lines and subtle forces across Britain, and elsewhere on spaceship Earth, understood and marked in prehistoric times by men of wisdom and cosmic consciousness."

Paul Screeton

REFERENCES
1. *A Welsh and English Dictionary* by Rev. Thomas Richards (Merthyr Tydfil, 1839).
2. *Archaeologia Cambrensis* (1911), p.319.
3. *Collecta Archaeologia* (1871), p.227.

Chapter 7

ARTHUR'S STONE, GOWER

"Give me a place to stand on, and a lever, and I will move the world."
Archimedes

The most famous prehistoric stone monument in Wales is a dolmen called Arthur's Stone. It is situated on the top of a long ridge called Cefn Bryn at Reynoldston in the old parish of Llanrhidian Lowr in West Glamorgan (SS 491905). The earliest mention of this ancient monument is in the Welsh Triads, where it is called Maen Ceti or the Big Stone of Sketty, and one of the wonders of Wales. Dating back, perhaps more than a thousand years, the Welsh Triads also celebrate Arthur's Stone as one of the three most stupendous works undertaken in Britain, of which Stonehenge is another and also Silbury Hill in Wiltshire.

Arthur's Stone (Maen Ceti), West Glamorgan.   *Chris Barber*

Amongst the ninety-four identified book references to this famous dolmen there are a variety of short descriptions and stories. The earliest written published record of the name Arthur's Stone seems to be in Camden's *Brittania*[1], then in *The Cambrian Directory*[2], where it is mentioned as being vulgarly called King Arthur's Stone and it is described as resting on six stones about 5 feet high.

Druidical Remains and Antiquities of the Ancient Britons, Principally in Glamorgan[3], refers to it as *"a large and notable cromlech, upwards of 20 tons weight, although there have been from time to time many pieces broken off for millstones. Now it appears probable that this cromlech was called Maen Ketti, from maen, a stone; ced, a gift, and tya, a house. Mr. Davies also gives the following explanation of Maen Ketti:— Ketti is a derivative of Ket and this must have implied ark or chest, for we still maintain its diminutive form Keten, to denote a small chest or cabinet. Wherefore Maen Ketti is the stone ark; and it could have been no other than the ponderous covering of that cell which represented the ark."* This is a typical statement of the fanciful and romantic writers of *represented the ark."* This is a typical statement of the fanciful and romantic writers of the early part of the last century who had some queer unfounded views about the Druids, who were then held responsible for the erection of all the ancient stone monuments. The only reliable contemporary reference to the Druids in Wales was made by Julius Caesar, who ruled Britain at least 2,000 years after Arthur's Stone and other similar prehistoric stone monuments were put in their places by a race of people who are not mentioned even in our earliest records.

Beale Poste, in *Brittanic Researches or New Facts and Rectifications of Ancient British History[4]*, mentions Arthur's Stone as standing over a fountain or spring and refers to the dolmen as Koetan Arthur. In *The Official Guide and Handbook to Swansea and its District[5]* the dolmen is given another name, for it states: *"But when all was said, there stands the Stone of Sketty and of Arthur — the unknown Sphinx of Gower — as much older as it is more mysterious than the famous riddle of Egypt."* A variation of Koetan Arthur is given in *The March and Borderland of Wales[6],* where the author calls the dolmen Arthur's Quoit, but in this case the word quoit is used instead of the Welsh word Coetan which means a quoit. Koetan is incorrect as the letter K is not used in the Welsh language and Coetan, which is sometimes used, is also wrong because there is no "a" in the correct Welsh word.

Some modern writers refer to the dolmen as Maen Ceti or Maen Cetti, so there are a number of variations or corruptions from the original name which might have been Coetan Arth Fawr or the Quoit of the Great Bear constellation.

The physical descriptions of Arthur's Stone which occur in various books during the last two centuries vary so much that one wonders if the authors ever saw the dolmen. The first mention of its weight seems to be in *The Tour Throughout South Wales and Monmouthshire[7]*, where it is mentioned as weighing twenty tons. Rev. J. Evans, in *Letters Written During a Tour Through South Wales[8]*, calls the dolmen the wonder of the world on Gower and mentions a large flat stone of several tons. By 1834 the weight had been put up to 25 tons in *The Graphic and Historical Illustrator, An Original Miscellany of Literary, Antiquarian and Topographical Information[9]* and this weight of 25 tons seems to have been accepted by subsequent writers. There is no record of any calculations to show how the weight of 25 tons has been assessed and it should be worthwhile for some able surveyor with the assistance of modern technology to arrive at a more accurate weight.

The number of supporting stones beneath the huge capstone vary from the six mentioned in *The Cambrian Directory,* referred to above, to six or seven given by J. T. Barber in this book mentioned above, to eight perpendicular supporters described in later books, but twelve supporters are mentioned in *A Topographical Dictionary of Wales[10]*. Chas. T. Cliffe, in *The Book of South Wales[11]*, refers to the above and writes that most of the published accounts of Arthur's Stone are very inaccurate. He states that the capstone of this dolmen actually rests on four stones, one of which is at the south-west end, the other three, the smaller of the whole and on which nearly all the weight falls, are below the centre.

There are only a few mentions of the capstone's length, breadth and depth in the many references to Arthur's Stone. For example, S. Baring Gould, in *A Book of South Wales[12]*, states that the capstone is about 14 feet long, 7 feet 2 inches in depth and 6 feet 6 inches in breadth. These are the measurements given by other writers and sometimes with a few minor changes.

The Rev. J. Evans in 1804, in *Letters Written During a Tour in South Wales* (mentioned above), says that the capstone was of a species of brescia which was of the same rock that the hill was principally composed. But in 1844, Samuel Lewis, in *A Topographical Dictionary of Wales[13]*, stated that it was composed of a different species of rock from any found in this part of the country, but consisted of the common pudding-stone or millstone grit which the local people had found totally unfit for use as a millstone. Such confusion is not helped by an amazing statement by a Welsh expert in a book published in 1965 where he states that the capstone is probably an erratic boulder and Arthur's Stone something of an accident. He may have expected his readers to believe that the glacial ice brought this huge capstone to rest neatly on top of a number of upright supporting stones.

The early illustrations of Arthur's Stone are also dubious. The first seems to be a rough drawing made in about 1830 which appears in the above mentioned *The Graphic and Historical Illustrator,* published in 1834. Nearly twenty years later appeared a vignette title engraving of Arthur's Stone in *The History of Wales*[14] showing four wild goats in a rural scene and these appeared to be more important than the dolmen.

Early illustration of Arthur's Stone.

Archaeologia Cambrensis[15] in 1866 had a sketch and in 1870[16] had a full description and a drawing of the dolmen made by Sir J. Gardner Wilkinson. This was reproduced in the well-known authorative work *Rude Stone Monuments in all Countries*[17] by James Ferguson, published in 1872 and is inaccurate for it can be confirmed by anyone who makes a careful observation of the area around Arthur's Stone. It will be noted that the background of the dolmen in the drawing is completely wrong and it is not likely to have changed very much during the last few hundred years.

The earliest photograph that has been noted of Arthur's Stone was published in *Harper's new Monthly Magazine*[18] in 1883. It accompanied an article by Wirt Sykes (p.17) and shows a man on the top of the capstone. In recent years it was reproduced in *Exploring the Wild Welsh Coast 100 years Ago*[19].

More different strange tales and legends are associated with this ancient stone monument than with any other megalithic site in Wales. The one of interest to dowsers who are able to detect underground streams coming out from beneath the capstones is mentioned by the Rev. J. Evans in 1804 as a stream ebbing and flowing with the tide beneath King Arthur's Stone and celebrated as Ffynnon Fair or Lady's Well. Today there is no visible sign of a spring or well at the dolmen and as the dolmen is at an altitude of 482 feet, any spring below is unlikely to be affected by the tide. Yet this story is still being mentioned by modern authors, none of whom give personal observations on the amount or times of the rise and fall of the water in a spring beneath the capstone.

There is, however, a spring called Lady's Well about ½ mile south-east of Arthur's Stone on the side of the main road (SS 498900) which is now enclosed in a small wooden building. The odd thing is that this spring is on a SCEMB line going south-east from Arthur's Stone through a large and prominent stone about 200 yards away from the dolmen and near a trackway. On the outer side of this can be seen the remains of a seven-pointed circle which is about 1 foot in diameter. This circle of seven points ⁚⁚ is a well-known sacred symbol used by some ancient civilisations and there are a number of clear examples of this shown on the mysterious large red clay disc called the disc of Phaestos, which was found in the north-east part of the Minoan Palace at Phaestos in Crete during the early part of this century and now has a special place in the museum at Heraclion. The SCEMB line continues through a standing stone site and ends at a tumulus near Penmaen Church (SS 532881).

Taliesin Williams, the over-zealous archdruid, often wrote under his bardic name Ab Iolo and in his *Iolo Manuscripts*[20], published in 1848, he says that Maen Cetti was by ancient tradition adored by the pagans; but St. David split it with his sword to prove that it was not sacred and he commanded a well to spring from under it, which flowed accordingly. A similar story is related in *A Handbook for Travellers in South Wales and its Borders including The River Wye*[21], where King Arthur is credited with striking off the rough stones near the dolmen in his detestation of idolatory.

The legend about Arthur's Stone going down to the sea to drink appears to have been first recorded in *Some Folk-lore of South Wales*[22], in 1898, where the author mentions that it is said that on certain nights of the year it goes down to Port Eynon, a few miles away, to drink of the sea and there were dim traces of a female presence which rode on the huge capstone. A. G. Bradley, in his book *The March and Borderland of Wales*[23], mentions that this is a common superstition in South Wales concerning cromlechs while C. J. O. Evans, in *Glamorgan — It's History and Topography*[24], p.397, gives the nights as Midsummer Night or All Hallows Eve.

A new legend reported in recent years can be found in *Folklore, Myths and Legends of Britain*[25]. It mentions local girls placing a honey cake soaked in milk on the stone at midnight when the moon was full. They would then crawl around the stone three times on their hands and knees, hoping to see their sweethearts. If they appeared, their fidelity was proved. But if not, then the girls knew that the boys did not intend to marry them. However, it is doubtful that any self-respecting Gower girl would be prepared to come forward to confirm that she had performed this ritual on a moonlit night.

Although Arthur's Stone is a well-known local landmark, it is only recently that postcards have been produced that depict the dolmen. One of these is an excellent colour picture taken by Roger Vlitas (Colourmaster Postcards of Dragon Publishing Ltd., Llandeilo, Dyfed). On the reverse side is the comment . . . *"Arthur is said to emerge from the cromlech when the moon is full and walk across the Gower."* Perhaps this Arthur is the Polar Force which may have something to do with the strange results on photographs taken of this stone.

Richard E. Roberts, of Cockett, Swansea, who has carried out investigations at Arthur's Stone for about thirty years, took some colour photographs on 20th March 1984 and 20th June 1985 with a 35mm camera which show feint downward beams of light in front of the dolmen against an overcast sky.

On 9th May 1987 John G. Williams took some colour photographs of the dolmen, also with a 35mm camera and one of them shows a clear white dot in thin cloud against a brilliant mid-day blue sky above the north end of the capstone. Two other pictures taken of the dolmen, from different positions, with the same camera and within minutes of each other, also show white dots in the sky over the capstone. It must be emphasised that they did not appear in any of the other photographs on the rest of the film.

These white dots in the sky have appeared in other photographs of dolmens, including one taken in Cornwall by someone who noticed nothing unusual in the photograph until it was pointed out to him. But even then he found it easier to accept the explanation that there was something wrong with his equipment rather than believe that his camera had recorded something in the sky which he had not noticed when he was taking the photographs.

It does seem that at certain times there are strange things in the sky above Arthur's Stone which can register on a sensitive photographic film when pictures are taken at fast speeds. These should not be dismissed as coincidence until a careful investigation has been undertaken, for there may be mysterious circumstances at this and other dolmens which can be uncovered and used for the benefit of mankind.

"We tend to assume that a photograph is something without life, yet recent radiaetheric research has shown that the negative emulsion absorbs something of the psychic energy of whatever is photographed."

Muz Murray

REFERENCES
1. *Brittania* by Camden (Gibson's Edition, 1695), col. 612.
2. *The Cambrian Directory* by J. Easton (Salisbury, 1801), p.31.
3. *Druidical Remains and Antiquities of the Ancient Britons, Principally in Glamorgan* by John G. Roberts (E. Griffiths, Swansea, 1842).
4. *Brittanic Researches or New Facts and Rectifications of Ancient British History* by Beale Paste (John Russell Smith, London, 1853), p.271.
5. *The Official Guide and Handbook to Swansea and its District* by S. C. Ganwell (British Association for the Advancement of Science Meeting at Swansea, 1880), book published at Swansea in 1880, p.187.
6. *The March and Borderland of Wales* by A. G. Bradley (London, 1905).
7. *The Tour throughout South Wales and Monmouthshire* by J. T. Barber (London, 1804), p.20
8. *Letters Written during a Tour Through South Wales* by Rev. J. Evans (London, 1804), p.178.
9. *The Graphic and Historical Illustrator, An Original Miscellany of Literary, Antiquarian and Topographical Information*, edited by Edw. W. Bayley, F.S.A. (J. Chidley, London, 1834), p.29.
10. *A Topographical Dictionary of Wales* by Samuel Lewis (London, 1844), Vol. II, p.85, under Llanrhidian.
11. *The Book of South Wales* by Chas. T. Cliffe (1847), p.179.
12. *A Book of South Wales* by S. Baring Gould (1905), p.136.
13. *A Topographical Dictionary of Wales* by Samuel Lewis (London, 1844).
14. *The History of Wales* by B. B. Woodward (George Virtue, London, 1853).
15. *Archaeologia Cambrensis* (1866), p.337.
16. *Archaeologia Cambrensis* (1870), pp.23 to 33.
17. *Rude Stone Monuments in all Countries* by James Ferguson (1872).
18. *Harper's New Monthly Magazine* (1883).
19. *Exploring the Wild Welsh Coast 100 years ago*, edited Stuart D. Ludlum (Thames and Hudson, London, 1985).
20. *Iolo Manuscripts* (Llandovery, 1848).
21. *A Handbook for Travellers in South Wales and its Borders including The River Wye* by John Murray (London, 1877), p.46.
22. *Some Folk-Lore of South Wales* by J. H. Thomas (W. N. Lewis, Cardiff, 1898), p.4.
23. *The March and Borderland of Wales* by A. G. Bradley (London, 1905).
24. *Glamorgan, Its History and Topography* by C. J. O. Evans (Cardiff, 1943), p.397.
25. *Folklore, Myths and Legends of Britain* (Reader's Digest, London, 1973), p.402.

Chapter 8

COETAN ARTHUR, NEWPORT, DYFED

"An important factor in manipulating the earth's subtle energies is the influence of the heavenly bodies, particularly the sun and moon, which throughout the day, varying with their respective positions, set up tides and currents within the terrestrial magnetic field."

John Mitchell

Coetan Arthur, Newport, Dyfed.   Chris Barber

Coetan Arthur is one of the most noted of the many dolmens in Wales and it is situated near the road leading from Newport to Berry Hill, just before it crosses the bridge over the Afon Nyfer and on the left-hand side in the middle of a group of new bungalows (SN 061395). The soft sylvan surroundings of this dolmen are in sharp contrast to the harsh rugged hills which stretch to the Preseli Mountains, where numerous prehistoric stone monuments are located in a lonely and hostile landscape. This particular dolmen is easily accessible to any traveller interested in prehistoric stone monuments. It is a favourite dolmen for John G. Williams, who has taken numerous photographs of it during a series of visits since July 1962. These now form an interesting and intriguing collection that is of historical importance.

There seem to be comparatively few early literary references to Coetan Arthur at Newport and some of them vary so much that one wonders if the writers actually examined this dolmen. The first mention appears to be in *Gentleman's Tour Through Monmouthshire and South Wales*[1], published in 1755 and the description seems to have been copied in *A Tour Through Monmouthshire and Wales*[2] (1781), which states that the upper stone of the dolmen is shaped like a mushroom and is upwards of 9 feet in diameter.

In *The Scenery, Antiquities and Biography of South Wales*[3], the dolmen is described as standing on three stones or pillars, two at the east end and one at the west, about 7 feet or 7½ feet high. The top stone supported by these is 18 feet long, 9 feet wide in the widest part and at one end between 2 and 3 feet thick. At the narrowest end, it is only about 4 feet thick. The mean breadth is 6½ feet which, multiplied by 18, gives 117 feet in its superfices. There is a different description in *A Handbook for Travellers in South Wales and its Borders Including the River Wye*[4] (1877), which describes the capstone as poised on two out of four upright stones and measures 10 feet in length by nearly 9 feet and is from 3 to 3½ feet thick. A more recent account in *The Prehistoric Chamber Tombs of England and Wales*[5] states that the capstone of Coetan Arthur at Penbont is 10 feet 7 inches by 8 feet 11 inches by 3 feet thick.

It is surprising to find that no illustrations of Coetan Arthur appear to have been published until 1895, when one was included in *Nooks and Corners of Pembrokeshire*[6], and the first photograph published seems to be in *Royal Commission of Ancient Monuments, Pembroke*[7], where there is both an illustration and a photograph.

Coetan Arthur, July 1962.   *John G. Williams*

On 8th July 1962, John G. Williams visited the site and photographed it for the first time. His results were so peculiar that in subsequent years he made regular visits to take further pictures in both monochrome and colour. But the first photograph, mentioned above, was taken at about mid-day on 8th July 1962 with a monochrome film in a 35mm camera when the weather was quite dull. The shutter speed was ⅟₆₀ second and it was taken from a distance of about 30 yards on the west side. It shows Coetan Arthur in a field against the background of a nearby hedge with a tree about 25 feet high. In the foreground of this photograph is a white blur which is thought to have been caused by a concentration of ultra-violet light, for similar results can be seen on other pictures of prehistoric stone monuments.

The next photograph was taken immediately afterwards on the same film and camera and shows the southern end of the dolmen with the southern upright supporting stone, and the photographer was about 20 feet away. There is a pronounced white blur over the bottom third of the picture. Nothing unusual was noticed when these two photographs were taken and it can be assumed that some unseen agency caused the white blurs to show where there may have been emissions of ultra-violet light which would not have been visible to the human eye.

John G. Williams visited Coetan Arthur again on 1st September 1962 and took six more monochrome photographs with his 35mm camera. Again nothing unusual was seen, but one of them taken from about 20 feet on the west side of the dolmen shows a vertical band of blurred light stretching from the bottom of the two northern upright supporting stones, up and over the northern part of the capstone and continuing upwards against the leaves of the trees in the background. Five colour photographs were also taken with another 35mm camera at the same time which seemed to give normal results, although the sky was shown in a strange pale orange-grey colour.

Coetan Arthur, September 1962.   *John G. Williams*

The next set of monochrome and colour photographs were taken on 21st July 1965. The colour photographs show that it was a dull, cloudy day and some of the monochrome prints show strange white dots above the ground against the background of the hedge. These were in fact overlooked until it was noted that some later photographs of prehistoric monuments showed above the ground and in the sky identical white dots, which were certainly not the fluff from a dandelion flower that had gone to seed!

A return visit was made in April 1969, but photographs taken on this occasion by John G. Williams showed nothing strange. By 23rd August 1973 building operations had commenced in the field where the dolmen still stands. Photographs taken on this date show a new road some distance to the south-west of the dolmen and in one of the pictures there are two large round black dots in the sky above Coetan Arthur to its right and left. Nothing unusual was seen in the sky when these photographs were taken.

Photographs taken in June 1978 by John G. Williams, with the same 35mm cameras, of Coetan Arthur were normal but reveal that some bungalows were being built in the field and the dolmen was still unenclosed. It was after this that some open wooden and wire fencing was erected around the monument and this is shown on a photograph taken on 2nd September 1978. It would seem that this ancient monument had been put in the care of the Welsh Office before September 1978 and a small green signpost and a wooden paling fence erected on the field sides.

On 7th July 1979 John G. Williams returned to the site and was dismayed to find two young girls and a young man excavating around the base of Coetan Arthur. He spoke to the young lady, who was from the National Museum in Cardiff and was in charge of the operation. She informed him that the dolmen was going to be moved to the National Museum at Cardiff. Then she showed him the concrete blocks which had been placed under the capstone and held together with mortar, which was done presumably to keep the capstone in place until the whole dolmen was moved in one huge piece by crane and then hauled away to Cardiff.

Coetan Arthur, July 1979.   John G. Williams

John expressed his views on the situation to the girl in charge but did not blame her for the work that had been ordered from a higher level. He also mentioned that there were stories about people who had dug under these ancient stones and suffered unpleasant after effects. The young lady seemed to have heard about these and she mentioned that her parents lived in Pembrokeshire and they had told her that the local farmers sometimes put lumps of quartz on their farm gateposts to keep evil influences away.

This unnecessary damage to one of our best prehistoric monuments surprised and annoyed John G. Williams so much that he only took two photographs on this occasion. Both of them show the greyish-black wall in the centre of the dolmen between the north and south supporting stones to the huge capstone and one of them features the usual kind of white blur at the bottom right-hand side of the picture across the south upright large stone on which one end of the capstone rests.

It seems, therefore, that the fluctuating concentration of ultra-violet light could still appear at the dolmen, although there had been excavations that may have caused some disturbances around the base.

When John paid his next visit to Coetan Arthur on 28th June 1980, he was pleased to note that the hideous concrete wall had been removed but noted that an area covering a patch extending at least 5 yards from the dolmen had been excavated to a depth of at least 1 foot. It seems that there must have been a rethink and a change of plans by the authorities, who wisely decided not to remove this remarkable monument to the National Museum at Cardiff. Photographs taken at this time show the results of the excavations and the new bungalows which have encroached on the rural scene.

One lady who used to play around Coetan Arthur when she was a child was shocked to learn of what had happened and thought that none of the local Newport people would have approved of the removal of their renowned prehistoric monument. This incident should put us on our guard against the desires of museum authorities to remove any of our ancient monuments from their natural surroundings, unless there is a pressing need for their preservation due to the site being used for large building operations or important roadworks.

Further visits to the site have been made since 1980 by John G. Williams and more photographs have been taken, but not one of these has shown anything unusual. This poses a number of questions for the consideration of the reader.

1. Did the excavations in 1979 have any effect on the unknown circumstances which seem to cause a concentration of ultra-violet light in the vicinity of the dolmen at certain undefined times?

2. Did the presence of the new bungalows and their inhabitants have any such effects?

3. Who was responsible for the change of plan relating to the removal of the dolmen and is there someone behind the scenes influencing these decisions?

4. Did the excavators find any trace of human bones within the dolmen which by some people is considered to be a burial chamber?

5. What is the explanation of the necessity to have such a huge and heavy capstone to cover what may have only been one burial at ground level?

This dolmen near the river has not previously received much notice and it is hoped that these observations will give an indication of some of the mysteries that can be investigated by any intelligent person. The name Coetan Arthur has been given to other dolmens which usually have some legend connecting them to the romantic hero of the early and middle ages of Welsh and English literature, but nothing seems to be on record in this respect as far as this Newport dolmen is concerned.

"The long unmeasured pulse of time moves everything. There is nothing hidden that it cannot bring to light."

Sophocles

REFERENCES
1. *Gentleman's Tour Through Monmouthshire and South Wales* (1755), p.92.
2. *A Tour Through Monmouthshire and Wales* by Henry Penruddock Wyndham (E. Easton, Salisbury, 1781), p.79. Another edition was also published in 1781 (J. Evans, London) and the description of Coetan Arthur is on p.93.
3. *The Scenery, Antiquities and Biography of South Wales* by Benjamin H. Malkin (London, 1807), Vol. II, p.230.
4. *A Handbook for Travellers in South Wales and its Borders Including the River Wye* by John Murray (London, 1877), p.209.
5. *The Prehistoric Tombs of England and Wales* by Prof. Glyn H. Daniel (Cambridge University Press, 1950), p.199.
6. *Nooks and Corners of Pembrokeshire* by H. J. Timmins (Elliot Stock, London, 1895), p.166.
7. *Royal Commission of Ancient Monuments, Pembroke*, p.269.

Chapter 9

MARKINGS ON THE STONES

"Evidence from times remote haunts us with past grandeur, mighty earthworks stand forlorn, gaunt stone monuments in wild places bear cryptic signs telling mute stories men cannot read."

Dr. Raymond Drake

The only signs of any markings on our prehistoric stones are those that have been incised by stone-cutting tools. There is no record of remnants of any paint or plaster being found on these stones which would indicate any very early decoration even on the long-protected insides of dolmens and burial barrows.

On prehistoric standing stones the incised markings that have been found are of four main types, namely Roman, Christian, Ogham and Prehistoric. Occasionally one may come across some initials carved on the top of a single upright stone, which on investigation often turn out to be the initials of the lord of the local manor or the landlord of the farm, and these were cut during the last one-hundred-and-fifty years to show his boundary limit. A good example may be seen at Tremaenhir in Whitchurch, Dyfed (SM 827264), which has *"J.G. 1860"* carved near the top of this 7-feet-high stone.

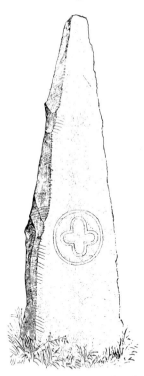

Bridell Stone, Dyfed.   *Chris Barber*   *Side view showing cross and Ogham letters.*

The early Christians converted some of the large standing stones by carving crosses on the upright faces to show that they had been taken over by the local church. One of the best examples of this is the Christianised standing stone, which is 7 feet tall and stands in the churchyard on the south side of Bridell Church in Dyfed (SN 177421). It is formed of the porphyrite greenstone of the Preseli Hills and has a large equal armed cross cut inside a circle on the centre of the stone. In addition, it has Ogham letters cut into its vertical edges and there are cup markings on its surface, so this is a unique Welsh specimen of a large standing stone being used by three separate cultures. The Ogham inscription reads, Nettasagru Maqui Mucoi Breci, which has been translated to mean:—

Nettasagus son of the descendants of Breci. It was most likely carved in the 5th-6th century A.D. A most unusual feature about Bridell Church is that it has no doors on the south or west sides, but there is a porch and a door on the north side.

Another ancient Christianised tall pillar stone is one called St. David Staff, which stands 7 feet high and is near the west end of the village church at Llandewi Brefi in Dyfed (SN 664553). It is said that Saints David and Dubricius leaned on the stone whilst preaching at the synod.

Maen Madoc, Powys.   *Chris Barber*

The Romans utilised a few of the large prehistoric standing stones for their own purposes and a good example is Maen Madoc at Plas-y-gors in Ystradfellte, Powys (SN 918157). It is an inscribed stone 11 feet high standing on the side of a mountain track and displays crude Latin capitals, some of which are reversed and read downwards. In 1940 it was moved and reset by the Ministry of Works. Wynford Vaughan Thomas, in his book *Wales a History[1]*, refers to it as a Roman milestone but it seems unlikely that the Romans put up the largest milestone in Wales in such a remote spot.

57

Ogham marks which are cut on the vertical edges of ancient upright stones are difficult to identify but the one in Bridell churchyard mentioned earlier is a good example. The best recorded prehistoric standing stones with the peculiar Ogham inscriptions are found in Southern Ireland and it would seem that none are known to exist in England.

The most difficult kinds of markings on prehistoric standing stones to identify are those which may be considered earlier than the Christian, Roman or Ogham inscriptions and are probably at least 2,000 years old, possibly dating back to the time of the original erection of these stones which may be another 4,000 years earlier. Welsh wind and rain will erode even the hardest stone and, if you look in any Welsh churchyard today, you will find very few gravestones over 200 years old with legible carved inscriptions, so one cannot expect to see much in the way of man-made markings on the ancient stones going back two-thousand years. The ancient people probably did not chisel any form of letters or hieroglyphics on their megaliths but it is apparent that they incised some symbols and small cup marks, varying in size from a couple of inches to 1 foot across, such as the large saucer-like depressions to be seen on the Penymarth Fish Stone in Cwmdu, Powys (SO 183199).

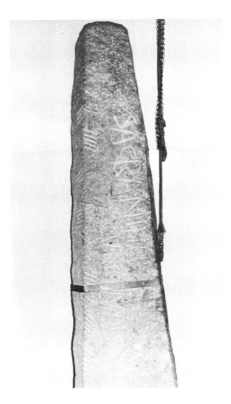

Stone in St. Dogmael's Church, Dyfed with Ogham and early Christian inscriptions.

Chris Barber

It is not surprising that the finest examples of these kind of markings are those that can be seen on the inside of a dolmen or burial barrow and have consequently been well protected from the elements. The finest example in Wales of such markings is inside the dolmen called Bryn Celli Ddu, which is situated in the Parish of Llandaniel Fab, Anglesey (SH 508702). The earliest book reference to Bryn Celli Ddu is in *Archaeologia Cambria*[2] (1847), which is the first page of the old and well respected Welsh archaeological journal. This and later yearly editions up to 1985 have a great deal of information, with plans and photographs relating to the site. An earlier reference, however, of little consequence can be found in *The Journeys of Sir Richard Colt Hoare Through Wales and England 1793-1810*[3], where it is mentioned as a carnedd overgrown.

Clynog Dolmen, Gwynedd, decorated with cup marks.

There are varying descriptions and photographs of these markings at Bryn Celli Ddu, which are formed by incised lines about ¼-inch deep and are considered to have been made by a pointed tool. One of the markings is an incised spiral on a pillar stone about 5 feet high which stands inside the chamber and some of the illustrations show other curious snake-like spirals. There has been no valid attempt at explaining the meaning of these markings, which are similar in form to those found at the ancient stone monument at New Grange in Meath, Ireland (0 007727), known as the Cave of the Sun.

Cup marks or small circular hollows are found cut into some prehistoric standing stones and these are generally acknowledged to be of pre-Christian date. But they are generally overlooked by most writers because there seems to be no acceptable explanation for their presence or purpose. A good example of cup marks is on the capstone of a dolmen called Bachwen Clynog at Clynog near Caernarvon (SH 40764947). These are not very clearly visible now due to weathering but there is a good early photograph of them in *Portfolio of Photographs of the Cromlechs of Anglesey and Caernarvonshire*[4]. There were supposed to have been 110 of these cup marks on the capstone according to *Royal Commission on Ancient and Historic Monuments, Caernarvon*[5] and Rev. P. B. Williams, in *The Tourist's Guide Through the County of Caernarvon*[6] (1821), thought the cup marks were possibly for some purpose of augury.

Some prehistoric standing stones have short lines of small hollows of about the same size and it is difficult to claim positively that these may have been cut on the stones in ancient times. In Powys, there is a large standing stone in the middle of a field between the River Wye and Llangoed Castle at Llyswen (SO 124398) which is about 7 feet high

59

and leans over at an angle of about 30°. On its unexposed site and about 4 feet above the ground there are a number of lines of these small hollows. They can easily be seen but they have not been recorded in any archaeological work.

Ty Illtyd Dolmen, Powys.   *Chris Barber*

There are a number of cases where the markings on prehistoric standing stones have been rather fancifully interpreted and these have been so obviously misleading that later writers have refrained from attempting to describe any doubtful markings on these ancient monuments. A good example is Maen Iltyd, a dolmen near Maneast Court at Llanhamlach in Powys (SO 098264), which was supposed to have been the hermit's cell of St. Illtyd and antique characters on the stones were believed to be the workmanship of the recluse. Sir Richard Colt Hoare, on p.238 of his above-mentioned book, says that the crosses and other figures cut into the stones on the inside of the cromlech are certainly only the playful handywork of those who have visited the hermit's cell.

Until such time that sensible explanations can be given for these markings, they are likely to be ignored by researchers. Yet no solutions can be expected unless a collection of reliable illustrations and photographs is compiled which can be carefully examined and compared in order that realistic deductions can be made regarding their meaning.

"The retrieving of these forgotten things from oblivion in some sort resembles the art of a Conjurer."

John Aubrey

REFERENCES
1. *Wales, a History* by Wynford Vaughan Thomas (Michael Joseph, 1985), p.43.
2. *Archaeologia Cambria* (1847), p.1.
3. *The Journeys of Sir Richard Colt Hoare Through Wales and England 1793-1810* by M. W. Thompson (Alan Sutton, Gloucester, 1983), p.268.
4. *Portfolio of Photographs of the Cromlechs of Anglesey and Caernarvonshire* by John H. Griffith (Bangor circa 1910).
5. *Royal Commission on Ancient and Historic Monuments, Caernarvon.*
6. *The Tourists Guide Through the County of Caernarvon* by Rev. P. B. Williams (Caernarvon, 1821), p.158.

Chapter 10

LEGENDS

"We may reject legends if we please, but history would be incomplete without them, for they represent the temper of the people by whom great institutions were founded and among whom they flourished."

Phillott

There are no contemporary written records relating to the erection of these ancient stones so the people who lived in their vicinity had to make up stories to explain the presence and purpose of these puzzling features of the rural landscape. Over the course of time these stories became legends and the ones that we hear today are like the fairy stories that used to be told to little children. Usually they relate to giants and magical powers and are not taken seriously by the average person today.

However, such legends are worthwhile examining as folklore stories have very often been known to contain a grain of truth, for the tales may be in the form of an allegory and perhaps told in a symbolic manner. Take for example the story related by Geoffrey of Monmouth in his book *History of the Kings of Britain*[1], written in about 1136. He refers to Stonehenge and says that the famous Welsh wizard, Merlin, himself took down the Giant's Round, a circle of standing stones on Mount Killaraus in Ireland and put them up in their present position at Stonehenge on the downs in Wiltshire. This was considered as one of Geoffrey's most incredible stories for nearly 800 years. Then in 1923 Dr. Herbert H. Thomas, a petrographer to the British Geological Survey, writing in *Antiquarian Journal*[2], shows that the inner standing stones of this amazing monument originated in the Preseli Hills in Dyfed, Wales, which is over two hundred miles away from Stonehenge. In addition, the Altar Stone seems to have come from the Cosherton beds of Old Red Sandstone on the shores of Milford Haven, also in Wales and not far from the Preseli Hills. Since then there have been numerous attempts to explain how these huge blocks of stone weighing over ten tons were transported from Wales to Salisbury Plain and then set up at Stonehenge. No credit has been given to old Geoffrey for being half correct as far as the distance that the stones were moved.

Carn Meini, Dyfed, where the Bluestones of Stonehenge were quarried.   *Chris Barber*

It is of particular relevance that in the Dark Ages the area around the Preseli Hills was colonised by the Irish. They were ruled by an Irish King and Goedelic was the spoken language. So this locality was just like a small part of Ireland in the time of Merlin, which could well explain the reason for Geoffrey of Monmouth's statement. The Blue Stones can only be found in an area of one square mile between the outcrops of Carn Meini and Foel Trigarn at the eastern end of the Preseli Hills.

There are a number of legends which describe how standing stones were thrown to their present sites by a giant who was many miles away. Before dismissing these stories as rubbish one should carefully check that the geological content of the particular monolith is not the same as the rock at the place from which the giant is supposed to have thrown it. If the ancient builders could move huge stones two hundred miles to Stonehenge, then is reasonable to assume that they could move large prehistoric standing stones from their place of origin, twenty or thirty miles, to where they now stand and have stood for thousands of years.

Out of over fifty legends relating to the ancient Welsh megaliths, twenty of them relate to the stones being thrown to their present position. These legends include the following:—

(1) Carreg Samson in the churchyard of Llanbadarn Fawr, Dyfed (SN 598810), was supposed to have been thrown there by St. Samson from Pen Dinas.

(2) Llech Gron near Nebo in Llansantfraed, Dyfed (SN 542649), was said to have been carried away by the Devil to the top of Trichrug Mountain and then thrown back to its present position.

(3) Carreg Samson, near Penlan in Llanfihangel Lledrod, Dyfed (SN 655697), was launched from Uwch Mynydd by a giant.

Barclodiad-y-Gawres, Gwynedd.   *Chris Barber*

(4) Barcliadiad-y-Gawres or "The Giantess's Apronful," a dolmen or carn in Caerhun, Gwynedd (SH 716717). These stones were dropped here by two giants travelling to the island of Mona (Anglesey).

Ffon y Cawr, Gwynedd.   *Chris Barber*

(5) A slender standing stone variously known as Ffon y Cawr, The Giant's Stick or Arthur's Spear, at Caerhun, Gwynedd (SH 739717), is supposed to have been thrown by a giant to this spot from Tal y Fan or Pen-y-Gaer.

(6) Coetan Arthur Cromlech, Ystumcegid Isaf in Llanystumdwy, Gwynedd (SH 498413), is supposed to have been thrown by Arthur from a hill near Beddgelert.

(7) Coetan Arthur Cromlech near Mynydd Cefn Amlwch, at Penllech, Gwynedd (SH 230346), which Arthur Gawr or Arthur the Giant cast from Carn Madryn, a hill a few miles away.

(8) Post-y-Wiber or Post of the Dragon near Aber Rhiadr in Llanrhaidr-ym-Mochnant, Clwyd (SJ 137248), was supposed to have come from Cwm Clothy, near the waterfall and was used for ridding the district of a dragon which had two haunts; one at Penygarnedd and the other at Bwlch Sychtyn in Llansillin Parish, adjoining on the north-east.

(9) A maenhir near the school at Llanrhaidr-ym-Mochnant, Clwyd (SJ 125260), which once did duty as a lamp-post being 10 feet high. Tradition says that it was brought from Rhos Maes Criafal in Maengwynydd about 2 miles to the north.

(10) Carreg March Arthur, near Llanfernes Bridge at Mold, Clwyd (SJ 202626), which is said to have been impressed with the hoof of King Arthur's horse when he landed here after leaping from the summit of Môel Farmmau. This is in direct alignment with the site of a destroyed standing stone in a field called Dol yr Orsedd at Pentrehobyn near Mold (SJ 245627).

(11) Arthur's Stone, the renowned dolmen on the summit of Cefn Bryn at Reynoldston, West Glamorgan (SS 491905). According to *Prehistoric and Roman Wales*[3] by Sir R. E. Mortimer Wheeler (1925), this was once a pebble in the shoe of King Arthur which he flung here from Carmarthenshire.

(12) Coetan Arthur dolmen remains at Pont Fadog, Llanddwye-is-y-Craig, Clwyd (SH 603228), was a quoit which Arthur threw from Moelfre Hill.

(13) Coetan Arthur or two dolmens adjoining the school at Dyffryn Ardudwy in the Parish of Llanenddwyn, Gwynedd (SH 589228). According to *Cambrian Mirror*[4] by Edward Parr (1847) these were thrown here by Arthur from the top of Moelfre Hill.

Maen Twrog, Gwynedd.   *Chris Barber*

(14) Maen Twrog, a standing stone in the churchyard of Maentwrog, Gwynedd (SH 664406), was thrown here from the top of Moelwyn Bach, three miles to the north, by St. Twrog. The marks of his fingers and thumb can still be seen on the stone!

(15) The Devil's Quoit at Llanfihangel near Rogiet in Gwent (ST 439881) was hurled from Portishead across the Bristol Channel by the Devil in a fit of temper.

(16) Harold's Stones just outside the village of Trellech in Gwent (SO 498052) were thrown to their present position by a giant from The Holy Mountain (Skirrid Fawr), about twelve miles away.

(17) Maengwyn Hir near Crugelwin at Llanfrynach, Dyfed (SN 238302), was thrown from the summit of Frenni Fawr by St. Samson.

(18) Coetan Arthur, a rocking stone on the south slopes of Mynydd Preseli in the Parish of Mynachlog-ddu, Dyfed (SN 135324), is said to have been hurled there by King Arthur from Dyffryn, two miles away.

Arthur's Stone, West Glamorgan.   *Chris Barber*

Coetan Arthur Rocking Stone, Dyfed.   *Chris Barber*

Carreg Leidr, Gwynedd, is a robber turned into stone for stealing the church Bible. The stone runs around the field every Christmas when the clock strikes twelve.   *Chris Barber*

(19) Llech y Tribed, a dolmen near Penlan at Molygrove, Dyfed (SN 101433), was hurled by St. Samson from the summit of Carningli, Newport, Dyfed.

(20) Caer Meini near Bedd Arthur in Mynachlog Ddu, Dyfed (SN 142326), according to *Mynachlog-Ddu, A Guide to its Antiquities*[5], has an Altar Stone called Coetan Arthur which was thrown by Arthur from Dyffryn, the farm near the noted Gors Fawr Stone Circle or from Duffryn Farm by another stone circle in Henry's Moat Parish, 5 miles away.

Nine of these legends have some connection with Arthur and four of them with St. Samson, which alternatively could be a corruption of the Welsh word Simson, meaning shaking and would be a more appropriate word to give to a dolmen capstone or rocking stone than Samson the Biblical strong man or the Cornish saint who had no churches dedicated to him in Wales.

The second most popular legend which is associated with our prehistoric standing stones is the one relating to the stone (or stones) going for a drink in a nearby river or pool and these include:—

(a) The Fish Stone at Penymyarth, Cwmdu, Powys (SO 183199), which is supposed to jump into the River Usk on Midsummer Eve and go for a swim.

(b) A standing stone in a field opposite the woollen factory at Llanwrtyd Wells, Powys (SN 885475), goes down to the nearby stream to drink at night.

(c) Maen Llia near Bryn Melin in the Parish of Senny, Powys (SN 924193), is supposed to love fresh water and goes for a drink in the River Nedd whenever it hears the crowing of a cock.

(d) Carreg Bica or Maen Brediran on Mynydd Drumau in Clydach, West Glamorgan (SS 725995), which is 13 feet high and is alleged to bathe in the River Neath once a year on Easter morning.

(e) Arthur's Stone, the noted dolmen on Cefn Bryn, Reynoldston, West Glamorgan (SS 491905), in 1804 was mentioned as having a spring which ebbed and flowed with the tide and in *Some Folk-Lore of South Wales*[6] (1893) is said on a certain night (or nights) of the year to go down to Port Eynon a few miles away to drink from the sea.

The Druidstone, Gwent.   *Chris Barber*

(f) Druidstone, a 10 feet tall standing stone near Began (perhaps Begwm in Welsh, meaning Pole of the Earth) in the Parish of Michaelstone-y-Fedw, Gwent (ST 235836), is another walking stone which when the cock crows at midnight goes down to the river to bathe.

(g) The Four Stones on the side of the road at Walton, near Presteign, Powys (SO 246608), according to local legend go down to drink at Hindwell Pool about 200 yards to the east when they hear the bells of Old Radnor church ring.

(h) The Dancing Stones of Stackpole Elidyr, Dyfed, which include the Devil's Quoit, near Sampson Cross at St. Petrocs (SR 962958), on a certain day are supposed to meet and go down to Saxon's Ford to dance in the water.

There is also a group of similar legends relating to sleeping at night under the capstone of a dolmen. One of them is related in *Mona, Enchanted Island*[7], and refers to Lliwy Dolmen or Arthur's Quoit at Penrhos Lligwy in Anglesey. In this story a fisherman fell asleep under the dolmen and dreamt that he rescued a beautiful maiden from the stormy sea. She turned out to be a witch and gave him a little golden ball containing a snake-skin charm which he had to wash in the sea once a year.

According to *Archaeologia Cambrensis*[8] (1888), anyone who sleeps under Coetan Arthur near Llanfair Hall in the Parish of Llanfair-Is-Gaer in Gwynedd (SH 515660) through the night of St. John's Festival would rise in the morning as strong as a giant or as weak as a dwarf. This is a very interesting dolmen because a photograph taken in about 1900 and published in *Portfolio of Photography of the Cromlechs of Anglesey and Caernarvonshire*[9] shows a noticeable patch of white below the capstone which might have been caused by a concentration of ultra-violet light and is the first recorded photograph of this strange phenomena.

The best known of this kind of legend is the one associated with Tinkinswood long barrow or dolmen at St. Nicholas in South Glamorgan (ST 082733). In *Prehistoric and Roman Wales*[10] is the statement that anyone who sleeps within the dolmen on a "spirit night" would suffer a calamity. He would either die, go raving mad or become a poet. It is not recorded so far that any sceptic has slept under the capstone of this dolmen for a night to prove that the above claims are wrong.

"Everything which has come down to us from heathendom is wrapped in a thick fog; it belongs to a space of time which we cannot measure. We know that it is earlier than Christendom, but whether by a couple of years or a couple of centuries, or even by more than a millenium, we can do no more than guess."

Professor Rasmus Nyerup

REFERENCES

1. *History of the Kings of Britain* by Geoffrey of Monmouth (Circa 1136) (Republished in Penguin Books 1966).
2. *Antiquarian Journal.* Vol., 3 pp.239-46.
3. *Prehistoric and Roman Wales* by Sir R. E. Mortimer Wheeler (1925), p.70.
4. *Cambrian Mirror* by Edward Parr (1847).
5. *Mynachlog-Ddu, A Guide to its Antiquities* by E. T. Lewis (E. L. Jones and Sons, Cardigan, 1972).
6. *Some Folklore of South Wales* by T. H. Thomas (W. N. Lewis, Cardiff, 1893), p.4.
7. *Mona, Enchanted Island* by Geoffrey Eley (The Priory Press Ltd., Royston, Hertfordshire, 1968), p.126.
8. *Archaeologia Cambrensis* (1888), p.58.
9. *Portfolio of Photography of the Cromlechs of Anglesey and Caernarvonshire* by John E. Griffith (Bangor circa 1910).
10. *Prehistoric and Roman Wales* by Sir R. E. Wheeler (1925), p.70.

Chapter 11

ARTHURIAN MONUMENTS

"During the centuries the legend grew in richness and wonder and Arthur himself somehow got submerged in it."

Rosemary Sutcliff

The prehistoric stone monuments of Wales have a variety of names, all of which can be said to be very old and their origins have been lost in the mists of distant time. Many of them are descriptive words used in the Welsh language but their English equivalents are used so much in modern times that the old Welsh name is replaced. Such descriptive names are Maen Hir, meaning Big Stone and Maen Llwyd, meaning Pale Grey Stone. Apart from these, there is only one really prominent name used in connection with our ancient stone monuments and that is Arthur.

It is generally accepted today that all our prehistoric stone monuments are at least four thousand years old, so they date back well beyond the time of the fifth-century British king and folk hero called Arthur. In ancient times, many boys would have been called Arthur because their parents revered and wished to honour some person who was called Arthur in the same way as some Christians today name their children after their favourite Christian saints. It is unlikely, therefore, that these large ancient stone monuments found in open countryside had any connection with the famous King Arthur and any attempt to prove such links would soon run into difficulties.

In a detailed list of nearly three-hundred prehistoric sites and place names with Arthurian connections in the British Isles, there are probably less than twenty which are mentioned in stories about King Arthur which appeared in print before 1800. On the other hand, there are very few stories published before 1800 A.D. about King Arthur which specify any prehistoric stone monument by name. Those that do mention him generally infer that the monument was already in existence at the time of King Arthur. One of these stories concerns the dolmen Arthur's Stone on Cefn Bryn, Reynoldston, West Glamorgan (SS 491905) and, according to *A Handbook for Travellers in South Wales and its Borders Including the River Wye*[1] (1877), the large fragments of stone near the huge capstone were sliced off by King Arthur in his detestation of idolatory. In *Some Folklore of South Wales*[2] (1898), we learn that King Arthur tried out his sword on Maen Ceti, whch is the Welsh name for the dolmen.

It is necessary, therefore, to look back into the dim past before the time of King Arthur for the Great Arthur whose name is so often associated with our prehistoric stone monuments and this, of course, is very difficult. There are no written records of such early periods but fortunately some help can be gained from the Welsh language, which is the oldest in Europe. Students of etymology realise that the important part of any language is the spoken word as phonetics change less than written words. In Welsh, Arth Fawr means Great Bear and the two words need only the slightest phonetic change to become Arthur. The Great Bear is the name of the well-known northern constellation of seven prominent stars, which are also called Ursa Major or The Plough, and it continually circles around the present North Pole star which is the nearest thing to a fixed point in the universe.

The Welsh Arth Fawr or Great Bear has connections with the polar regions of the northern skies, which go back beyond any period of recorded time in Welsh history. In Welsh folklore, Ursa Major was called Aradr Arthur, that is Arthur's Plough, while the constellation of stars we now call Lyra was known as Telyn Arthur or Arthur's Harp and the prominent line of stars which are said to form the belt of Orion were called Llath Arthur or Arthur's Wand. There seem to be no stories explaining how these groups of stars obtained their Arthurian names, which is in direct contrast to the fanciful Greek myths which are related to the appellations given to the main constellations of the northern heavens and recognised as proper names for particular groups of stars by Western cultures.

There must have been some very early Welsh stories relating to the origins of these

Arthurian groups of stars which were probably suppressed by leaders of later cultures because they were inconsistent with their views. These early stories may have told something about the uses of Polar Forces and there seem to be a few vague references to this in some of the earliest Arthurian legends.

One fact in support of the above is the use of the Welsh word Pegwn in connection with several sites which can be regarded as being of pre-Christian date. According to *A Welsh and English Dictionary* by Rev. Thomas Richards (Merthyr Tydfil, 1839) the word "Pegwn" means an axle tree; an imaginary line drawn from one pole to another; also either of the two poles. One of the prehistoric sites associated with this name is the pair of stone circles on Mynydd Bach in the Parish of Trecastle, Powys (SN 833311).

Y Pigwn, Powys.   *John G. Williams*

These stone circles adjoin the rectangular-shaped remains of a Roman encampment, which on some maps is marked as Pigwn which is a Welsh word meaning a round heap. This is not appropriate for either the Roman remains or the two circles of standing stones, so it is reasonable to consider that Pegwn might have been the original name. There is a SCEMB line running from Twyn Henwen (Ancient White Tump) on the south which goes through to a probable standing stone at nearby Cefn Arthen across the valley on the north.

At Llanidloes in Powys is Pegwn Bach tumulus near Waunddubarthog (SO 018807) and this Welsh name refers to the Mound of the South Pole. To the north-east of this, also near Waunddubarthog, is Pegwn Mawr tumulus, meaning the Mound of the Big or North Pole (SO 026813) and there is a SCEMB line going through these two large mounds from Crugyn Gwydde (SO 920687) to a moat at Newtown which is joined at the angle of 47° by another SCEMB line, which suggests that there is some solar connection.

There is also Castell Pigyn or Pegwn (Fort of the Pole) near Carmarthen (SN 435223), which is of pre-Roman date and is on SCEMB lines with some of the Arthurian sites.

In Wales, there are numerous dolmens which have Arthurian names and most of these have their huge heavy capstones, some of which weigh twenty tons, placed with their main longest axis running north to south. These capstones were originally placed over three or more upright stones according to some general plan and appear to have been so delicately balanced that they could have been rocked in a to-and-fro motion along their main axis.

The north and south alignments and the up-and-down motions of these huge capstones suggest a possible use of the Polar Forces which includes what we call polar magnetism. Electricity relies on polar magnetism, which is not generally recognised as a very important part of the everyday life of people who live in the modern-day Western culture. If there was no Polar Force, nearly all our lights would go out and a lot of machines would come to a grinding halt.

All the old religions had their sky gods and some defied the Polar Forces and made their chief god a symbol of the Pole Star. One of these in ancient Egypt was the early supreme god called Horus, who was represented by an equilateral triangle and sometimes shown at the top of seven steps which may have been an allusion to the seven prominent stars in the Great Bear constellation. Ancient traditions suggesting the use of electricity long ago are now generally accepted as true according to *Cosmic Continents*[3] by Dr. W. Raymond Drake, who mentions that in 1938 Wilheim Konig, a German archaeologist, was rummaging in vaults below the museum at Baghdad, where he discovered clay vases at least two-thousand years old excavated at the village of Kujit Rabua. The practical Konig was astounded to recognise our electric-pile, a battery duplicated in identical fashion with acid generated electricity.

The Mabinogion[4] is a strange collection of Welsh legends which have mainly been handed down by word of mouth for many centuries and has been altered, amended and added to so much that it is not possible to ascertain the original story. Folk memory is said to preserve the essentials of ancient legends and an example of this perhaps can be found in the puzzling story about Peredeur, son of Efrawg, out of the north, who visited a hall where he saw three bald-headed swarthy youths playing gwyddbwyll, an ancient form of chess. And, after they had cleared the board of the pieces, a big black one-eyed man came in. The next morning, Peredeur was given arms by one of the maidens at the hall and he fought against the big black one-eyed man, who was forced to ask quarter.

This Peredeur was prepared to do on condition that his opponent would tell him who had plucked out his eye. The reply was *"Lord I will talk; fighting against the Black Worm of the Barrow. There is a mound that is called the Dolorus Mound and in the mound there is a barrow, and in the barrow there is a worm, and in the worm's tail there is a stone, and the virtues of the stone are that whosoever should have it in the one hand, what he would desire of gold he should have in his other hand; and it was fighting against that worm I lost my eye. And my name is the Black Oppressor."* Later Peredeur went to the Dolorus Mound and slew the worm.

In this story is a suggestion of the great knight of the north in conflict with a worm or serpent in a dolmen or burial barrow which has an important virtuous stone. This might be a reference to the Polar Forces activating the capstone of a dolmen. A clearer non-technical reference to the powerful and mysterious forces emanating from the region of The Great Bear constellation, which have only been partly rediscovered by our scientists during the past few centuries, cannot be expected to be found in any literature. It is hoped that our Welsh scholars will take note of this new Arthurian aspect and will carefully examine all the available Welsh legendary sources to find points of confirmation of the knowledge and perhaps use of the Polar Forces in ancient times here in the British Isles.

"When the stars appear in the purple skies, aged folk will point out one of their constellations as 'Telyn Arthur', 'Arthur's Harp', the Lesser Bear and 'Arthur's Plough' and Orion's Belt as 'Arthur's Yards'.

Marie Trevelyan.

REFERENCES
1. *Handbook for Travellers in South Wales and its Borders Including The River Wye* by John Murray (London, 1877), p.46.
2. *Some Folklore of South Wales* by T. H. Thomas (W. N. Lewis, Cardiff, 1898).
3. *Cosmic Continents* by Dr. W. Raymond Drake (Madras, India, 1986), p.173.
4. *The Mabinogion* translated by Lady Charlotte Guest (London, 1877) (facsimile edition published by John Jones Cardiff Ltd., 1977).

Chapter 12

THE CHURCH AND THE STONES

"Unto you is given to know the mysteries of the kingdom of God: but to others in parables, that seeing, they might not see, and hearing they might not understand."

Luke VIII.10

Today there appears to be no official policy of the Church in Wales or of any of the Welsh non-comformist churches relating to the presence of prehistoric standing stones on property belonging to the churches or situated near the churches. There are not now many cases where this can arise, but in ancient times these remnants of what was thought to be of pagan worship were objects of abhorence which were supposed to have been destroyed by the early followers of Christianity. The early Roman Catholic Church issued instructions to their priests to destroy these ancient monoliths, yet there are still a few left which are directly related to certain churches.

Kilgwrrwg Church, Gwent.   *Chris Barber*

In *Byways in British Archaeology*[1] we read that early Christianity was both antagonistic to and tolerant of pagan custom and belief. Under the rule of Constantine, the tendency was to destroy heathen temples and their idols but by the Edict of Theodosius (A.D. 392) pagan shrines were to be dedicated as Christian churches. Later, an Edict of Honorius (A.D. 408) definitely forbade the demolition of heathen temples.

Constantine's instructions were not fully carried out as Pope Gregory the Great in 601, when sending a letter to Abbot Mellitus, who was then about to visit Britain, commanded that, while idols were to be destroyed, the temples themselves were to be preserved. This causes one to wonder how many of our prehistoric stone monuments were completely destroyed and how many ancient churches still have the remains of some of these stones in their foundations which either can not now be seen or else have not been noted by modern writers. It was obviously not advisable for the church men to mention these pagan relics at times. When one looks at the stonework of an old country church which has undergone recent extensive repairs or alterations, it is not unusual to notice large stones of different colours and geological types. It could be that the builder of the original church saw the large lumps of stone from a prehistoric standing stone that had been destroyed many years before and decided it would be convenient to incorporate them in the stone walls of the church or in some cases the stone walls that enclosed the churchyard.

The 'pointed stone' built into the north porch wall at Corwen Church, Clwyd.

Chris Barber

The surviving examples of single prehistoric standing stones or stone circles on land immediately adjoining a church are to be found on the south or south-east side of the church. To appreciate the original situation, we must put the matter the other way round and say that the Christian fathers built their first old churches to the north or north-west of the ancient stones that they found sticking out of the ground in a lonely landscape. We should bear in mind that at the time of the erection of these churches there was plenty of space available so that we can assume that there must have been a special reason for the churches being placed north or north-west of the prehistoric standing stones. This may have been to negate some force or power that was flowing to these stones from the north or north-west and could include the Polar Force and the different powers that may be identified by dowsers and sensitives at these sites.

It should also be noted that, where there are old preaching crosses which probably pre-date the erection of a church, these carved, comparatively recent stone monuments, are found to the south of the church. Some of these preaching crosses could have been erected on the sites of prehistoric standing stones by the early church leaders after they had destroyed and broken up the original stone, or sometimes the prehistoric stone itself was re-shaped to form a cross of simple or intricate design. These early church leaders probably realised that the isolated upright stones marked something special under the ground and they could have found out that underneath these prehistoric standing stones there were two underground streams of water flowing at different levels and crossing immediately below the upright stones.

The heathen temples mentioned above probably referred to small prehistoric stone circles. According to some dowsers, these stone circles have an underground spring near their centre from which flow a number of subterranean streams. The early church leaders probably knew about this and the special effects caused by and in these stone circles, so they built their early churches over the north-west portion of the circle. In some very old churches, dowsers have detected an underground spring underneath the south end of the altar situated in its usual place at the east end of a church. From this underground spring, in some cases there appears to be a stream flowing under the south side of the aisle towards the west end of the church.

There are probably other examples of single stones near the south or east sides of churches in the old preaching crosses, but most of these have been built up in tiers of stones so that the original megalith would not be recognised.

Preaching Cross, Trellech, Gwent.   *Chris Barber*

It is possible for a person standing inside a prehistoric circle of standing stones and over the underground spring to experience a peculiar change of consciousness. This may, therefore, happen in the south-east corner in one of the oldest churches, which may have been erected on a heathen or pagan site which may originally have been part of a prehistoric stone circle. In this respect, it is interesting to note in the Communion Services of the Church in Wales that the priest washes his hands at the credence, a small table placed in the south-east corner of the church, before he places the bread on the paten and pours out the wine for communion. An impartial investigation of this could reveal important things that have been long forgotten by our present church authorities.

Early Celtic Cross, Kilgwrrg Church, Gwent.   *Chris Barber*

A blocked-up doorway in the north wall of a church is often known as the Devil's Door.   *Chris Barber*

Sometimes these ancient churches have been enlarged or extended so that the original south-east corner has changed in appearance and it is advisable to mark this particular spot by a special feature. This seems to have been done by positioning an important tomb such as that of Jasper Tudor in the Cathedral of St. David's and there also seems to be one of these in the church of St. John at Glastonbury in Somerset.

The most fascinating and interesting example of a connection between the church and our stone monuments can still be seen in the churchyard of Bridell near Pembroke. Here is a 7 feet high stone standing on the south side of the parish church (SN 177421), with prehistoric cup markings on the side of the stone followed by Ogham incisions perhaps made thousands of years afterwards. Then, in the 4th or 5th century, a large Greek cross inside a circle was cut into its south face, probably by the earliest of the Christian leaders.

This Christianised standing stone is on at least two crossing SCEMB lines. The first one goes due north from an unrecorded standing stone about 5 feet high which is used as a gatepost in a lane leading from the main road at Crymych Arms, Llanfyrnach, Pembroke (SN 182387), towards Fron Llwyd and adjoins a low carn called Crug Bach, which means little rock and could refer to this standing stone; through the Bridell stone to the site of a dolmen on the side of a road from Cardigan to Tygwyn and golf links at Cardigan (SN 175482). This dolmen is mentioned in *Archaeologia Cambrensis* (1848), p.311, and Vol. II of *The Scientific Journey Through England and Wales and Scotland* by Thomas Walford (John Booth, London, 1818) under Cardigan, where it is called Llech y gawres, which means the slate stone of cry or shout, or it could originally have been Llech y cawrs, meaning the slate stone of the giants.

The crossing SCEMB line is from Coetan Arthur or Pentre Ifan dolmen at Nevern (SN 099369), which goes north-east through the Bridell Stone to the site of a standing stone which it is believed stood at Crug Cae on the side of the main road near Sarnau at Tresaith, Cardigan (SN 307507).

The early Christian fathers may have known the significance of the prehistoric standing stone at Bridell, the underground streams of water and these SCEMB lines. They had taken over the ancient stone by carving their symbols on its south face and their next move to lessen the stone's influence was to build a church. This they did on its north side and it is interesting to note that, if the original church had the same basic design as the present one, they then built a doorway on the north side of the structure and not the west or south sides as are usually seen in churches today. This anomaly can be seen in the porch on the north side of the church, while there are no signs on the south or west sides.

This may have been an attempt to negate or divert the Polar Force or powers flowing north to south along the SCEMB line into the body of the church. The superstition concerning the northern or Devil's Door of the church is quite common and well authenticated according to Walter Johnson in *Byways in British Archaeology*, p.336, and there was a prevalent belief that the Holy Spirit entered the church by the south door, while the devil departed through the opening opposite which was known as the Devil's Door. The prejudice against burial on the north side of a church can be traced beyond the advent of Christianity. It is one of those clinging faiths and fears which beset the early folk of these islands.

During the last 1,500 years, many of these prehistoric standing stones in churchyards or nearby have been removed and destroyed. However, there are still a few remaining examples in Wales. These include:
  (1) Llanwrthwl, Powys (SN 975637).
  (2) Llanarth, Powys (SN 423577).
  (3) Llanbadarn Fawr, Powys (SN 598810).
  (4) Llandewi Brefi, Powys (SN 664553).
  (5) Llandawke, Dyfed (SN 283112). This is sometimes called the Ogham Stone. See Archaeologia Cambrensis (1867), p.269.

(6)   Llanbedr y Cenin, Gwynedd (SH 585269).
(7)   Llangain, Gwynedd (SH 297289).
(8)   Cilcain, Clwyd (SJ 177652).
(9)   Maentwrog, Clwyd (SH 664406).
(10) Bryngwyn, Powys (SO 187496).

Yspytty Cynfyn, Dyfed.   *Chris Barber*

Evidence of the use of prehistoric stone circles by the early builders of Christian churches is difficult to find on the ground, but there is a good example at the church of Yspytty Cynfyn in the Parish of Llanbadarn Fawr, Powys (SN 752791). Here there are at least four large stones in the churchyard wall, the largest of which is 11 feet high. *Archaeologia Cambrensis*[2] (1980) suggests that the circle was erected about 1807, but the earliest reference in *The Scenery, Antiquities and Biography of South Wales*[3] (1807) mentions large upright stone monuments in the churchyard, with the characters entirely defaced.

The connections between the Church and our prehistoric standing stones have been largely covered up, but a serious and patient investigator can still find some unexplained and interesting features in the dormant stones.

"The earth is not a dead body, but is inhabited by a spirit that is its life and soul. All created things, minerals included, draw their strength from the earth spirit."

Basilus Valentinus

REFERENCES
1. *Byways in British Archaeology* by Walter Johnson (Cambridge, 1912), p.25.
2. *Archaeologia Cambrensis* (1980), pp.138-146.
3. *The Scenery, Antiquities and Biography of South Wales* by B. H. Malkin (1807), Vol. II, p.103.

Chapter 13

DESTRUCTION

"The great tragedy of megalithic civilisation occured when men lost touch with the spirit."

John Mitchell

It is amazing how many Welsh prehistoric stone monuments still remain to be seen in whole or part when one considers that they were erected perhaps more than 5,000 years ago. John G. Williams has an index of over one-thousand-four-hundred existing or destroyed, or possible sites of megaliths, which come into the general classification of standing stones, stone circles, dolmens (or cromlechs/burial barrows) for Wales alone and these represent about ten per cent of the original stone monuments that must have existed. So at a rough estimate there must have been over ten thousand in Wales.

When you look around in rural Wales and see the number of stone circles, standing stones and dolmens and the greater number comparatively of ancient camps, earthworks, carns, mounds and tumuli which were probably set up in most cases around at about the same time, then you can picture busy local communities and an impressive number of people who erected and utilised these mysterious remnants of ancient times.

These stone monuments must have served a very important purpose for the original builders and they would have been carefully protected, but as generation succeeded generation the secrets of their uses were lost. But the ancient stones were still held in veneration and not often damaged or destroyed by the local population. Some of the stones would have been so large and heavy that it would have been too awkward and inconvenient for them to have been moved by the local residents.

It would not have been until the coming of Christianity, when the early Christian fathers treated these ancient stones as the idols of the pagans and caused the first deliberate damage and destruction of these megaliths. They left no records of the ones which were destroyed but one may surmise that some of them were replaced by church sites or wayside Christian crosses, as remains of ancient stones have been found in the older churches and some single standing stones have been cut into the shape of the so-called Latin cross used by the western churches.

During the last century, modern man has lost his respect for these ancient stones and the rapidly increasing urbanisation of the Welsh countryside has partly been the cause of him changing his views. He has no regard for an awkward block of old stone that may spoil the use of a commercial site and with the assistance of powerful mobile machinery he has the means of moving the heaviest of these ancient stones. There have been a few cases in Wales where a farmer wanting a few more square yards of land for crops, or wishing to make it easier to move his tractors and implements in one of his fields, has dug around the base of a prehistoric standing stone and then pushed it over with a tractor or bulldozer before towing it away to be dumped in a nearby hedge.

The first Ancient Monuments Act was passed in 1882 and under this the landowners of property on which there were ancient monuments could ask for state protection of that monument or ask the relevant government department to buy the site. However, the landowners could not be forced to sell their ancient sites to the government and this was highlighted in 1899 when Sir Edmund Antrobus offered to sell Stonehenge and 1,300 acres of farmland around it to the nation for £125,000. This was a ridiculous price in those days and it was not until 1918 that Stonehenge came into the ownership of the British government when it was donated by Sir Cecil Chubb. It should be borne in mind that the majority of Welsh prehistoric sites are in private hands, which means that many of them have no form of protection from damage or destruction if the landowners consider these lumps of rock to be a nuisance.

Very few of the prehistoric monuments listed in this book are scheduled as ancient monuments under the control of the Department of the Environment. There have been many cases where some of those that are scheduled have been damaged or even destroyed with considerable time passing before the matter is brought to the attention of the responsible officials, who probably then realise that it is too late to repair any of the damage.

In Wales, the stone circles are usually not as large as those in England, but there is plenty of evidence to show that they have been damaged or destroyed. The worst example is Meini Gwyn or The White Stones at Castell Garw in the Parish of Llandyssilio East in Dyfed (SN 142266), where Edward Llwyd in *Gibson's Britannia*[2], writing in 1695, reports that Buarth Arthur or Meiniu Gwyr on a mountain near Kil y Maen Llwyd is one of that kind of circular stone monuments our English historians ascribe to the Danes and had fifteen standing stones. Only two stones, about 3 feet and 4 feet high, were seen when John G. Williams visited the site in July 1962, although there appeared to be some prostrate stones in the long grass.

Rocking stones or Logan stones are akin to dolmens with their movable capstones and there have been a number of these in Wales, but only the Pontypridd stone still rocks. One of the best known Logan stones is Maen Sigl or Shaking Stone, which is positioned on the brow of the hill overlooking Whitesands Bay at St. David's in Dyfed (SM 730278). *The Cambrian Directory*[3] (1801) says *"We understand it was thrown off its balance, by order of the farmer to prevent the curious from trampling on his grounds."* It was marked Maen Sigl on the One Inch O.S. map of 1919 but it seems that there are now no remains of this huge stone, which may have been broken up and rolled down the hillside into the sea.

Most of the Welsh dolmens have either been damaged or in many cases completely destroyed and a large number of them have had their capstones toppled to one side and their upright supporting stones removed. In recent years one was completely destroyed in the Parish of Talgarth, Powys. Known as Croes Llechan or Slate Cross (SO 167364), it was on the right-hand side of the main road from Talgarth to Three Cocks and Hay-on-Wye. It was marked as Croes-Llechau on the One Inch O.S. map of 1831, and Rev. T. Rees in *A Topographical and Historical Description of South Wales*[4], writes — *"About 2 miles to the eastward of the town, in a field called Croesllechau, there is a very remarkable cromlech. It is not particularly distinguished by its size but from the circumstance of a hawthorn having sprung up at one end of it, so near as to grow against the covering stone and gradually, by its increasing bulk, to raise it some inches above its original seat."*

There is an illustration of this dolmen in an old school text book about the County of Brecon which was published in about 1900. Sometime between that date and 1950 the dolmen was demolished, as there was no sign of it in position in 1967, although a nearby stone gatepost was noted and photographed. This gateway was moved due to road widening in 1984.

Single prehistoric standing stones are very likely to be moved, broken up and lost. One of these is the standing stone which was 6½ feet high, located on Ffinant Farm in the Parish of Trefeglwys, Powys (SN 975911). It was marked as an erect stone on the One Inch O.S. of 1836, and as Standing Stone on the O.S. scale 1:25,000 of 1961. The old county volume (Montgomery) of Royal Commission of Ancient Monuments, on p.172, says that the field in which it stood is called Cae y Garreg and is south of the main road bridge over a small stream. In 1959 John G. Williams made a search for it and noticed a few large lumps of stone in the stream below the road and according to local information this was part of the standing stone.

Sometimes it is difficult to positively identify a large stone as a genuine prehistoric standing stone. One such case was the 7 feet high, 4 feet wide and 1 foot thick dark grey slaty stone jutting out of a farm wall across the road from the south end of the extensive churchyard in the village of Mathry, Dyfed (SM 880320). The stone was of a different type to that used in the long and high farm walls and stuck out rather prominently. This stone was first noted and photographed by John G. Williams in 1962, but in June 1980 it was found that it had been taken down and a concrete foundation had been laid for a new wall to be built in the farmyard. A young man at the farm said that "the john", which is the local name for a slab stone, had been moved.

This last case shows that, if an ancient stone is not scheduled as an ancient monument or the ancient stone is not shown on the Ordance Survey map as a prehistoric stone circle, dolmen or standing stone, or has not even been recorded by an acknowledged authority as being an ancient and historically interesting monument, then there is nothing one can do to prevent a landowner knocking down and breaking up what he may think is just a large uninteresting stone in his farm wall.

Those sites which are not scheduled under the various Ancient Monuments Acts, and there are hundreds of these in Wales, are at much greater risk. The landowner can knock down, break up and remove these prehistoric stones without any fear of legal action against him.

The worst case of destruction of a stone circle is at the largest one in the world; namely the Avebury Stone Circle in the county of Wiltshire in England (SU 102700). *The Graphical and Historical Illustrator, An Original Miscellany of Literary, Antiquarian and Topographical Information*[1] (1834), mentions that Dr. William Stukeley, in 1743, enumerates 652 stones constituting the entire layout of the temple which covers about 22 acres. Most of the standing stones were demolished before 1820 and there are copies of old prints in some published books showing how the huge stones were heated and split up for use as building materials. Most of the modern writers mention that only twenty-seven standing stones remain on the circumference of the immense stone circle out of what had been well over one-hundred standing stones.

There is also another kind of more sinister damage that may occur at the more isolated sites of prehistoric monuments by the evil persons who practice black magic. This may sound sensation seeking to some readers, but as recently as June 1985, at a large standing stone on a lonely moor in Dyfed, a peculiar arrangement of stones was noted. There were twelve stones around this monolith in a circle of about 10 feet in diameter. The stones varied in size from about 6 inches roughly square and none probably weighed more than 30lbs, but they had obviously recently been placed in their positions on the grass. The evil people who put the stones in the circle may have been trying to utilise for their own selfish purposes the forces and powers that are connected with these ancient monuments, but they could find that these will get out of control and cause their own destruction.

REFERENCES

1. *The Graphical and Historical Illustrator, An Original Miscellany of Literary, Antiquarian and Topographical Information.* Edited by Edward W. Brayley (J. Childe, London, 1834), p.113.

2. *Gibson's Britannia.*

3. *The Cambrian Directory* by John Easton (Salisbury, 1801), p.54.

4. *A Topographical and Historical Description of South Wales* by Rev. T. Rees (Sherwood, Neely and Jones, London, 1815), p.138.

Chapter 14

PRESERVATION

"We do not know the extent of Megalithic man's knowledge of geometry and astronomy. Perhaps we never shall. He was a competent engineer. Witness how he could set out large projects to an accuracy approaching 1 in 1,000 and how he could transport and erect blocks of stone weighing up to 50 tons."

A. Thom, 1971

It is extremely important that much greater efforts should be made to preserve and protect the many prehistoric stone monuments in Wales. We need to prevent their needless destruction and damage by commercial interests that have no regard for our priceless heritage and by mindless vandals who inflict damage without any motive because their intelligence level is so low they are a menace to our modern society.

When we consider the money and effort that has been spent during the last twenty years to preserve and resite the ancient monuments in Egypt due to the building of the Aswan Dam, where the benefits were cancelled out by the loss of fertilising silt in the Nile delta and huge sums had to be spent on artificial fertilisers and compare this with our attempts to maintain an equally important example of ancient construction work by early intelligent man, then the inevitable conclusion is that we are doing far too little. It is probable that more money is spent on books and films about our ancient British monuments than is spent on the maintenance and preservation of the monuments themselves during the last decade.

Coetan Arthur, Dyffryn Ardudwy. Gwynedd   *Chris Barber*

Most of the prehistoric stone monuments that are in public ownership are reasonably well maintained and preserved when one considers that they were all ruined to a large extent when they were taken into public ownership. The main problem to be faced is that they might become too popular with the general public and become overvisited.

This could result in damage to the stones by the deliberate action of vandals or the excessive wear of the approaches, such as footpaths and tracks. This would mean that the authorities would be obliged to put up strong wire fencing with steel posts and restrict the right of access, as has happened at Stonehenge, where a serious visitor problem has developed during the last twenty years.

The majority of the Welsh prehistoric stone monuments are on private land and in these cases, even when the ancient stones are scheduled as ancient monuments, there is little or no effort made to protect and preserve them. It would help if landowners were encouraged to take a greater interest in these valuable assets and persuaded that they can do something useful to prevent their total destruction.

Once modern man begins to realise that the builders of our ancient stone circles, standing stones and dolmens were not ignorant savages but were very skilful engineers and highly intelligent in the use of the natural polar and solar forces, then there will be a greater desire to rediscover such knowledge in the hope that it may be of service in our modern world. The first thing we have to do is to retain all the prehistoric monuments that still exist in Wales and then take steps to stop their deterioration by implementing sensible methods of preservation, which does not include surrounding them with tall iron railings. The rural nature of the surroundings of these monuments should be retained as far as possible and no ploughing, digging or building should be allowed to take place within 10 yards of any ancient monument.

A thorough and careful examination should be made by the officials of Cadw* of all possible stone monuments that may now be considered to be of pre-Christian origin in Wales and a series of photographs taken from different angles which should relate to a detailed description of each monument on specified dates. These photographs should be checked on the sites at regular intervals to see if any damage has been done to the stone monument since the last inspection.

All these monuments should be scheduled under the Ancient Monuments Act and at the same time new and stricter regulations brought into force to prevent any further damage to these sites. Cadw should be given full rights of access and the power to do any work that may be necessary to protect those ancient monuments that are on private land.

There is also a need to maintain a record of all written and photographic works relating to all the Welsh prehistoric stone monuments and details from this record should be made freely available to all genuine researchers into the works of our ancient ancestors. A search should be made for any old descriptions, engravings, drawings or even paintings of these ancient stone monuments for the purpose of comparing these with what can be seen at the sites today. There are hardly any full descriptions that can be helpful that are more than two-hundred years old. They vary so much that one wonders if the different writers were in fact referring to the same ancient stone monument.

This will be particularly apparent when looking at the various descriptions of stone circles, as the old writers more often than not gave a different number of stones in certain stone circles. Unless this source of reliable data is obtained it is useless trying to solve the many mysteries and problems relating to our prehistoric monuments of stone and earth that only partially remain.

The freeholders or long leaseholders of the lands on which these ancient monuments are situated should be given every encouragement to retain and preserve them, either by the government giving annual grants based on some kind of scale relating to the type of monument, its size and other relevant factors, or by allowing income tax deductions or concessions for money spent on any works at these monuments which may be considered reasonable for their protection or for improving access to them. In addition, the owners of these ancient monuments should also be allowed to charge as an expense against their personal income tax, any amounts that they spend on the provision and sale of booklets, leaflets and postcards of the monuments on their land. These would provide the visitor with useful material when visiting these sites.

Income from the sale of such items could be used by the owner as a fund towards maintaining the monuments in their true rural surroundings, so that visitors can form a better idea of the original monument and its local background. There would then be no need for the government to take over these sites and fence them in with iron railings or wooden posts, which always spoil their appearance.

Fortunately it has been found that generally there has been no difficulty in obtaining access to these sites. If a local farmer is around, then he should be courteously approached and permission sought to take photographs. It is important to stress that the usual code of behaviour in the countryside should be observed. Gates should be shut and disturbance of livestock in the field where the ancient monument stands should be avoided. Very often, if a serious interest is expressed to the farmer regarding the ancient stones in his field, then it will normally be appreciated and he may even relate some local stories about the stones which may never have been recorded in any books, but handed down by word of mouth through the ages.

There is no record of any charges being made to photograph any prehistoric standing stone in Wales and this is appreciated by the genuine researchers as being of great help. It is hoped that this situation will continue and that access to these ancient stone monuments will be freely available to all people, but there should be some sensible restrictions which would, for example, prevent a group of holidaymakers crossing a farmer's field of standing corn to visit a prehistoric stone in the middle of the field.

Some restrictions on access to these ancient monuments will be necessary as already there are problems over the use of some of our rural footpaths, bridleways and tracks which can alienate country people. Vehicles of all kinds should be excluded from all the tracks and it may even be necessary to restrict access to some monuments to certain times of the year. Although this would not be popular with some town dwellers, it would be much better than having lines of concrete or tarmac paths leading to these ancient stones.

Consideration should also be given to the inevitable damage caused by visitors to farmland and crops and some kind of adequate compensation for this should be paid to the farmers affected who would then be more than willing to allow people to cross their land.

*Cadw carry out the statutory responsibilities of the Secretary of State for Wales in protecting, conserving and presenting monuments and historic buildings in Wales.

84

Chapter 15

DOWSING

"Every megalithic site is over a centre or channel of the terrestial current whose emanations are detected by the dowser's rod."

John Mitchell

The discovery of underground streams beneath large stones has been known and acknowledged since ancient times. There are two clear references to this in the Bible. Exodus 17.6 reads *"Behold I will stand before thee thereupon the rock in Horeb, and thou shalt smite the rock and there shall come water out of it, that the people may drink. And Moses did so in the sight of the elders of Israel."*

Numbers 20, 7-11 refers to this in more detail. *"And the Lord spake unto Moses, saying. Take the rod and gather thou the assembly together, thou and Aaron thy brother, and speak ye unto the rock before their eyes: and it shall give forth his water, and thou shalt bring forth to them water out of the rock: so thou shalt give the congregation and their beasts drink.*

And Moses took the rod from before the Lord, as he commanded him. And Moses and Aaron gathered the congregation together before the rock, and he said unto them. Hear now ye rebels; must we fetch you water out of this rock?

And Moses lifted up his hand, and with his rod he smote the rock twice and the water came out abundantly, and the congregation drank, and their beasts also."

This is probably the first record of a dowser at work and it should be noted that the rock must have been large as the congregation were gathered together before the rock. Also, the water course must have originally been underground as there was no mention of any water being present until Moses struck the rock, apparently in a particular place.

It is not surprising, therefore, to learn that modern dowsers claim to be able to detect underground streams of water passing immediately below our prehistoric standing stones. The earliest record of dowsing at a Welsh prehistoric standing stone occurs in the works of Alfred Watkins, the Hereford photographer and Secretary of the Woolhope Field Club. In 1930 he visited The Four Stones at Walton, near Presteigne, Powys (SO 246608), with a local water diviner who went blue in the face whilst dowsing at these stones and claimed there were two underground streams at different levels crossing below the four stones.

During recent years other dowsers have had similar results and it is now believed by some that there are always two underground streams crossing at different levels below all single prehistoric standing stones. These underground streams are usually believed to be 20 or more feet below the surface of the ground where the stone is standing and this means that it is not possible to prove these claims of the dowsers, for no landowner is likely to permit anyone to drill or dig holes of more than 20 feet deep by a standing stone. The result is that many people will reject the findings of the dowsers, who normally show no wish to prove what they have detected to non-believers who are prejudiced in their thinking.

If the dowsers are correct in only some cases of undeground streams passing directly under these ancient upright stones, then it raises a number of questions of great importance which modern man finds hard to grasp. Were these large prehistoric stones placed in position where there were crossing streams of underground water or were the underground streams, in fact, diverted to cross beneath the stones?

This of course raises many other questions concerning the reasons for such a complex system, its uses, and by no means least, the kind of users that lived in this land when these ancient stones were erected. Here is a new field for the proposers of fanciful theories which one day they will exploit!

Dowsers find that the underground streams do not seem to pass underneath the individual stones in a stone circle, but there do seem to be some streams which start inside a stone circle and below ground and pass out in between some of the individual stones on the diameter of the stone circle. When dowsers operate at dolmens they sometimes find that above the two crossing underground streams there is another underground stream which flows in a southerly direction.

Sensitive persons like dowsers sometimes detect different kinds of vibrations or powers at these sites if they are in their original positions. These are difficult to define but it is thought that there are seven different kinds of power bands of which three operate below ground level and the other four can be ascertained by some people on the sides of these stones above the ground. It seems that the first five power or wavebands can be experienced on all prehistoric standing stones but the top two bands, numbers six and seven, can only be felt on the taller standing stones, which are over 5 feet high. This is a new field of study which has shown some interesting and promising results.

John G. Williams dowsing the 5th Waveband.   *Chris Barber*

The fifth waveband up from the bottom of the stone, which has been called spiral power, is the easiest one for an open-minded person to experience. Unfortunately many people through modern scientific teaching believe that these things are not possible and they make up their minds not to experience any reaction when it is explained to them how it is possible to contact this curious natural power. This is done by placing the palms of both hands on the face of the prehistoric standing stone at about 5 feet above ground level on the north or east sides of the stone during the hours of daylight. If the hands are placed firmly against the stone, after a short while a responsive person will experience a peculiar sensation of being pushed away from one side of the stone. But if either palm is taken away from the face of the stone, then this sensation ceases immediately.

This strange spiral power pushes a person away from the standing stone either to the right or the left. If it pushes him away to the right and he then crosses over his hands and puts his palms flat on the face of the stone so that his hands swop positions, then

John G. Williams detecting the 7th wave band at Great Oak Standing Stone, Powys. Chris Barber

the spiral will act in a reverse direction and push him away to the left. This is something like reversing an electrical circuit and indicates that the movement of the person away from the face of the upright stone is caused by some kind of power and is not the result of the person's imagination.

It has been found that this spiral power waxes and wanes in a twenty-eight day cycle so there are times when the spiral power is less effective than at others. At the end of the cycle the power is reversed so that it moves a person to the right on one day then 28 days later it will move the same person to the left. Some people who experience this spiral power feel afraid of the unknown and just want to forget about it. Others, because of the variable factors mentioned above, think that they have been misled in some way because they may not be able to repeat the experience when the power potential has become low when approaching a change-over time.

A few dowsers can detect seven different power bands at these prehistoric standing stones but it seems that the top two power bands, numbered for convenience six and seven, are only found on the taller stones that are over 5 feet high. The seventh waveband seems to have some connection with ultra-violet light and can be contacted by some people when they touch the top of one of these taller stones with the finger tips of both hands. This may cause a violent muscular contraction and may therefore be dangerous to people who suffer from heart disease.

It is thought that these seven different waveband powers correspond to the lowest divisions of what has been named The Sacred and Secret Pi design. This was known to the 17th century Welsh mystical poet Henry Vaughan and in *Silex Scintillions*, which was published in 1650, there is a poem called "The Stone", in which he has written the following strange lines:—

> "But I (Alas)
>
> *Was shown one day in a strange glass*
> *That busie commerce kept between*
> *God and his Creatures, though unseen*
> *They hear, see, speak*
> *And into loud discoveries break*
> *As loud as blood.*

87

Chapter 16

QUARTZ

"The structure of quartz possibly converts earth currents. If quartz is linked to underground water-courses, a conversion from hydrostatic pressure into static electricity may occur."

Randall N. Baer and Vicki V. Baer

The ancient stone monuments of pre-Christian times in Wales can be found in all kinds of shapes, sizes and colours, but they cannot be classified into specific types. These ancient stones of a seemingly endless variety have had their shape affected by age and weathering, which frustrates any attempts at finding common features which could be useful starting points for lines of serious research. However, the only common point relating to these stones is that they all seem to contain granules of quartz. Not all stones found in our rural landscape contain quartz, so one may infer that quartz was one of the necessary elements required in the mysterious stones chosen by the ancient erectors.

Lumps of quartz in one of Harold's Stones, Gwent.
Chris Barber

Quartz can be found in these stones either in small sparkling crystals or in larger groupings of crystals, which sometimes appear as noticeable white veins running through the rock hewn out to form the larger ancient monoliths.

It is therefore necessary to make a careful examination of the chemical components of quartz and their joint distinctive and peculiar physical characteristics which prove to be most unusual. In modern times, there is an increasing use of quartz crystals and silicon chips in the expanding computer industry and projects relating to space research. This new attention given to the priorities of quartz opens up all kinds of possibilities which would astonish archaeologists of the old school.

Quartz is a clear crystal which is usually colourless and is made up in a chemical form of one atom of the element silicon and two atoms of oxygen. It is given the chemical abbreviation Si.0.2. The atoms forming any kind of recognised crystalline mineral are always arranged in certain patterns and these determine the structure and symmetry of the crystal. There are six main crystal systems and quartz belongs to the one called Hexagonal because the crystals have four different axis, of which three are equal and horizontal and make angles of 120° with each other while the fourth and vertical axis is at right-angles to the plane of the horizontal axis and is of a different length to the other three axis.

The hexagonal prisms of quartz in its natural state are terminated by hexagonal pyramids. The solid corners are often truncated by tetrahedral faces placed either to the right or left as the crystal is properly orientated, giving rise to the right and left-handed varieties respectively. In some forms, the prism faces are suppressed and crystals consist of a double hexagonal pyramid. These quartz crystals are found in a positive and negative formation which is unlike the formation of any natural crystal. There may be some connection here between this peculiarity and the Spiral Power of the Fifth Wave Band felt or experienced at prehistoric standing stones by some dowsers, when their bodies are moved either to the right or the left when they are holding the palms of both hands of the vertical surface of the upright stone about 5 feet above ground level (see page 86).

In 1880, the famous French scientists Pierre and Jaques Curie, who discovered radium, were measuring the conductivity of quartz and they observed that pressure on the testplates on which they were working produced a measurement on a sensitive electrometer. They had discovered what is now known as the piezoelectric effect. This shows that mechanical pressure on a crystal will produce a measurable voltage and conversely an electrical voltage applied to a crystal will produce mechanical movement. It was found that, when alternating electrical current is passed through a crystal plate, the charges oscillate back and forth at the resonant frequency of the crystal. This now forms the basis for the crystal oscillator components used in electronics which has recently led on to the silicon revolution of the computer age, which is now progressing so fast that the average person is often amazed at the results that can be obtained from the most up-to-date computers and robots.

Some time before 1980, two dowsers made a small collection of quartz-bearing stones which included some of the peculiar blue stones from the Preseli Hills in Dyfed (from whence the famous Blue Stone megaliths were quarried and transported over two-hundred miles to be erected in the stone circle at Stonehenge in Wiltshire). They used these pieces of quartz-bearing rock for the purpose of some experiments which involved advanced dowsing techniques. Their results indicated that some kind of power was being radiated from the pieces of stone containing quartz crystals, in narrow rays which seemed to be travelling outwards in straight lines from the sides of the stones at various angles. These rays of power seemed to vary at different times and, if a stone was either moved around on the place where it stood or was moved to another place, the power rays seemed to change and could not then be detected by the methods used by the two dowsers.

They found these variations frustrating, for no reliable results could be obtained from which any kind of sensible conclusions could be drawn. However, one surprising result was obtained which did seem to be constant. When a small piece of amber was held about 6 inches away from the quartz crystals in the stone, on the line where they had detected one of the narrow power rays being emitted from the stone, it seemed to deflect this power ray in a completely different direction.

In due course they began to realise that the presence of these quartz-bearing stones in the house and their strange experiments were adversely affecting the health of one of the dowsers. So they decided to discontinue the experiments and removed the stones from the house. The health of the affected dowser improved after this had been done. They had been experimenting with dangerous unknown powers and readers who might try their own lines of research are warned of these potential dangers, for a great deal more should be known about the peculiar properties of quartz before they consider embarking on any similar experiments.

Experiments were begun in 1988 by the authors of this book involving the use of small transistor radios in the close vicinity of prehistoric standing stones. The hand-held radios were tuned into a radio station on the medium wave and slowly carried around the standing stone. Although the stones chosen for the experiment were a considerable distance from any houses, machinery, motor cars and electric pylons, it was found that in each case there were a few limited areas of less than a foot across where the radio set was subject to some kind of radio interference. These interesting results have been obtained at a number of prehistoric standing stones in Wales and it is thought that the radio interference is probably caused by a power ray emitted from the quartz embedded in the ancient stones.

Initial results from this new line of research indicate what a great deal more needs to be done in this field which will open up all kinds of exciting possibilities. It is hoped that others may try these simple experiments and that there will be co-ordination to gather information so that a proper evaluation of this form of radio interference can be made.

The importance of the presence of quartz in connection with our ancient stone monuments to their builders thousands of years ago is shown in the archaeological records of the finding of considerable amounts of quartz-bearing stones or chippings inside some of the prehistoric dolmens or burial barrows of Wales. At one of the best-known Welsh sites, namely Bryn Celli Ddu dolmen at Llanddaniel Fab in Anglesey (SH 508702), it is mentioned in *Royal Commission of Ancient Monuments, Anglesey*[1] that when the chamber was excavated thoroughly in 1928 the outer chamber, which was filled by the original blocking of earth and stones, was found to have a barrier of water-worn and deliberately broken pebbles of white quartz, such as were found all over the site.

By 1935, the excavators of these ancient sites had become more meticulous and did not throw out pieces of stone containing quartz because, when Ty Newydd dolmen at Llanfaelog, Anglesey (SH 344739) was excavated, the pieces of quartz found there were carefully collected and counted. The *Royal Commission of Ancient Monuments, Anglesey*[2] reports that over the entire floor of the dolmen there was a deposit of black earth containing much charcoal about 2 inches thick, and scattered in this layer were one-hundred-and-ten pieces of broken white quartz. No explanation for the presence of so many pieces of white quartz (which can be assumed were purposely placed there either by the original builders of this huge ancient monument or its subsequent users) has been given.

There are still quite a number of dolmens in Wales that have not been properly excavated. When any work of this nature is done at one of these dolmens, particular attention should be paid to the presence and position of any pieces of quartz-bearing stone and these should be carefully examined by an expert. Such stones may have been the equivalent of our silicon chips to the ancient builders, whose techniques of moving huge stones showed that they had much more intelligence than is usually attributed to the ancient Britons.

In recent years, some researchers in California have shown considerable interest in the use of crystals and quartz in particular. A recent book, *Windows of Light, Quartz Crystals and Self-Transformation*[3], gives much interesting and useful information about quartz and deals with its uses for healing purposes. Reading this book makes one wonder about the large amounts of white quartz which may have originally been in all Welsh dolmens and it opens up new and intriguing areas of research into the knowledge of our remote ancestors which could prove beneficial to modern man.

"A sharp blow to a quartz crystal under pressure can cause thousands of volts of electricity to be discharged from it."

David D. Zink

REFERENCES
1. *Royal Commission of Ancient Monuments, Anglesey*, p.44.
2. *Royal Commission of Ancient Monuments, Anglesey*, p.65.
3. *Windows of Light, Quartz and Self-Transformation* by Randall N. Baer and Vicki V. Baer (Harper and Row, San Francisco, U.S.A., 1984).

Chapter 17

STRANGE LIGHTS AND OBJECTS

"Fogging on photographs has been allied to the quartz composition of many standing stones or to the current transmitted by them."

Paul Screeton

Our prehistoric stone monuments are regarded by many people as large lumps of sterile and useless stone which are merely blots on the rural landscape. There are hardly any notable paintings of these Welsh monuments before 1900 and some of the pencil or charcoal drawings of them have been found to be unreliable representations. So unfortunately there is no real basis for comparing the results of some recent photographs which show strange patches of light or unexplained objects in the sky. The few available photographs of these monuments taken before 1900 involved long-time exposures and the printed results generally lack detail. Since 1900 photography has greatly improved and some pictures showing strange light effects have been obtained. Unfortunately these have often been discarded and destroyed by the photographers who dismissed them as dud results. It should be realised that the camera, operating at very fast speeds and having a greater range of vision than the average human being, is capable of recording something that is not visible to the naked eye.

A second look should be given to the local legends which feature movement of these prehistoric stones or odd things happening in their vicinity. Usually they are treated as humorous, but silly folklore, but it is possible that these tales may help to provide an explanation for the increasing number of photographs taken which show things that the photographer did not observe when he took the picture. On seeing the results, the immediate reaction is that there is a fault with the camera or the film.

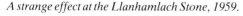

A strange effect at the Llanhamlach Stone, 1959.   *Justin Delair*

The first definite indication that there may be something physical at these sites was recorded on a sunny afternoon in October 1959 when Justin Delair and John G. Williams were taking photographs of a standing stone in a roadside hedge opposite Peterstone

91

Court, in the Parish of Llanhamlach, near Brecon, Powys (SO 089267). This was traditionally the spot from which St. Peter once preached when travelling this way. The stone is of a greyish colour and 4 feet 6 inches high and about 2 feet wide. Both men took photographs with different cameras at about the same time and nothing unusual was noted.

When Justin Delair's photographs were developed and printed in monochrome, one of them was most peculiar. It showed a white blur between the stone and John G. Williams, who was standing about 3 feet away. The blur of light extended from the bottom to the top of the stone, where it tapered slightly and this was seen against the background of the nearby hedge. This result would have been dismissed as a freak, because there was no sensible explanation for the white blur apart from camera or film fault, had it not been for two colour photographs taken at the same time by John G. Williams with a 35mm camera. They both showed a dark purple-blue around the base of the stone which faded away towards its top.

It was reasonable to suppose that whatever had caused the strange result on the monochrome photograph of Justin Delair had also showed up as a dark purple-blue colour on the two colour transparencies taken at the same time by John G. Williams. In such situations the photographic experts usually blame a bad film or camera leaking light for something that they cannot explain. It is thought that the films, in both cameras, were registering a concentration of ultra-violet light which would not be visible to the human eye in the outdoor surroundings without wearing special glasses. Unfortunately the negative of Justin Delair's photograph was lost when he moved house. One of the colour slides was sent to The Ministry of Defence for an opinion and was mislaid. The other one was sent to an architect in London and was stolen when his office was burgled.

This incident at Llanhamlach opened up a new line of research and many more photographs of prehistoric stone monuments were taken in the hope that the certain conditions, that seemed to be necessary to obtain similar kinds of photographs, could be ascertained. Interesting results were slow in coming, but a few unusual photographs were obtained in England and Wales over the following years to reward the patience of the photographers. In Wales, the best photographs to show ultra-violet light at prehistoric standing stones were at the following sites.

(1) Coetan Arthur Dolmen at Newport, Dyfed (SN 061395) on 8th July 1962.

(2) Lligwy Dolmen in the Parish of Penrhos Lligwy, Anglesey (SH 501861) in May 1965.

(3) An unrecorded standing stone named Warrior Stone in the Preseli Hills in the Parish of Meline, Dyfed (SN 138330) in July 1977.

(4) Maen Hir called St. Arfan's Stone at Llanfon Fawr in Powys (SN 975552) in June 1966.

(5) Arthur's Stone, the noted dolmen on Cefn Bryn at Reynoldston, West Glamorgan (SS 491905), in March 1984.

A systematic search was made in all books which showed prehistoric standing stone photographs to see if any featured signs of unusual light patches which may have been caused by a concentration of ultra-violet light. Only two examples were found, but these are significant as strong independent evidence to support the view that at certain times there are strange lights in the vicinity of these ancient monuments.

The first was in a rare booked called *Portfolios of Photographs of the Cromlechs of Anglesey and Caernarvonshire*[1] (1900), which has an excellent collection of photographs of dolmens or cromlechs and some standing stones, but there is a lack of detail of the whereabouts of some of these. The pages and photographs are not numbered and on the one photograph entitled *Coetan Arthur Cromlech (W. View) near Caernarvon*, which is in the Parish of Llanfair-Is-Gaer, Gwynedd (SH 515660), there is a clear patch of light at the bottom right of the huge capstone which cannot be explained as sunlight judging from the position of the shadows in other parts of this photograph. It is of interest that this illustration indicates that the phenomena of concentrated ultra-violet light was occuring before 1900.

Coetan Arthur, Gwynedd, showing patch of light at the bottom right of the huge capstone.

J. E. Griffith (1900)

Another example of a published photograph showing a strange light at a prehistoric stone dolmen is in *Prehistoric Heritage*[2] and there is something very strange about this one. On p.156, photograph No. 107 is captioned "The Kemp Stones near Dundonald in Northern Ireland" and shows the Kemp Stones dolmen at Dundonald in County Down (J 445736) with a distinct white patch of light on the top part of the capstone, which was probably caused by a concentration of ultra-violet light. This book was originally published as *Zeugen der Vorneit* and was copyright 1976 by Econ Verlag GmbH, Dusseldorf and Vienna. When it was published by Charles Scribner's Sons in New York, in 1979, the photograph No. 107 had been altered and did not show the white patch on the capstone of the dolmen. Enquiries were made about this in 1982 after the American edition was purchased, but no reply was received.

The most astounding appearance of a strange light and object happened in July 1977, when BBC Wales were filming for a Welsh Children's programme at The Great Oak Standing Stone, Crickhowell, Powys (SO 223185). Richard Williams, then aged fifteen years, first demonstrated the effects of the spiral power by placing the palms of both of his hands on the vertical side of the standing stone and was filmed being pushed to one side. John G. Williams then showed the effects of the power of the seventh wave band by placing the finger tips of both of his hands on the top of the stone, which is about 6½ feet high and was violently thrown backwards. This was only done once for medical reasons and was filmed at a fast speed.

In due course the film was screened by BBC Wales in a series called Ty Bedd and at least five viewers reported seeing an object rapidly coming out of a cloud in the background. At Llandaff studios, BBC Wales ran the film at a slow speed and magnified it on a large screen with the result that a small yellowish-white oval object could be observed coming out of a cloud immediately above the stone. It was some distance away and flashed across a patch of blue sky to disappear into clouds just above the horizon. It was filmed at 24 frames a second (which is very fast), according to a letter later received from the producer, Brynmor Williams. Somebody at Llandaff did some calculations on the speed of the object and estimated it to be travelling at an amazing 16,000 miles an hour.

Although the object appeared small on the film, it probably came out of a cloud which was in front of a mountain less than 3 miles away to the south so the object could have been at least 10 feet long. If it had continued its rapid descent along the same line as shown in the film, then it should have hit the ground within a few miles of the Great Oak standing stone and made a very noticeable large hole. Nothing unusual like this was reported in the Crickhowell area at about that time and most people find it convenient to forget the incident. However, it is significant that some recent photographs of prehistoric stone monuments taken at fast camera speeds have also shown small spots in clear skies which may not be conventional aircraft or faulty development and printing of the film.

There have been a few coloured photographs taken which show a red or orange kind of halo around the top part of a standing stone. They seem to fade on the photograph after a while and this tends to make the photographer wonder if he really did see that strange colour when he looks at the picture a year later. One of these was taken at the 12 feet high standing stone on Llwyn y fedwen farm at Cwmdu, near Crickhowell, Powys (SO 157204). It was at this stone, on 7th November 1975, that Professor John Taylor and Francis Hitching did some filming for *Earth Magic* and used a magnometer up and down the face of the stone to show different readings.

On 21st March 1984, Richard Roberts, of Sketty, Swansea, a well-known amateur astronomer and researcher of Arthur's Stone, Reynoldston, West Glamorgan (SS 491905), took some colour photographs with his 35mm camera and found that they showed shafts of white light in parallel extending from the grey sky background to the south end of Arthur's Stone. These were the most puzzling pictures that he had taken in over thirty years investigations at this noted prehistoric monument.

None of these photographs are suitable for reproduction in book form, for they would need to be touched up to show the relevant detail and this would automatically invite accusations of fraud. However, they are all contained in a collection of over three-thousand photographs of prehistoric stone monuments in the British Isles in the possession of John G. Williams, which have been numbered and referred to in an Index of over 4,200 of these monuments in England, Wales, Scotland and Ireland, under counties and parishes, with Ordnance Survey references.

The keen reader should try taking photographs of these ancient monuments at camera speeds of 1/250th of a second or faster under clear bright skies and then look carefully at the results to see if anything unusual is shown in the sky on the photographs.

"Desmond Leslie has written of visiting Stonehenge in 1954, and on all of the photographs he took a column of light like a searchlight can be seen rising into the cloudswept February sky from the very centre of the Trilithon."

Paul Screeton

REFERENCES

1. *Portfolio of Photographs of the Cromlechs of Anglesey and Caernarvonshire* by John E. Griffith F.LS, of Bangor, North Wales (Bemrose and Sons Ltd., of Derby and London, 1900).

2. *Prehistoric Heritage* by Felix R. Paturi, translated by Tania and Bernard Alexander (Macdonald and Janes of London, 1979).

3. *Earth Magic* by Francis Hitching (Cassell & Co. Ltd., 1976).

Clynog Dolmen, Gwynedd, showing a remarkable streak of unexplained light near the base of the dolmen.   *Chris Barber*

Interior picture of Clynog Dolmen taken on the same occasion and also showing a strange blur of light.   *Chris Barber*

This amazing picture shows John G. Williams dowsing the 7th Waveband and it was taken at the exact moment that his fingers touched the top of the stone. The negatives on either side of this frame on the FP4 film were completely normal. Without a doubt this is proof that the camera can record strange effects that are not visible to the human eye.

Chris Barber

Chapter 18

THE FUTURE

"If the doors of Perception were cleansed every thing would appear to man as it is, infinite. For man has closed himself up, till he sees all things thro' narrow chinks of his cavern."

William Blake

Before considering the future of the Welsh prehistoric monuments, it is necessary to briefly assess the present position in relation to the numerous theories for their purpose that have been put forward during the last four-hundred-years, a period of time which is less than one-tenth of their existence in their present positions.

The earliest mentions of the British megalithic monuments attributed their erection of the Danes of the 9th century and Walter Charlton, writing in *Chorea Gigantum* in 1643, considered that Stonehenge was the ancient coronation place of the Danish kings. Later the Romans were given credit for the erection of these monuments and in the early part of the last century the romantic school of Druidic thought emerged. This referred to Temples of the Sun, Sacrificial Stone Slabs and Stones of Prophecy and was very popular until doubts were cast on the sources of the so-called Druidic lore. When this period faded, it was replaced by the scientific view which claimed that our ancient stone monuments were erected by the earliest ignorant people to inhabit Wales and gives the impression of people laboriously chipping away at huge stones to construct large burial chambers for their dead, or erecting tall stones to mark the burial spots of their chiefs.

None of these views should be considered today, as many of the stubborn facts remain in the landscape without any proper explanation. There are huge masses of stone of 20 tons or more placed carefully in position that would test the skill of our best engineers

Meini Hirion, Gwynedd. *Chris Barber*

and builders. Also, there are the SCEMB alignments of three or more ancient sites stretching over the landscape for 10 miles or more; in many cases with a precision equal to that of the surveyors in our highly competent Ordnance Survey department. These things must be accepted in the future before there is any hope of moving on to find the answers to the many puzzles posed by these silent masses of stone which have been erected in such orderly alignments.

During the last ten years, there has been more popular literature published about prehistoric stone monuments than during the previous thirty years and still new books on this subject continue to appear on the shelves of our best book shops. This is an indication of the growing public interest in these ancient mysterious monuments and this is likely to increase in future years. During the past few centuries, the views of the experts on our ancient history have been accepted without question, but today many people realise that often there are considerable differences of opinion about our prehistoric stone monuments in particular and they need to examine the available evidence and draw their own conclusions.

When one looks around for hard and uncontestable facts about our megaliths, it is easy to see that there is a substantial amount of relevant information that is lacking. For instance, one thing that is conveniently overlooked is that there is no firm evidence to show the places of habitation used by the builders of these large and very heavy stone monuments. One could expect that the ancient people who skilfully handled masses of stone weighing 20 tons or more would have no difficulty in erecting a large stone dwelling for at least one of their leaders, but it seems that such buildings were never constructed.

This means that quarrying, working, moving and placing these huge stones in their specially selected positions was extremely important for the inhabitants of Wales over 5,000 years ago. The reasons for this may not have been religious ones, as our knowledge of the ancient religions at the time of the erection of these prehistoric standing stones is based on pure speculation. For example, the versions of the Celtic and Druidic religions portrayed by Iolo Morganwg, the noted Archdruid and other similar writings are very dubious. It is necessary, therefore, to consider the possibility that these ancient stones served some kind of practical purpose which in present times is unknown.

Future researchers must make greater efforts to investigate all possible kinds of uses for these ancient stones and this can only be done by a careful and thorough examination of all the available data, regardless of the fact that some details will come from sources which are not regarded as orthodox by most present-day archaeologists. This data is at the moment very scattered throughout the literature of the last two or three centuries and it will sometimes be found that quite a number of the large prehistoric stone monuments have little or no mention in the accepted works of reference or books dealing with the pre-Roman sites in Wales. One of the reasons for compiling this book is to make available to a larger public the knowledge of the exact position of those generally recognised prehistoric stone monuments.

This collection of data should be stored in a central non-government office and information from it via computers should be made available to any genuine person on the payment of a scale fee which could be used to finance the enterprise. A collection of photographs of British prehistoric standing stones should also be made by the data centre and new ones should be continually added to the collection. Where possible, full notes about the photographs, giving dates, weather, distance, position, camera aperture and speeds, should be supplied. Special equipment should be used to compare similar photographs taken approximately from the same position but at different times, with different cameras and by different photographers, to see if there has been any material change in the ancient stones over a period of time.

The advisability of doing the above can be easily noted when one looks at a good modern colour photograph of one of our more popular ancient stone monuments and then compares it with a monochrome photograph in a printed book. Then compare both with a drawing of that monument made in the last century. You are likely to wonder if you are really looking at the same ancient stone monument.

Standing stone near Llanfechell, Gwynedd, where a pylon carrying lines stretching from Wylfa Nuclear Power Station makes an interesting contrast in time and perhaps the transmission of energy.
Chris Barber

Geologists and chemists should examine all these ancient sites and report on their geological composition and give their opinions on where the particular stones were quarried before erection by early man. It is known that some of these megaliths have been moved a considerable distance from where they were quarried. The Blue Stones of Stonehenge, Wiltshire, which originated in the Preseli Mountains, Dyfed, is not an isolated case.

Anomalies have been found in the vicinity of some of these sites in the reception of the vibratory bands of heat, light and sound which are usually dismissed as being merely a coincidence. No serious research has ever been done in this matter, partly due to financial reasons of setting up and constantly maintaining a lot of complicated and sensitive equipment over a long period of time. If only a fraction of the vast amounts now paid to astronomers to look for signs of life in outer space was spent on trying to find a solution to some of the mysteries relating to these ancient stones, then it is likely that the rewards would more than repay the money spent.

We must always remember that the immense and mighty natural forces of the universe were not created by man but by God and it is only now that we are in the space age that we begin to realise how far-reaching are the potentials of the countless different vibrations that come within the scope of what we logically call light, heat and sound because they cause reactions to our senses of seeing, touching and hearing.

Henry Vaughan the Silurist, in *Silex Scintillians,* published in London in 1650 in his poem *The Stone,* wrote:

> *"They hear, see, speak*
> *And into loud discoveries break*
> *as loud as blood."*

If this was a reference to a prehistoric standing stone, then he may have known some of the secrets that elude us today. A new approach needs to be made towards all our ancient stone monuments dating back from Christian times and all the old ideas and theories should be questioned and tested, for some of them will be found to be very flimsy and lacking any firm foundation. The genuine seeker of truth can then go into new fields of research where there are likely to be ample and fascinating rewards. These will give a much better kind of understanding of the way of life of the ancient builders and provide many useful lessons for our present generation and bring changes for the benefit of the whole of mankind.

"To listen more closely to the ancient stones. They can stir up in us a healthy sense of wonder at our past, a sense of perspective on our present, and a sense of hope for our future."

David D. Zink

Bodafon Dolmen, Gwynedd

GAZETTEER

This gazetteer of the Welsh prehistoric stone monuments is set out under the present Welsh seven counties which were reformed in 1974 from the old thirteen counties, followed by the name of the parish or community and then the name of the monument and a short description of the locality. This is followed by the Ordnance Survey reference number, which consists of two letters and either six or eight figures. The Ordnance Survey maps of recent years of scale one inch or 1:50,000 provide a diagram showing 100Km squares and the letters used to designate them. For North Wales the letters are SH and SJ, and for South Wales they are SM, SN and SO with small parts in the squares SS and ST.

The first three or four numbers when eight are used are taken from the top of the map, reading left to right and indicate that the site of the monument is exactly below this number. The last three or four numbers when eight are used are taken from either the right or left side of the map, reading downwards and indicate the site of the monument is exactly opposite this number. When the two sets of numbers are co-ordinated, then the exact position of the monument can be found on the map.

Most of the prehistoric sites listed in the Gazetteer are shown in words printed in Gothic letters on the Ordnance Survey maps. But not all the sites listed are marked on certain editions of the maps.

The earliest editions of the Ordnance Survey maps dating from the early part of the last century show more prehistoric sites than those covering the same areas of recent date and sometimes it will be found that a few of the prehistoric monuments marked on these early maps have disappeared and there is not even a written record of their existence.

After the Ordnance Survey reference number there is occasionally in the entry the letters A.C., which refers to *Archaeologia Cambrensis,* the acknowledged authorative Welsh archaeological journal, with the date of issue and page number which mentions that particular site. In addition, there are references to other books which are of importance, particularly if they are of an early date (i.e. prior to 1850).

R.C.A.M. is the abbreviation for volumes of the *Royal Commission of Ancient Monuments.* All other important references are given in full.

There are many other prehistoric stone monuments which are not recognised as such by some archaeologists, so any monuments of a dubious nature have been omitted from this gazetteer, although the authors may have some records of these sites.

As an abbreviation for John Godfrey Williams, whose name frequently occurs, the letters J.G.W. have been used.

Upper Cromlech,
Cors-y-Gedol, Gwynedd.

CLWYD

1. CEFN
   Cist near Ysgubor Newydd House (SJ 0072 7246). A.C. (1869), p.197.

2. CERRIG Y DRUIDION
   Stone circle near Alwen Waterworks, by road leading to Denbigh (SJ 9438 5338). A.C. (1855), p.268. The site is now covered by the Alwen Reservoir.

3. CHIRK
   Standing stone in a field called Cae Carreg Lwyd (SJ 270405). This stone is 5 feet high and is mentioned in *Clwyd Archaeological Record* Ref. 01138.

Penbedw Park Stone Circle.   *Chris Barber*

4. CILCAIN
   Stone circle in Penbedw Park, near railway and main road at Tardd-y-dwr (SJ 1712 6793). A circle of five stones of millstone grit conglomerate, which are between 3 and 5 feet high and situated in an oak copse.

5. CYFFYLLIOG
   The Queen's Chair on Cadair y Frenhines. It is a stone resembling an armchair and was removed during the last century from Llys y Frenhines (The Queen's Court) (SJ 065552). A.C. (1854), p.240. The stone was erected in Pool Park, Ruthin, by Lord Bagot in 1804.

6. GWYDDELWERN
   Maen Gwynhidw is a dolmen situated near the church (SJ 080472). Edward Llwyd, in *Papochalia* (1695-8), ii.50, provides a sketch of this dolmen which has been destroyed.

8. LLANDRILLO
    Stone circle on the slopes of Cadair Bronwen near carns (SJ 056372). It is marked
    as 𝕾𝖙𝖔𝖓𝖊 𝕮𝖎𝖗𝖈𝖑𝖊 on the Ordnance Survey map. *Parochialia,* by Edward Llwyd (1698),
    Part II, p.87, has sketch plan and there is a good photograph of the site in *Sun,
    Moon and Standing Stones* by John Edwin Wood (Oxford, 1978), p/t.10. *The Royal
    Commission on Ancient Monuments* No. 225 gives the diameter of the circle as 39
    feet with forty-one stones.

9. LLANGOLLEN RURAL
    Carreg-y-Big, a 9 feet high standing stone near Llety Ifan and Ffynnon Arthur,
    close to a road junction (SJ 224397). R.C.A.M. No. 415 of Denbigh.

10. LLANRHAIDR-YM-MOCHNANT
    A maenhir in a field called Erw-y-Garreg belonging to Maes Mochnant Isaf
    (SJ 13692482). Marked as 𝕾𝖙𝖆𝖓𝖉𝖎𝖓𝖌 𝕾𝖙𝖔𝖓𝖊 on recent Ordnance Survey maps. A.C.
    (1855), p.267, and (1894), p.153, refers to a fine maenhir 12 feet high called Post
    y Wiber (Post of the Dragon). There are legends relating to it being used for
    ridding the county of dragons. The local people are said to have draped it with a
    scarlet cloth to allure and excite the flying serpent. R.C.A.M. No. 487 of Denbigh.

11. LLANRHAIDR-YM-CINMERCH
    Maen Cleddau or "The Stone of the Sword" near Hen Ddinbych and Hafoty Wen
    (SH 993564). A.C. (1878), p.107.

Capel Garmon Cromlech, Clwyd.   *Chris Barber*

12. LLANRWST RURAL
    Capel Garmon Cromlech near Capel Garmon Church (SH 818544). Marked as
    𝕭𝖚𝖗𝖎𝖆𝖑 𝕮𝖍𝖆𝖒𝖇𝖊𝖗 on Ordnance Survey maps before 1960. A.C. (1856), p.91; (1888),
    p.60; (1871), p.97; (1927), pp.1-43. It has a huge capstone and the western end
    was used as a stable in the 18th century.

13. LLANRWST RURAL
    Maen Pebyll, the remains of standing stones at Nebo (SH 844566). Marked as 𝕸𝖆𝖊𝖓
    𝕻𝖊𝖇𝖞𝖑𝖑 on Ordnance Survey maps. A.C. (1856), p.93; (1909), p246; (1923), p.143.
    R.C.A.M. No. 507 of Denbigh.

Hendre Waelod Cromlech, Clwyd. *Chris Barber*

14. LLANSANTFFRAID-GLAN-CONWY
Hendre Waelod Cromlech, near the banks of the River Conway, below Bryniau (SH 793748). It is marked as **Cromlech** on early Ordnance Survey maps and **Burial Chamber** on later ones. A.C. (1865), p.278 with illustration. R.C.A.M. No. 542 of Denbigh. It is known locally as Allor Moloch or as Morloch's Altar.

Pillar of Eliseg, Clwyd. *Chris Barber*

15. LLANTYSILIO-YN-IAL
Pillar of Eliseg, near the remains of Valle Crucis Abbey (SJ 203445). On Ordnance Survey maps it is marked as **Pillar of Eliseg** and is supposed to have been erected in memory of Eliseg, Prince of Powys, killed in 603 but considered by some writers

to be more ancient than this period. It was originally at least 12 feet high and was moved from its original position in 1779 and again later. A.C. (1851), p.295; (1865), p.133; (1938), pp.41-6. R.C.A.M. No. 567 of Denbigh. *The Pillar of Eliseg,* by C. A. Raleigh Radford (H.M.S.O., 1953), has a number of useful references and details of the inscription, which is no longer legible.

16. LLANYCIL
Meini Hirion, which used to stand 250 yards north-west of a cottage called Meini Hirion in Cwm Glan-llafor, Maestron (SH 8666 3535). R.C.A.M. No. 481 for Merioneth. *History of Merioneth,* by E. G. Bowen and C. A. Gresham (Llandyssul, 1967), Vol. I, p.283, says that a stone on this site was destroyed in 1873 and previously there had been three stones on the site.

17. MOLD
A standing stone 3 feet high near Llanferres bridge on the old Flint county boundary (SJ 202626). R.C.A.M., p.61, of Flint mentions that it is beneath an archway of stonework and bears an impression not unlike a huge horseshoe and is thus called Carreg Carn March Arthur or The Stone of Arthur's Horse's Hoof.

18. NANNERCH
A standing stone due north of Moel Arthur near Bryn Garreg (SJ 1432 6703). Marked as 𝕾𝖙𝖆𝖓𝖉𝖎𝖓𝖌 𝕾𝖙𝖔𝖓𝖊 on the one inch Ordnance Survey map of 1961. R.C.A.M. No. 197 of Flint says that it is 6 feet high and 6 feet square.

Maen Huail, Clwyd.   *Chris Barber*

19. RUTHIN
Maen Huail, a standing stone which is a rude block of limestone situated near Barclays Bank in the centre of the town. Some years ago, it was removed from its original site to make room for a car park (SJ 125584). A.C. (1855), p.267. Legend states that on this stone King Arthur once beheaded Huail, who was one of the sons of Kaw of Brydyn and the brother of Gildas the historian of those times.

20. TREUDDYN

Carreg-y-Llech, a standing stone about ¼-mile WNW of the parish church (SJ 2487 5853). A.C. (1873), p.202, states that it is a monolith of sandstone 6 feet high leaning towards the west. Edward Llwyd, in *Parochiala* (1969), Vol. I, p.92, says that Carreg-y-Llech might be a shortened form of Carreg-y-Llech Lafar, meaning "The Stone of the Echo or Speaking Stone".

Maen Achwynfon, Clwyd.   *Chris Barber*

21. WHITFORD

Maen Achwynfan, a Christianised standing stone at the junction of some ancient tracks in the corner of a field at Whitford (SJ 129787). It is marked as 𝔐𝔞𝔢𝔫 𝔄𝔠𝔥𝔴𝔶𝔫𝔣𝔞𝔫 on up-to-date Ordnance Survey maps. A.C. (1865), p.364; (1891), p.75. R.C.A.M. p.95 under Flint refers to it as a wheel cross called Maen Chwyfan and has four good photographs which show that it might have been carved from a standing stone in situ. Maen Chwyfan, or "The Stone of Lamentation", is 12 feet high. It was mentioned in an old deed dated 1388 according to *Gibson's Camden*. Carved with ornate Celtic designs on all sides, it is the tallest wheel cross in Wales, being an impressive 11 feet 3 inches high. Sometimes it is called St. Cwyfan's Stone.

22. ABERGWILI
A standing stone at Pant y glien in a field called Parc y maen Llwyd (SN 457218).
It is about 5 feet high and has white quartz embedded in it. R.C.A.M. No. 3
of Carmarthen.

23. ABERGWILI
Merlin's Stone stands in a field called Parc y maen Llwyd at the foot of Merlin's
Hill (SN 453215). A.C. (1876), p.286; (1877), p.137. R.C.A.M. No. 7 of
Carmarthen. It is also called Carrg Myrddin or Carreh Fyrddin. There is a tradition
that Merlin Ambrosius once prophesied that a raven would one day drink a man's
blood off it. Perhaps his words came true, for in the 19th century a young man
was digging under this stone in the hope of finding buried treasure when the stone
fell over on top of him and he was killed. The stone was subsequently re-erected
by the landowner.

24. ABERGWILI
Pentre Ynis standing stone, on a farm of that name near Sarnau (SN 429248). It
is marked as Standing Stone on recent Ordnance Survey maps and Stone on earlier
editions. R.C.A.M. No. 4 of Carmarthen.

25. AMBLESTON
A dolmen at Garn Tarne, rocks by the roadside on boundary with St. Dogwells
(SM 980273). Marked as Burial Chamber on recent Ordnance Survey maps and
Cromlech on old ones. A.C. (1898), p.281. R.C.A.M. p.1 for Pembroke refers to it
as having been destroyed but there are photographs of it in 1930.

26. AMBLESTON
Parc y Llyn Dolmen near Cromlech Lodge and Parc y Llyn (SM 982266). On
Ordnance Survey maps of 1919 and before it is marked as Cromlech and as Burial
Chamber on later ones. R.C.A.M. No. 1 of Pembroke.

27. AMROTH
A 6-feet-high maenhir at Longstone near Luddchurch (SN 145095). It is marked
as Longstone on some Ordnance Survey maps. R.C.A.M. No. 6 of Pembroke.

28. ANGLE
Devil's Quoit or Newton Cromlech on Broomhill Burrows above high water mark
(SM 887008). Marked as Devil's Quoit on recent Ordnance Survey maps.
A.C. (1865), p.281, with illustration and (1926), pp.1-3. R.C.A.M. No. 18 of
Pembroke mentions that it is 12 feet long.

29. BETTWS
Llech yr Halen or "Slate Stone of the Sun" on Mynydd Bettws near the old county
boundary (SN 670105). R.C.A.M. No. 40 of Carmarthen says that it was
sometimes called Llech yr Aberth or "The Stone of Sacrifice". *A History of*

Carmarthenshire, by Sir John E. Lloyd (1935), p.49, says that it is also called "Pillar of Salt".

30. BRIDELL
This Christianised standing stone is in the churchyard on the south side of the parish church (SN 177421). It is 7 feet high and is one of the most interesting stones in Wales because it bears evidence that it has been used by three different cultures. On its face are cup markings made by prehistoric man; on its edges are Ogham letters cut by the early Celts and there is also a large cross inside a circle which was carved by the later Christians. An unusual feature about the church is that it has a door on its north side but none on the west or south sides. A.C. (1860), p.314; (1872), p.249; (1873), p.103; (1889), p.309. R.C.A.M. p.31 of Pembroke.

31. BURTON
The Hanging Stone, a dolmen between Sardis and Thurston (SM 973083). It is marked as 𝔅urial 𝔠hamber on recent Ordnance Survey maps and as 𝔠romlech on earlier ones. A.C. (1864), p.346; (1872), p.125; (1885), p.142. R.C.A.M. No. 83 of Pembroke.

32. CELLAN
This large standing stone known as Brynvaen is on the boundary between the old counties of Cardigan and Carmarthen near Byrfaen (SN 625465). It is marked as 𝔅rynfaen on the earliest Ordnance Survey map of 1833. It is 9 feet high and is near another large standing stone called Hir Faen.

33. CENARTH
Cilfod Fach Maen Hir, near Bwlch Melyn, opposite the farmhouse (SN 265403). R.C.A.M. No. 57 of Carmarthen.

34. CILMAENLLWYD
Coynant Maen Hir on Coynant Farm (SN 161250). R.C.A.M. No. 84 of Carmarthen.

35. CILMAENLLWYD
Two stones 6 feet high, standing in a field called Parc y maen, are known as Meini Hirion (SN 152252). A.C. (1974), p.41. R.C.A.M. No. 86 of Carmarthen.

36. CILMAENLLWYD
A standing stone in a hedge of a field near Nebo Cottage (SN 138254). It is marked as 𝔖tanding 𝔖tone on recent Ordnance Survey maps.

37. CILYCWM
A standing stone on Cefn Gwenffrwd above Troed y rhiw-hir (SN 756473). It is marked as 𝔖tanding 𝔖tone on recent Ordnance Survey maps and as 𝔐aenhirion on older editions. R.C.A.M. No. 78 of Carmarthen refers to it as an ancient boundary stone.

38. CILYCWM
Standing stones on Mynydd Mallaen with Crugiau Merched nearby (SN 736447). On recent Ordnance Survey maps the site is marked as 𝔖tanding 𝔖tone. R.C.A.M. No. 76 (1) of Carmarthen states that one of the stones is 65 inches high.

39. CONWYL ELFED
Known as Arthur's Quoit or Crug, this is the remains of a dolmen at Nant y Clawdd (SN 378325). On the 1952 Ordnance Survey one inch map, it is marked as a 𝔅urial 𝔠hamber. A.C. (1877), p.82, under Cerrig Llwydion.

40. CONWYL ELFED
Carreg Wen standing stone near Triolmaengwyn (SN 399340). R.C.A.M. No. 99 of Carmarthen describes it as over 6 feet high and containing much white quartz. It is believed to have been blown up before May, 1963, for a forestry plantation fence to be erected.

Bridell Stone, Dyfed.   *Chris Barber*

41. **CONWYL ELFED**
The remains of a dolmen called Cerig Llwydion near Clyn Coch on the banks of the Afon Bele (SN 375325). It is marked on the first edition Ordnance Survey map as 𝕮𝖗𝖔𝖒𝖑𝖊𝖈𝖍. A.C. (1877), pp.81-6; (1878), p.325. R.C.A.M. No. 97 of Carmarthen.

Lady Stone, Dyfed.   *Chris Barber*

42. **DINAS**
Lady Stone on side of main road from Fishguard to Newport in a field (SN 008388). On recent Ordnance Survey maps it is marked as 𝕷𝖆𝖉𝖞 𝕾𝖙𝖔𝖓𝖊 and as 𝕾𝖙𝖆𝖓𝖉𝖎𝖓𝖌 𝕾𝖙𝖔𝖓𝖊 on 1919 edition and before. R.C.A.M. p89 of Pembroke states that it is 8½ feet high. It is also known as the Black Horse Inn Stone.

43. **GOODWICK**
Penrhiw Dolmen stands above the harbour village (SM 943392). It is marked as 𝕮𝖗𝖔𝖒𝖑𝖊𝖈𝖍 on Ordnance Survey map of 1843 and as 𝕭𝖚𝖗𝖎𝖆𝖑 𝕮𝖍𝖆𝖒𝖇𝖊𝖗 on later editions. A.C. (1883), p.343; (1884), p.139. R.C.A.M. No. 548 (a) of Pembroke states that the capstone measuring 14 feet by 8 feet has been overthrown. There is a photograph of the dolmen taken in about 1865 in Carmarthen Museum.

44. GOODWICK
Three dolmens in a row behind the Council houses at the harbour village just below Garn Wen (SM 950390). Recent Ordnance Survey maps mark the site as **Burial Chamber** and it is shown as **Cromlech** on 1912 and earlier editions. A.C. (1883), p.343. R.C.A.M. p183 of Pembroke.

45. HAROLDSTON WEST
On the side of the main road to Haverfordwest is Hang Davy Stone (SM 895146). It is about 4 feet 6 inches high and is marked on recent Ordnance Survey maps as **Hang Davy Stone**. A.C. (1858), p.213, refers to it as Martin Davy's Stone. There is a local tale about a man being hung there.

46. HAROLDSTON WEST
Harold Stone at Broad Haven in a field adjoining the main road (SM 862148). It is marked as **Harold Stone** on recent Ordnance Survey maps but it is now believed to have been destroyed. R.C.A.M. No. 985 of Pembroke.

47. HAYSCASTLE
A standing stone in a field between Haycastle Tump and Rhyndaston Fawr near a tumulus (SM 896244). The Ordnance Survey maps of 1981 and 1983 show it as a **Standing Stone** but it is apparently not mentioned in any book.

48. HENRY'S MOAT
Budloy Stone in a field called Parc Maen Hir at Budloy (SN 064286). On the Ordnance Survey map of 1983 it is marked as a **Standing Stone**. A.C. (1911), p.298. R.C.A.M. p.118 of Pembroke mentions that it is 7 feet high and has been worked with a tool on the west side.

49. HENRY'S MOAT
Known as Duffryn Stones, the remains of a stone circle near Bernards Well (SN 059285). On Ordnance Survey maps up until 1919 the site was marked as **Circle** and after this date as **Carn Circle**. A.C. (1911), p.296. R.C.A.M. No. 313 of Pembroke states that it has a diameter of 65 feet and there are thirteen stones up to 5 feet high.

50. HUBBERSTON
Long Stone near a road junction where one road goes to St. Botolphs (SM 893073). It is marked as **Long Stone** on 1983 Ordnance Survey map and earlier. No. 78 of *Map of South Wales showing the Distribution of Long Barrows and Megaliths* (published by the Ordnance Survey, Southampton, 1936).

51. KIDWELLY
Two pointed stones on the south side of the road between Penlan Uchaf and Rogerlay (SN 413084). The site is shown as **Standing Stone** on the Ordnance Survey map of 1981.

52. LITTLE NEWCASTLE
Colston Cromlech on the side of road near railway and Colston (SM 983282). It is marked as **Cromlech** on Ordnance Survey maps before 1919 and as **Burial Barrows** on later maps. R.C.A.M. No. 396 under Pembroke mentions Colston Cromlech and remains of a second. There is a pointed stone about 50 yards due south which stands 40 inches above the ground.

53. LLANBADARN FAWR
This roughly shaped cross known as Carreg Samson used to stand in the churchyard (SN 598810). *The History and Antiquities of the County of Cardigan*, by S. R. Meyrick (1808), p.393, has a descripton and illustration. It was 7 feet 8 inches high and was decorated with carvings. *Walks and Wanderings in County Cardigan*, by E. R. Horsfall Turner (Bingley, Yorks, N.D. c.1903), p.75, has an illustration and describes it as perhaps the tallest, thinnest and most perfect in the country and was of grey graphite 8 feet above the ground. Legend says that St. Samson threw the stone from Pen Dinas with another that he was using as a flail.

54. **LLANBADARN FAWR**
Stone circle in the churchyard wall of Yspytty Cynfyn (SN 752791). The wall surrounding Yspytty Cynfyn churchyard contains at least four large standing stones, the tallest of which is 11 feet. A.C.. (1849), p.12; (1946), pp.140-1; (1980), pp.138-146. *The Scenery, Antiquities and Biography of South Wales,* by B. H. Malkin (1807), Vol. II, p.103, mentions large upright stone monuments in the churchyard, with the characters entirely defaced.

55. **LLANBOIDY**
A dolmen at Cross Hands is known as Arthur's Table or Bwardd Arthur (SN 194231). It is marked as a 𝔅urial 𝔈hamber on 1952 Ordnance Survey maps but as a 𝔖tanding 𝔖tone in 1983. A.C. (1865), p.91; (1871), pp.133-6 with illustration on p.152. It is also called Gwal y Filiast.

56. **LLANBOIDY**
Gwal y Filiast Dolmen, on the bank of Afon Taff, near Glyntaff House (SN 170256). Before 1920 it was marked as 𝔈romlech on Ordnance Survey maps and as 𝔊wal y 𝔉iliast 𝔅urial 𝔈hamber on later editions. A.C. (1865), p.91; (1871), p.152; (1872), p.81 and 133-6; (1875), p.409; (1884), p143 and (1911), p.328. R.C.A.M. No. 215 of Carmarthen.

57. **LLANDEWI BREFI**
Inside the church is an ancient pillar stone called David's Staff (SN 664553). A.C. (1861), p.311, mentions it as a tall thin stone 7 feet high. *A Book of South Wales,* by S. Baring Gould (London, 1905), p.27, calls it St. David's Staff wherewith he slew the beaver.

58. **LLANDDOWROR**
Castell Standing Stone in a field called Parc Newydd on the farm of Castell (SN 253145). It is 5 feet 8 inches high and leans slightly to the east. On recent Ordnance Survey maps it is marked as Standing Stone. R.C.A.M. No. 245 of Carmarthen.

59. **LLANDEFAELOG**
A standing stone known as Maen Llwyd which stands on the side of the road between Iscoed Uchaf and Cwmbury (SN 386128). It is shown as 𝔐aen 𝔏lwyd on the 1981 Ordnance Survey map and as a pointed stone called 𝔐aen 𝔏lwyd on the one inch Ordnance Survey map of 1831.

60. **LLANDEFAELOG**
Three pale grey standing stones known as Meinillwydi near Llech Dwni (SN 432102). They are marked as 𝔖tanding 𝔖tones on recent Ordnance Survey maps and shown as three stones marked 𝔐eini 𝔏lwydion on the one inch Ordnance Survey of 1831. A.C. (1974) mentions two stones 8 feet 6 inches and 6 feet high. R.C.A.M. No. 303 of Carmarthen.

61. **LLANDELOY**
Treffynnon Cromlech near Ty llwyd and Treffynnon (SM 856287). Marked as 𝔅urial 𝔈hamber on recent Ordnance Survey maps and as 𝔈romlech on 1919 and before. R.C.A.M. No. 435 of Pembroke.

62. **LLANDILO**
Cefn Cethin Maen Llwyd, near Plasbach on the side of road to Ammanford (SN 627192). It is marked as 𝔐aen 𝔏lwyd on some Ordnance Survey maps. A.C. (1893), p.152, says that it is 8½ feet high. R.C.A.M. No. 253 of Carmarthen.

63. **LLANDILO**
Sythfaen, a standing stone in a hedge on the side of a road going to Capel Gwynfi near Waun Hir (SN 670225). It is marked as 𝔖ythfaen on Ordnance Survey maps from 1831 to 1947, then as 𝔖tanding 𝔖tone. R.C.A.M. No. 252 of Carmarthen states that it had been broken and the pieces joined together again and it is 6½ feet high.

Yspytty Cynfyn Stone Circle, Dyfed.   *Chris Barber*

64. **LLANDYBIE**
A stone circle near Capel Hendre called y Naw Carreg (SN 592115). R.C.A.M. No. 292 of Carmarthen has a plan showing a circle 60 feet in diameter with nine stones.

Meini Gwyn, Dyfed.   *Chris Barber*

65. **LLANDYSSILIO EAST**
Buarth Arthur or Meini Gwyn near crossroads at Castell Garw (SN 142266). It is marked as 𝕸𝖊𝖎𝖓𝖎 𝕲𝖜𝖞𝖗 on early Ordnance Survey maps and as 𝕸𝖊𝖎𝖓𝖎 𝕲𝖜𝖞𝖓 on maps after 1952. A.C. (1911), p.323. R.C.A.M. No. 321 (1) of Carmarthen. Only two stones of the circle of seventeen now remain. Edward Llwyd in 1695 says in *Gibson's Britannia*, Col. 628, that fifteen stones were standing.

66. **LLANDYSSILIO EAST**
Dolwilim Dolmen near main road at Carn Besi (SN 156276). Marked as 𝕭𝖚𝖗𝖎𝖆𝖑 𝕮𝖍𝖆𝖒𝖇𝖊𝖗 on recent Ordnance Survey maps and as 𝕮𝖗𝖔𝖒𝖑𝖊𝖈𝖍 on 1919 map. R.C.A.M. No. 321 (V) of Carmarthen.

67. **LLANEDY**
Brynrhyd Stone on the farm of Brynryd is a greyish-red stone about 8 feet high containing white quartz (SN 589084). R.C.A.M. No. 326 of Carmarthen.

68. **LLANGADDOCK**
Coitan Arthur, a somewhat ovate boulder lying in the bed of Sawdde Fechan at Pont yr Aber (SN 738227). A.C. (1874), p.89. R.C.A.M. No. 426 of Carmarthen. It is said to have been thrown here by King Arthur from Pen Arthur Issa, a farm 1½ miles to the north-west, where there is Cerrig Pen Arthur.

69. **LLANGADDOCK**
A standing stone on the east side of some large earthworks on the north side of the main road from Llangaddock to Bethlehem (SN 695260). It is rather strange that there is no reference to this greyish coloured stone, which is over 6 feet high and has two supporting stones, because it is quite prominent from the road and is a long distance from any kind of stone building or wall.

70. **LLANGADDOCK**
Sythfaen, a standing stone near Llwyndu and Fair Fach (SN 676245). It is marked as 𝕾𝖞𝖙𝖍𝖋𝖆𝖊𝖓 on Ordnance Survey maps with the exception of those after 1981. R.C.A.M. No. 425 of Carmarthen mentions that it is nearly 10 feet clear of the soil.

71. LLANGAIN
Three large stones known as Meini Llwydion which stand close together in a field near Llangain School (SN 378154). They are marked as Meini Llwydion on modern Ordnance Survey maps. A.C. (1875), p.404; (1974), p.41. R.C.A.M. No. 440 of Carmarthen features a photograph. The stones are also known as Myrddin's or Merlin's Quoits.

72. LLANGAIN
Two large stones in a field adjoining the main Carmarthen to Llanstephan road near Rhyd Lydan and Gilfach (SN 380160). They are marked as Myrddin's Quoit on recent Ordnance Survey maps. A.C. (1875), p.404. R.C.A.M. No. 439 of Carmarthen refers to Rhyd Lydan cromlech.

73. LLANGELER
The remains of a dolmen can be found to the south of Blaennantrhys (SN 409361). It is known as Coetan Arthur but marked as Crugiau on Ordnance Survey maps dating from 1831. The capstone, which is about 7 feet long, has been thrown off its supporters which are lying near a boundary hedge. R.C.A.M. No. 26 of Carmarthen.

74. LLANGELER
A standing stone between Pencastell and Brafle. It is on a moated mound in a field called Parc Garreg Llwyd at Pencastell Farm (SN 400378). R.C.A.M. No. 466 of Carmarthen states that it is 10 feet high.

75. LLANGENDEIRNE
Known variously as Arthur's Table, Bwrdd Arthur and Gwal y Filiast, the remains of a dolmen can be seen on the north-east side of Mynydd Llangendeirne (SN 465177). These are two groups of megaliths set against outcrops of quartzite. R.C.A.M. No. 483 of Carmarthen.

76. LLANGENDEIRNE
Maen Lwyd, a standing stone near the road between Ffrwd and Fan (SN 453122). On the Ordnance Survey map of 1831 it is shown as a Pointed Stone and marked as Maen Llwyd. It is marked as Standing Stone on the 1981 map.

77. LLANGENDEIRNE
A standing stone between Pontantwn and Cloigyn Fawr (SN 439138). On early maps this site is marked as Maen Hir and the Ordnance Survey map of 1966 shows it as Standing Stone.

78. LLANGENDEIRNE
Two standing stones in a field adjoining the farmhouse at Coed Walter (SN 453150) are marked as Maen Hirion on the 1946 Ordnance Survey map and Standing Stones on later editions. R.C.A.M. No. 484 of Carmarthen. The stones are 5 feet high and there is a third one nearby.

79. LLANGOEDMOR
Llech yr Ast or The Bitch's Stone stand in a field known as Canllefas (SN 216485). A.C. (1859), p.329; (1855), p.280. It is mentioned by George Owen in *Pembrokeshire* (1603) as near Blaen Porth.

80. LLANGYNOG
A dolmen variously known as Arthur's Table, Bwrdd Arthur or Twlc y Filiast stand alongside a stream about 200 yards south-west of Ebenezer Chapel (SN 337162). It is shown as Twlc Filiast or Cromlech on Ordnance Survey maps. R.C.A.M. No. 505 of Carmarthen.

81. LLANHOWELL
Lecha Dolmen is on the side of a stream between Lecha and Ysgeifiog (SM 812272). Recent Ordnance Survey maps indicate a Burial Chamber but, before 1919, the site is marked as Cromlech. R.C.A.M. p.171 for Pembroke records that the capstone was 15 feet by 11 feet by 4 feet.

82. **LLANLLAWDOG**
Known as Meini Gwyn, three large monoliths of quartz stand in a field called Cae'r Garreg close to Dolgwm House and near Beili Glas (SN 458277). R.C.A.M. No. 512 under Carmarthen.

83. **LLANLLAWER**
A dolmen on the side of the road near Tre-llwyn-uchaf below Mynydd Llanllawer (SN 007364). It is marked as **Cromlech** on early Ordnance Survey maps. A.C. (1855), p.272. R.C.A.M. No. 510 for Pembroke.

Parc y Merw Stone Row, Dyfed.   *Chris Barber*

84. **LLANLLAWER**
Seven large standing stones at Parc y Merw (The Field of the Dead) near Tre-llwyn (SM 998359). The site is marked as **Standing Stones** on early Ordnance Survey maps and as Stone Row on later editions. A.C. (1868), p.177, has an illustration. R.C.A.M. p.173 for Pembroke refers to an alignment of seven large stones with the tallest one 12½ feet high. It is the longest megalithic alignment in Wales and some writers mention eight stones.

85. **LLANLLAWER**
A standing stone on the left side of the main road to Newport near Rhos Isaf and Ty Meini (SM 997377). It is marked as **Standing Stone on** Ordnance Survey maps and is about 8 feet high. *The Pembroke Historian,* Vol. II (1966), p.14.

86. **LLANON**
Brynmaen pillar stone stands on the side of the road to Pontardulais (SN 556069). On the 1947 Ordnance Survey map it is marked as Bryn Maen. R.C.A.M. No. 533 of Carmarthen. It is 15 feet high and of local red sandstone.

87. **LLANPUMPSAINT**
Ffos y Maen Standing Stone is in a field called Parc y maenllwydd (SN 413277). Its position is marked on the one inch Ordnance Survey map of 1831 as **Stone.** R.C.A.M. No. 539 (1) of Carmarthen says that it is 8 feet high.

88. LLANRHIAN

Near Tregynon is Llain y Sibedau, the remains of a stone circle (SM 825309). It is marked as 𝕷lain y 𝕾ibedau on the Ordnance Survey map of 1980 and as 𝕾tone 𝕮ircle on the 1950 map. R.C.A.M. p.177 of Pembroke. Richard Fenton, in *Historical Tours Through Pembroke*, p.35, describes them as Stonehenge in miniature and mentions that it was a heap of stones 60 feet in circumference, most of which were small blocks of white quartz.

89. LLANSADWRN

Maen Cilau is a massive monolith over 9 feet high just within the entrance gate to Abermorlais Park. It is also known as Carreg Fawr standing stone (SN 695293). On the Ordnance Survey map of 1831 it is marked as 𝕮arregfawr; on the 1920 and 1925 maps as 𝕮arreg 𝕱awr; on 1947 and 1952 as 𝕮arreg 𝕱awr and as 𝕮areg 𝕱awr on later ones. R.C.A.M. No. 547 of Carmarthen calls it Abermorlais Stone.

Llech Gron, Dyfed.   *Chris Barber*

90. LLANSANTFRAID

A standing stone known as Llech Gron is near Rhos Harminiog and Nebo (SN 542649). It is shown by this name on Ordnance Survey maps and is about 14 feet high. One legend says that it was carried by the Devil from the top of Trichrug Mountain.

91. LLANSTEPHAN
Fron Uch Dolmen stands in a field immediately north-west of a reservoir (SN 348110). It has a capstone over 9 feet long and two remaining supporting stones. R.C.A.M. No. 568 of Carmarthen.

92. LLANSTEPHAN
Maen Llwyd near Maes Gwyn stands on the side of a track (SN 360136). It is marked as Maen Llwyd on some Ordnance Survey maps and as Standing Stone on the 1966 map. R.C.A.M. No. 572 of Carmarthen.

93. LLANSTEPHAN
Maen Melyn, standing in a field hedge by a road junction near Maes Gwyn (SN 347128). It is marked as Maen Melyn on some Ordnance Survey maps and as Standing Stone on others. R.C.A.M. No. 570 of Carmarthen describes it as a fine red sandstone monolith 85 inches high and 150 inches in girth.

94. LLANSTEPHAN
Two standing stones known as Maenau Llwydion in a field opposite a farmhouse (SN 314140). On Ordnance Survey maps they are shown as Maenau Llwydion in 1831, Maen Llwyd in 1946, Standing Stones in 1966 and Meini Llwdion in 1981. R.C.A.M. No. 248 of Carmarthen. They are two large greyish stones and one was 5 feet high when seen in 1963.

95. LLANSTEPHAN
Pant yr Athro Maen Llwyd situated near Pilgrims' Rest and the banks of Afon Cywyn where the ground is very marshy (SN 313148). On some Ordnance Survey maps it is marked as Maen Llwyd while the 1966 edition shows Standing Stone. R.C.A.M. No. 571 of Carmarthen says it is of red sandstone 52 inches high.

96. LLANFIHANGEL ABERCYWYN
A large standing stone known as Maen Llwyd can be seen on the banks of the Afon Cynon near Lower Court, St. Clears (SN 312145). It is marked as Maen Llwyd on the Ordnance Survey map of 1981. R.C.A.M. No. 381 of Carmarthen calls it Lower Court Stone.

97. LLANFIHANGEL AR ARTH
Cwm Cathern Maenhir stands in a field called Caegarreg wen which belongs to the farm of Cwm Cathern (SN 424375). R.C.A.M. No. 392 of Carmarthen says that it is a white quartz boulder 5 feet high.

98. LLANFIHANGEL GENAU-Y-GLYN
A dolmen known as Bedd Taliesin is situated near Gwar cwm uchaf on the side of the mountain above the Dovey Estuary (SN 672912). It is marked as Bedd Taliesin on Ordnance Survey maps. A.C. (1847), pp.356-7; (1854), p.210; (1873), p.292. *A Gentleman's Tour Through Monmouthshire and Wales*, by Henry P. Wyndham (T. Evans, London, 1781), p107, states *"The spurious sepulchre of the Bard Taliesin, who flourished in the 6th century and one which stood near the highway, has, within these five years, been entirely plundered and the broken stones are now converted into gateposts."*

99. LLANFIHANGEL LLEDROD
Near Penlan is the remains of a dolmen called Carreg Samson (SN 655697). It is marked as Llech Mihangel on the one inch Ordnance Survey map of 1833 and shown as a pointed stone between Penlan and Bryn garw. A giant is supposed to have thrown it from Uwch Mynydd and it still bears his finger marks, which have been described as the shape of a horse shoe cut deeply into a Druidical altar slab.

100. LLANWINIO
A standing stone at Pantymaen near Cwmbach on the side of the road (SN 267257). It is marked as Standing Stone on modern Ordnance Survey maps. R.C.A.M. No. 585 of Carmarthen says that it is an erect and somewhat pointed monument of white quartz, 85 inches high with a girth of 105 inches.

Bedd Taliesin, Dyfed.   *Chris Barber*

101. LLANWNDA

Carreg Samson or Carn Wnda Cromlech stands on the west side of Carn Wnda (SM 933394). It is marked as Burial Chamber on modern Ordnance Survey maps but as 𝕮romlech on the 1919 edition and before. A.C. (1848), p.283; (1855), p.274; (1865), p.282; (1872), p.135; (1882), p.105; (1883), p.343; (1888), p.132. R.C.A.M.. No. 548 (11) of Pembroke says that capstone was 11½ feet long.

102. LLANWNDA

Gyllwch Dolmen is situated at Garrigilfach near Ysgubor Gaer (SM 909389). On modern Ordnance Survey maps it is marked as 𝕭urial 𝕮hamber and 𝕮romlech on the 1843 map. A.C. (1848), p.283; (1855), p.274; (1865), p.282; (1872), p.135; (1882), p.105; (1883), p.343; (1888), p.132. The capstone is 13½ feet long on four supporters.

103. LLANWNDA

Parc Hen Stone stands between Hennen School and Carn Wnda in á field (SM 933391). It is marked as 𝕾tanding 𝕾tone on the 1980 Ordnance Survey map. R.C.A.M. p.185 of Pembroke states that it is about 7 feet high.

104. LLANYBYTHER

A standing stone known as Carreg Hir is situated near crossroads between Mynydd Llanbyther and Banc Melyn (SN 543396). It is shown as 𝕾tone and marked 𝕮arreg 𝕳ir on the one inch Ordnance Survey map of 1831. R.C.A.M. No. 604 of Carmarthen.

105. LLANYCRWYS

On the old county boundary between Cardigan and Carmarthen is a tall standing stone known as Hirfaen. It is just below the summit of Bryn Hirfaen (SN 624464). On recent Ordnance Survey maps it is marked as 𝕳irfaen. A.C. (1861), p.309, says that is is about 16 feet high. R.C.A.M. No. 611 of Carmarthen says that it is 15 feet high.

106. MAENCLOCHOG

Near Cornel Bach is the remains of a cromlech known as the Cornel Bach Stones (SN 082276). A.C. (1974), p.42, mentions two stones both 6 feet high. *A Topographical Dictionary of Wales,* by Samuel Lewis (London, 1844), Vol. II, p.198, refers to a large stone several tons in weight, so nicely poised on three small upright stones as to vibrate on the slightest touch and upon it being struck sounded like a bell. It was destroyed by the inhabitants, who blew it up with gunpowder.

107. MAENCLOCHOG

Parc y Tywood Maenhir stands between Hafod-ddu and Galchen (SN 098282). It is marked as 𝕾tanding 𝕾tone on the 1983 Ordnance Survey map. R.C.A.M. p.205 of Pembroke states that it is 8½ feet high.

108. MAENCLOCHOG

The remains of a cromlech can be found between Eithbed and Westland (SN 080286). On the Ordnance Survey map of 1843 it is marked as 𝕮romlech and as 𝕭urial 𝕮hamber on recent maps. A.C. (1910), p.486; (1911), p.300. R.C.A.M. No. 635 of Pembroke.

109. MANORBIER

King's Quoit is a ruined dolmen on the side of a cliff path at Old Castle Head (SS 060973). It is marked as 𝕶ing's 𝕼uoit on modern Ordnance Survey maps. A.C. (1977), p.12. R.C.A.M. p.210 of Pembroke under No. 648 says the capstone is 15 feet by 9 feet.

110. MANOROWEN

Two standing stones known as the Brwynant Stones, situated in fields north-east of Brwynant Farmhouse (SM 930357). R.C.A.M. p.209 of Pembroke states that they are 5 feet 9 inches and 6 feet 3 inches high. One of the stones seems to have an Ordnance Survey bench mark cut into it.

Carn Wnda Cromlech, Dyfed.   *Chris Barber*

King's Quoit, Dyfed.   *Chris Barber*

111. MARROS

Two dolmens positioned above the sea shore at Morfa Bychan (SN 223076). They are marked on recent Ordnance Survey maps as 𝕮𝖍𝖆𝖒𝖇𝖊𝖗𝖊𝖉 𝕮𝖆𝖎𝖗𝖓𝖘. A.C. (1870), p.42; (1918), p.64. R.C.A.M. No. 618 of Carmarthen.

Carreg Samson, Dyfed.   *Chris Barber*

112. MATHRY

Carreg Samson or The Longhouse Cromlech is situated between Abercastle and Castle-coch in a field adjoining Long House near the sea (SM 838336). Marked as 𝕮𝖗𝖔𝖒𝖑𝖊𝖈𝖍 on the one inch Ordnance Survey map of 1843 and from 1952 as 𝕭𝖚𝖗𝖎𝖆𝖑 𝕮𝖍𝖆𝖒𝖇𝖊𝖗 until 1980, when it was marked as 𝕮𝖆𝖗𝖗𝖊𝖌 𝕾𝖆𝖒𝖘𝖔𝖓. The amazing St. Samson is supposed to have lifted the capstone in place with his little finger. About 500 yards north-west of the cromlech is a small islet on which is a mound called "The Grave of Samson's Finger". A.C. (1872), p.140; (1883), p.237 and p.345; (1925), p.422; (1926), p.190. R.C.A.M. p.219 of Pembroke says that the capstone is 15 feet long and 9 feet wide.

113. MATHRY

Penlan Dolmen is located between Penfeidr and Penlan, near Castell (SM 889300). It is marked as 𝕮𝖗𝖔𝖒𝖑𝖊𝖈𝖍 on the earliest Ordnance Survey maps and as 𝕭𝖚𝖗𝖎𝖆𝖑 𝕮𝖍𝖆𝖒𝖇𝖊𝖗 on later editions. R.C.A.M. p.320 of Pembroke calls it Penlan Mabus Cromlech.

114. MATHRY

Ty Newydd Grug Stone stands 30 yards south of a tumulus between Bryn Cleddau and Ty Cant (SM 925287). It is marked as 𝕿𝖞 𝕹𝖊𝖜𝖞𝖉𝖉 𝕲𝖗𝖚𝖌 on 1980 Ordnance Survey maps and as 𝕾𝖙𝖆𝖓𝖉𝖎𝖓𝖌 𝕾𝖙𝖔𝖓𝖊 on later maps. R.C.A.M. p.220 of Pembroke states that it is 8 feet 9 inches high.

115. MATHRY

Walter Llwyd Dolmen is situated between Mathry village and Rehoboth (SM 866317). On Ordnance Survey maps up until 1919 it is marked as 𝕮𝖗𝖔𝖒𝖑𝖊𝖈𝖍 and on subsequent editions as 𝕭𝖚𝖗𝖎𝖆𝖑 𝕮𝖍𝖆𝖒𝖇𝖊𝖗. A.C. (1872), p.139. R.C.A.M. No. 668 of Pembroke records that the capstone is 11 feet by 10 feet.

116. MELINE

Bedd Arthur is an enclosure of stones, rectangular in shape, positioned on Mynydd

Preseli about 300 yards north-west of Carn Arthur (SN 131324). It is marked as 𝔅𝔢𝔡𝔡 𝔄𝔯𝔱𝔥𝔲𝔯 on Ordnance Survey maps. A.C. (1898), p.74; (1984), p.52, and plan p.62 which shows fifteen stones. This is one of the many supposed burial places of King Arthur.

117. MELINE

Beddyfanc Dolmen is situated on the slopes of Mynydd Preseli near Brynberian (SN 107347). On the one inch Ordnance Survey map of 1843 it is marked as 𝔅𝔢𝔡𝔡-𝔶𝔯-𝔄𝔣𝔞𝔫𝔤𝔠; 𝔅𝔢𝔡𝔡-𝔶𝔯-𝔄𝔣𝔞𝔫𝔠 on the 1919 map and 𝔅𝔢𝔡𝔡𝔶𝔯𝔣𝔞𝔫𝔠 𝔅𝔲𝔯𝔦𝔞𝔩 ℭ𝔥𝔞𝔪𝔟𝔢𝔯 on the 1952 map. R.C.A.M. No. 681 describes it as twenty-five to thirty stones around a mound whose name means "Beaver's Grave" or perhaps "Dwarf's Grave".

Llech y Tribedd Dolmen, Dyfed.   *Chris Barber*

118. MOYLGROVE

Llech y Tribedd Dolmen is located near the coast above Penlan (SN 101433). It is marked as 𝔏𝔩𝔢𝔠𝔥-𝔶-𝔡𝔯𝔦𝔟𝔢𝔡𝔡 on Ordnance Survey map of 1843, ℭ𝔯𝔬𝔪𝔩𝔢𝔠𝔥 on 1919 and 𝔅𝔲𝔯𝔦𝔞𝔩 ℭ𝔥𝔞𝔪𝔟𝔢𝔯 on the 1952 map. A.C. (1847), p.373; (1864), p.311; (1885), p.142 with illustration. R.C.A.M. p.256 of Pembroke refers to it as "The Tripod supported on Triangular shaped stone, 9 feet 8 inches long by 9 feet broad standing on three supporters". A legend says that it was hurled from the summit of Carningli, Newport, by one Samson.

119. MYDDFAI

Standing stones on the slopes of Mynydd Myddfai near Fedw Fawr and River Usk (SN 807285). They are marked as 𝔐𝔞𝔢𝔫 ℌ𝔦𝔯 on the Ordnance Survey map of 1831 and as 𝔖𝔱𝔞𝔫𝔡𝔦𝔫𝔤 𝔖𝔱𝔬𝔫𝔢 or 𝔖𝔱𝔞𝔫𝔡𝔦𝔫𝔤 𝔖𝔱𝔬𝔫𝔢𝔰 on later maps. The tallest stone is 7 feet high and the smallest one is about 2 feet high. R.C.A.M. No. 606 of Carmarthen.

120. MYNACHLOG DDU

A rocking stone known as Arthur's Quoit or Carn Arthur is located on top of an outcrop about 30 feet high on the south slopes of Mynydd Preseli (SN 135324). This large rock is marked as ℭ𝔞𝔯𝔫 𝔄𝔯𝔱𝔥𝔲𝔯 on the 1819 Ordnance Survey map and as ℭ𝔞𝔯𝔫 𝔄𝔣𝔯 on 1919 and 1952 maps. A.C. (1898), p.74, states that on Carn Arthur is a great stone known as Arthur's Quoit which is said to have been hurled by the king from Duffryn, 2 miles away. This is in Henry's Moat Parish, where there is a stone circle.

121. MYNACHLOG DDU

Cerrig Meibion Arthur or The Stones of the Sons of Arthur are two erect standing stones on Mynydd Preseli near Cwm Garw (SN 118310). They are marked as 𝕾𝖙𝖆𝖓𝖉𝖎𝖓𝖌 𝕾𝖙𝖔𝖓𝖊𝖘 on Ordnance Survey maps of 1919 and 1952. A.C. (1898), p.74; (1911), p.308; (1974), p.142 and photograph plate XVI. R.C.A.M. No. 729 of Pembroke.

122. MYNACHLOG DDU

Gors Fawr Stone Circle is positioned on moorland to the west of the main road near Llan (SN 135295). It is marked as 𝕲𝖔𝖗𝖘-𝖋𝖆𝖜𝖗 𝕾𝖙𝖔𝖓𝖊 𝕮𝖎𝖗𝖈𝖑𝖊 on Ordnance Survey maps, with the exception of the 1983 map which shows it as 𝕾𝖙𝖔𝖓𝖊 𝕮𝖎𝖗𝖈𝖑𝖊.

123. MYNACHLOG DDU

A cromlech below Crug-yr-hwch near the road and Llainbanol (SN 165329). It is marked as 𝕭𝖚𝖗𝖎𝖆𝖑 𝕮𝖍𝖆𝖒𝖇𝖊𝖗 on modern Ordnance Survey maps and as 𝕮𝖗𝖔𝖒𝖑𝖊𝖈𝖍 on the 1919 map. R.C.A.M. No. 728 of Pembroke mentions a 12-feet-long capstone that has been destroyed.

124. MYNACHLOG DDU

Waun Llwyd Standing Stones on the slopes of Mynydd Preseli at Dolau Maen below Bedd Arthur (SN 158312). They are shown as 𝕿𝖜𝖔 𝕾𝖙𝖔𝖓𝖊𝖘 on the one inch Ordnance Survey map of 1820 and marked as 𝕾𝖙𝖆𝖓𝖉𝖎𝖓𝖌 𝕾𝖙𝖔𝖓𝖊𝖘 on later maps. A.C. (1974), p.42, with photograph plate XVI. R.C.A.M. No. 730 of Pembroke says that they are 9 feet and 7 feet high. There may have been other standing stones here which gave the name of the locality; Glyn Saithmaen (Valley of Seven Stones).

Trellyfant Cromlech, Dyfed.   *Chris Barber*

125. NEVERN

Trellyffant Cromlech, near the coast between Trellyffant and Trefwrdan (SN 083426). It is marked as 𝕮𝖗𝖔𝖒𝖑𝖊𝖈𝖍 on Ordnance Survey maps up to 1919 and as 𝕭𝖚𝖗𝖎𝖆𝖑 𝕮𝖍𝖆𝖒𝖇𝖊𝖗 on subsequent editions. A.C. (1871), p.230; (1872), p.132. R.C.A.M. No. 760 of Pembroke states that the capstone is 6 feet 10 inches by 6 feet. This capstone is particularly interesting, for it has over thirty cup marks. According to Giraldus Cambrensis in 1188, the cromlech was called Trellyffant (Toad's Town) because the chieftain inside was eaten by toads.

Pentre Ifan Dolmen, Dyfed.   *Chris Barber*

126. NEVERN
Pentre Ifan or Coetan Arthur Dolmen near Pentre Ifan and Carnedd Meigion Owen (SN 099369). This is one of the best-known prehistoric stone monuments in Wales and was marked as 𝔆𝔯𝔬𝔪𝔩𝔢𝔠𝔥 on the one inch Ordnance Survey map of 1843, as 𝔓𝔢𝔫𝔱𝔯𝔢 𝔈𝔟𝔞𝔫 𝔆𝔯𝔬𝔪𝔩𝔢𝔠𝔥 on the 1919 edition and as 𝔓𝔢𝔫𝔱𝔯𝔢 𝔈𝔟𝔞𝔫 𝔅𝔲𝔯𝔦𝔞𝔩 𝔆𝔥𝔞𝔪𝔟𝔢𝔯 on later maps. A.C. (1847), p.313 and p.374; (1855), p.274; (1859), p.284; (1865), p.284; (1872), p.128; (1874), p.59; (1883), p.342; (1884), p.136; (1885), p.72; (1905), p.163; (1926), p.190; (1949), pp.3-23. R.C.A.M. No. 759 of Pembroke. *The History of Little England Beyond Wales,* by Edward Laws (Geo. Bell and Sons, London, 1888), says that the capstone is 18 feet by 9 feet and on p.302 there is a copy of a drawing of the dolmen made by George Owen on 18th May, 1603.

127. NEVERN
Standing stones on Mynydd Preseli near Brynberian at Tafarn-y-bwlch (SN 080339). The site is marked as 𝔖𝔱𝔞𝔫𝔡𝔦𝔫𝔤 𝔖𝔱𝔬𝔫𝔢 or 𝔖𝔱𝔞𝔫𝔡𝔦𝔫𝔤 𝔖𝔱𝔬𝔫𝔢𝔰 on Ordnance Survey maps. R.C.A.M. of Pembroke, p.258, refers to these stones as Waun Mawr Stone Circle which had a diameter of 150 feet.

128. NEVERN
Two standing stones about 400 yards south of Carnedd Meibion Owen and about the same distance north of Penparke (SN 091358). These stones are about 5 feet high and 15 feet apart lying north and south. The site is marked as 𝔆𝔯𝔬𝔪𝔩𝔢𝔠𝔥 on the Ordnance Survey map of 1919. *The Pembroke Historian* (1966), p.16, refers to them as the Penparke Stones.

129. NEVERN
Y Garreg Hir Standing Stone between Tre-fach and Gelli Fawr (SN 064351). It is marked as *Standing Stone* on the Ordnance Survey maps of 1912 and 1952. R.C.A.M. p.258 of Pembroke says that it is 9 feet high.

130. NEWPORT
Arthur's Stone, alternatively called Carreg Coitan, Carreg Coitan Arthur or Quoit Stone, is a dolmen on the banks of the Afon Nyfer near a bridge and the coast

(SN 061395). It is marked as **Cromlech** on the Ordnance Survey map of 1843 and as Careg Coetan on 1951. A.C. (1847), p.313 and p.374; (1872), p.140; (1926), p.190. R.C.A.M. p.269 of Pembroke has an illustration and a photograph.

Bedd Morris, Dyfed.

131. NEWPORT

Bedd Morris, a large standing stone on the parish boundary with Llanychlwydog and positioned on the side of the road (SN 038366). It is marked as **Morris's Grave** on the 1819 Ordnance Survey map, **Bedd Morris** on 1843 map, **Standing Stone** on 1919 and **Bedd Morris** on 1951 and later. A.C. (1875), p.306.

132. NEWPORT

Cerrig y Gof, a circle of the remains of five small dolmens on a low mound near Holme House (SN 037389). The site is marked as **Carreg y cof** on the one inch Ordnance Survey map of 1843, **Cerrig y Gof** on the 1919 map, **Crug y Gof** on 1952 and 1965 maps and as *Burial Chamber* on later editions. A.C. (1847), p.373; (1851), p.307; (1872), p.140; (1923), p.400. R.C.A.M. No. 811 of Pembroke gives a full description of the site.

133. NEWPORT

Llech y Drybedd, a circle of stones close to the main road near Newport Church (SN 058394). A.C. (1847), p.313, mentions a capstone on three upright stones. *Letters Written During a Tour Through South Wales*, by Rev. J. Evans (London, 1804), refers to *Gibson's Camden* and mentions a circle of stones consisting of several stones pitched on end in a circular form. In the midst of the circle, which measures 50 feet in diameter, was a rude flat stone supported by eight pillars; it however then rested on but three. The length was 18 feet and breadth 9 feet.

134. PUNCHESTON

Fagwyr Fran West Standing Stone, 150 yards north of the farmhouse of that name (SN 005315). It is in the middle of a field and about 9 feet high when visited by J.G.W. in July, 1962. R.C.A.M. p.299 of Pembroke. *The Pembrokeshire Historian II* (1966), p.14.

135. PUNCHESTON

Quoit Stone or Carreg Quoitan next to Parc Carreg (SN 008300). R.C.A.M. p.298 of Pembroke says that it is 7 feet 3 inches high. *The Pembrokeshire Historian II* (1966), p.16.

136. PUNCHESTON

A standing stone west of the village and Capel Smyrna. When J.G.W. visited the site in July, 1962, he found a large grey stone standing in the garden of a council house (SN 006297). R.C.A.M. p.298 of Pembroke. *The Pembrokeshire Historian II* (1966), p.14.

137. ROCH

Cuffern Dolmen on Cuffern Mountain near Roch Farm (SM 900222). It is marked as 𝔠𝔯𝔬𝔪𝔩𝔢𝔠𝔥 on the one inch Ordnance Survey map of 1919 and as 𝔅𝔲𝔯𝔦𝔞𝔩 𝔠𝔥𝔞𝔪𝔟𝔢𝔯 on 1952. R.C.A.M. p.312 of Pembroke.

138. ST. DAVID'S

Coetan Arthur, a dolmen on the rocky headland at St. David's. It is marked as 𝔠𝔯𝔬𝔪𝔩𝔢𝔠𝔥 on the 1843 Ordnance Survey map, 𝔠𝔬𝔢𝔱𝔞𝔫 𝔞𝔯𝔱𝔥𝔲𝔯 on the 1912 and 1919 editions, 𝔅𝔲𝔯𝔦𝔞𝔩 𝔠𝔥𝔞𝔪𝔟𝔢𝔯 on 1952 and 𝔠𝔬𝔢𝔱𝔞𝔫 𝔞𝔯𝔱𝔥𝔲𝔯 𝔅𝔲𝔯𝔦𝔞𝔩 𝔠𝔥𝔞𝔪𝔟𝔢𝔯 on the 1981 map. A.C. (1865), p.283 with illustration; (1872), p.143; (1899), p.130. R.C.A.M. p.321 of Pembroke states that the capstone is 12 feet long and 8½ feet wide. It is also called Arthur's Quoit and is yet another location where King Arthur is said to be buried.

Maen Dewi, Dyfed.   *Chris Barber*

139. ST. DAVID'S

Maen Dewi, a standing stone 8 feet high situated behind a cottage called Drws Gobiath (The Door of Hope) on the edge of Dowrog Common (SM 775275). It is marked as 𝔪𝔞𝔢𝔫 𝔡𝔢𝔴𝔦 on Ordnance Survey maps from 1912. R.C.A.M. p.321 of Pembroke. According to a local story the stone disappeared one night.

140. ST. DAVID'S

Maen Sigl or Shaking Stone, which used to stand on the brow of the hill overlooking Whitesands Bay (SM 730278). On the Ordnance Survey map of 1919 it is marked as 𝔪𝔞𝔢𝔫 𝔰𝔦𝔤𝔩. R.C.A.M. No. 939 of Pembroke has a description and a good photograph of this now-destroyed rocking stone.

141. ST. DAVID'S
Stone circle in the ancient camp on St. David's Head, sometimes called Hut Circles
(SM 723279). A.C. (1899), pp.105-131. R.C.A.M. p.324 of Pembroke states that
the circle is 21 feet in diameter and consists of ten or twelve low stones, some with
flat tops.

142. ST. DAVID'S
Trecenny Standing Stone, in the middle of a field alongside the road near
Glasfrynin (SM 767257). The stone is marked as *Stone* on Ordnance Survey maps
of 1912, 1919 and 1965, and as *Standing Stone* on others. R.C.A.M. p.322 of
Pembroke says that it is 7 feet high.

143. ST. DAVID'S
Two dolmens on the steep sides of Carn Llidi near an old gun emplacement
(SM 735279). They are marked as *Burial Chambers* on 1981 Ordnance Survey maps.
A.C. (1863), p.73.

144. ST. DOGWELLS
Broad Moor Stone in a field known as Gwerglodd y Garreg near Wolf's Castle
(SM 952276). It is marked as *Standing Stone* on Ordnance Survey maps of 1981 and
1983. R.C.A.M. p.363 of Pembroke says that it is 8 feet high.

145. ST. EDRINS
The remains of a dolmen between Weary and Walterstone near Treddiog
(SM 898289). It is marked as *Cromlech* on the one inch Ordnance Survey maps of
1843, 1912 and 1919 and *Stone* or *Standing Stone* on later maps. R.C.A.M. p.366 of
Pembroke refers to Clunffrwrn Stone which stands 5 feet high.

146. ST. EDRINS
Tre Hywel Dolmen near a road junction at Pen-lan and Castell (SM 889296). It is
marked as *Cromlech* on the one inch Ordnance Survey map of 1843. R.C.A.M. p.366
of Pembroke states that only three uprights 6 feet high remain. Four stones about
3 feet high were seen near the road hedge in September 1984.

147. ST. EDRINS
Penlan Ole Maenhir near Blaen Llyn and Penlan (SM 883296). R.C.A.M. No. 667
of Pembroke states that it was only 4 feet high but at one time was 7 to 8 feet in
height. *Map of South Wales showing the Distribution of Long Barrows and
Megaliths* (published by The Ordnance Survey, Southampton, in 1936) under No.
72 calls it Penlan Mabus Uchaf Burial Chamber.

148. ST. ELVIS
A dolmen near the coast at St. Elvis Farm and near the ruined church of St. Teilo
(SM 812239). On the Ordnance Survey maps of 1919 and before it is marked as
Cromlech and *Burial Chamber* on 1951 and subsequent editions. R.C.A.M. No. 1030 of
Pembroke says that there are two capstones, the longer being 12 feet by 10½ feet
and the other 8 feet by 5 feet. Some large stones in the nearby fences may have
come from the dolmen (observed by J.G.W. in July, 1986).

149. ST. ISHMAELS
Long Stone near Mabesgate and castle mound. It is 10 feet high of laminated
sandstone (SM 827076). On the Ordnance Survey map of 1980 it is marked as
Standing Stone. R.C.A.M. p.371 of Pembroke states that there are three stones in
this locality called Long Stone.

150. ST. NICHOLAS
A dolmen situated between Carn Segan and Ffynon-y-druidion (SM 919368). It is
marked as *Cromlech* on the Ordnance Survey maps of 1912 and 1919 and as
Burial Chamber on later maps. A.C. (1872), p.139. R.C.A.M. No. 1063 of Pembroke
has a photograph and a description. The remains of the capstone and supporters
were seen in an overgrown hedge in June, 1985.

151. ST. NICHOLAS
Rhos y Clegyrn Stone Circle and Standing Stone near Trefelgarn (SM 913355).The one inch Ordnance Survey map shows 𝕮𝖎𝖗𝖈𝖑𝖊 in 1843 while later maps show 𝕾𝖙𝖆𝖓𝖉𝖎𝖓𝖌 𝕾𝖙𝖔𝖓𝖊 and 𝕮𝖎𝖗𝖈𝖑𝖊. A.C. (1974), pp.13-42. R.C.A.M. p.378 of Pembroke.

152. ST. NICHOLAS
Standing Stone between Trefelgarn and Ffynnon Druidion beside the road (SM 922366). It is marked as 𝕮𝖗𝖔𝖒𝖑𝖊𝖈𝖍 on one inch Ordnance Survey map of 1843 and as 𝕾𝖙𝖆𝖓𝖉𝖎𝖓𝖌 𝕾𝖙𝖔𝖓𝖊 on later maps. *The Pembrokeshire Historian II* (1966), p.14, calls it Ffynnon Druidion Stone.

153. ST. NICHOLAS
Trellys Cromlech on the side of the road near Tre-llys-y-coed (SM 905349). Until 1912 it was marked as 𝕮𝖗𝖔𝖒𝖑𝖊𝖈𝖍 on Ordnance Survey maps and then as 𝕭𝖚𝖗𝖎𝖆𝖑 𝕮𝖍𝖆𝖒𝖇𝖊𝖗 although in 1951 on the scale of 1:25,000 it was marked as 𝕱𝖋𝖘𝖙 𝕾𝖆𝖒𝖘𝖔𝖓. A.C. (1883), p.345. R.C.A.M. No. 1064 of Pembroke calls it Ffst Samson and has a description and photograph. *The Queen's Wales, South Wales,* by H. L. V. Fletcher (Hodder and Stoughton, London, 1956), p.115, calls it Samson's Quoit.

154. ST. PETROCS
Harold Stone between Sampson and Stackpole Warren (SR 968958). It is marked as 𝕳𝖆𝖗𝖔𝖑𝖉 𝕾𝖙𝖔𝖓𝖊 on Ordnance Survey maps of 1952 and 1956. R.C.A.M. p.381 of Pembroke mentions that this is the second of the Devil's Quoits. There are three of these in a direct alignment ending at the Devil's Quoit at Angle. On a certain day in the year the Dancing Stones at Stackpole are supposed to meet and go down to Rhyd Sais (Saxon's Ford) to dance and, when they are tired, the three stones return to their individual sites.

Devil's Quoit, Dyfed.   *Chris Barber*

feet high called Sampson's Farm Stone and it is one of the three Devil's Quoits in the vicinity which are supposed to meet and go down to the water to dance. R.C.A.M. p.381 of Pembroke.

156. STACKPOLE ELIDYR

Devil's Quoit on Stackpole Warren, above Fish Ponds (SR 980950). R.C.A.M. p.387 of Pembroke says that it was 6 feet above the shifting sands and leaning slightly to the west. It was apparently moved in 1881 and on its site was built a conical stone monument about 8 feet high which was called Lady Cawdor's Seat. *The Pembrokeshire Historian II* (1966), p.16, lists it as Stackpole Warren Stone. This is supposed to be one of the three Devil's quoits which meet annually to dance at Rhyd Sais.

Strange Rocks at Treffgarn, Dyfed.   *Chris Barber*

157. TREFFGARN

Stone circles or hut circles below the rocks of Maiden Castle (SM 955251). On Ordnance Survey maps from 1952 the site is marked as Hut Circles. There are many large stones of strange shapes scattered in this area.

158. WHITCHURCH

Standing Stone at Nine Wells, Solva, near Llanungar Fawr (SM 791250). On the Ordnance Survey map of 1919 it is marked as Cromlech. R.C.A.M. p.410 of Pembroke. This stone was probably destroyed before 1962 during the construction of the Royal Naval Air Station. *The History of Solva,* by F. W. Warburton (London, 1944), p.9, states that it was 7 feet high.

159. WHITCHURCH

Tremaenhir Standing Stones in a field beside the road at Tremaenhir Farm near Gaerwen (SM 827264). They are marked as Maen Hir on one inch Ordnance Survey maps of 1912 and 1919 and as Standing Stones on 1951 and later. A.C. (1974), p.42, says that two stones are over 6 feet high. R.C.A.M. No. 1165 of Pembroke. *The History of Solva,* by F. W. Warburton (London, 1944), p.9, states that there were formerly three maenhirs at Tremaenhir of which two remain, the other having been built into the fireplace of the farmhouse.

GWENT

Gwern-y-Cleppa Dolmen, Gwent.   *Chris Barber*

160. DUFFRYN

Gwern-y-Cleppa Dolmen in a field adjoining Maes Arthur and to the north of the M4 near Tredegar Park, outside Newport (ST 272860). A.C. (1909), p.271; (1913), p.83. *Historical Traditions and Facts Relating to Ancient Gwent or Siluria,* by W. N. Johns (W. N. Johns, Newport, 1897) Pt. I, p79, states that three of the uprights were in situ and of siliceous grey sandstone.

The Langstone, Gwent.   *Chris Barber*

161. LANGSTONE

The Langstone in fields to the east of Langstone Court (ST 380898). *Monmouthshire Sketchbook,* by Fred J. Hando (Newport, 1957), says that it is an unusual stone, shaped in plan like a bishop's mitre and there is a sketch on p.9.

162. LLANDDEWI SKIRRID

Maen Llwyd, a standing stone that stood in a field on the side of a trackway leading from a place called Maen Llwyd to Parsonage Farm (SO 344156). It is marked as 𝕸aen 𝕷𝖑𝖜𝖞𝖉 on the one inch Ordnance Survey map of 1831 and on the Ordnance Survey 1:25,000 scale map of 1956.

Gaer Llwyd Dolmen, Gwent.   *Chris Barber*

163. LLANGWM

Gaer Llwyd Dolmen, which stands in a field near crossroads on the B4235 Usk to Chepstow road (ST 445968). It is marked as 𝕭urial 𝕮hamber on recent Ordnance Survey maps. A.C. (1846), p.277, with illustration under Newchurch; (1855), p.122, calls it Gwal y filiast; (1909), pp.27 and 266. The dolmen is sometimes called Garnllwyd Dolmen and the capstone is 12 feet in length.

164. LLANGYBI

A standing stone in the middle of a field between Llangybi Church and the River Usk (ST 381965). It is marked as 𝕾tanding 𝕾tone on Ordnance Survey maps of 1951 and 1953. *Mysterious Wales,* by Chris Barber (David and Charles, Newton Abbot, 1982), pp.12-13, has a photograph of this 6-feet-high stone which is the only published illustration available.

165. LLANFAIR DISCOED

The remains of a stone circle on the south-east side of Gray Hill near Penhein (ST 445933). 𝕾tone 𝕮ircle is marked on recent Ordnance Survey maps. The earliest mention of this circle is in *Historical Traditions and Facts Relating to Ancient Gwent or Siluria,* by W. N. Johns (W. N. Johns, Newport, 1897), Pt. I, p.76, where it is said to have been destroyed twenty years before.

166. LLANFAIR DISCOED

A stone circle on the south side of Gray Hill, above Caerwent (ST 438935). It is marked as 𝕾tone 𝕮ircle on the one inch Ordnance Survey map of 1953. A.C. (1909), p.277. It is 32 feet in diameter with thirteen stones.

Llangybi Stone, Gwent.   *Chris Barber*

167. LLANFIHANGEL NEAR ROGIET

A standing stone called the Devil's Quoit, between the church and Upper Grange (ST 439881). It is marked as 𝔖tanding 𝔖tone on 1981 Ordnance Survey maps. *Historical Traditions and Facts Relating to Ancient Gwent or Siluria,* by W. N. Johns (W. N. Johns, Newport, 1897), Pt. I, p.91, says that it is 7 feet high and was supposed to have been hurled from Portishead across the Bristol Channel in Somerset.

The Devil's Quoit, Dyfed.   Chris Barber

168. LLANFIHANGEL NEAR ROGIET

A standing stone in the middle of a field west of the church (ST 448876). The Ordnance Survey map of 1981 shows this as 𝔖tanding 𝔖tone. It is 6 feet high and is known as the Devil's Quoit, having been hurled to this spot from Portishead, Somerset, by the Devil in a fit of temper.

169. MICHAELSTONE-Y-FEDW

A standing stone in a private garden at Druidstone House, St. Mellons, near Began (ST 235836). It is marked as 𝔖tanding 𝔖tone on the one inch Ordnance Survey map of 1947. A.C. (1909), pp.267 and 272; (1915), p.282. *Mysterious Wales,* by Chris Barber (David and Charles, Newton Abbot, 1982), p.17, with photograph, states that it is 10 feet 6 inches high. When a cock crows at midnight the stone uproots itself and goes down to the river for a swim.

170. PORTSKEWETT

Heston Brake Dolmen on the brow of a hill near Black Rock (ST 506887). It is marked as 𝔏ong 𝔅arrow on the Ordnance Survey maps of 1953 and 1981. A.C. (1855), p.17, refers to nine upright stones. *Proceedings Clifton Antiquarian Club II* Pt. I (1888-9), pp.64-6, mentions excavations in 1888 which indicated that the mound had been opened and examined at an earlier period.

171. TRELLECH

Harold's Stones in a field adjoining the road to Chepstow at the south end of the village. These are three very large stones, 9, 12 and 15 feet high (SO 498052). The most recent Ordnance Survey maps have them marked as 𝔥arold's 𝔖tones. A.C. (1855), p.120; (1857), p.415; (1861), p.59; (1940), p.169. These are the most notable prehistoric standing stones in Gwent. See Chapter 4 for a detailed description.

The Druidstone, Gwent.　　　　　　　　　　　　　　　　　　　　*Chris Barber*

GWYNEDD

172. ABERECH

A dolmen at Four Crosses near the road leading to Pwllheli (SH 3991 3849). It is marked as 𝔅urial 𝔠hamber on the 1952 Ordnance Survey map. A.C. (1849), p.4; (1855), p.179; (1937), pp.165-7. R.C.A.M. No. 1515 and Fig. 50 of Caernarfon.

173. ABERECH

A standing stone near Four Crosses on level ground (SH 4001 3899). R.C.A.M. No. 1514 (1) describes a large monolith 5 feet 6 inches high.

Din Dryfal Dolmen, Gwynedd (1900).   *John E. Griffith*

174. ABERFFRAW

Din Dryfal Dolmen situated to the west of the village and to the east of Bodfeirig (SH 348686). A.C. (1871), p.308; (1908), p.8. R.C.A.M. p.2 of Anglesey has a photograph and plan. *Portfolio of photographs of the Cromlechs of Anglesey and Caernarvonshire*, by John E. Griffith (Bangor N.D., c.1900), has a photograph and calls it Dinas Dindryfal and mentions a huge upright stone 11 feet high.

175. AMLWCH

A standing stone near Werthyr to the west of the parish church and near a road junction (SH 415928). It is marked as 𝔐aen 𝔥ir on the Ordnance Survey map of 1841 and as 𝔖tanding 𝔖tone on the 1953 map and later editions. R.C.A.M. p.3 of Anglesey says that it is 9½ feet high.

176. BODEDERN

Presaddfed Dolmens at the south end of Llyn Llywenen (SH 347809). The site is marked as 𝔠romlech on the Ordnance Survey map of 1841 and as 𝔅urial 𝔠hamber on later maps. A.C. (1855), p.25; (1871), p.283; (1908), p6; (1985), p.267. R.C.A.M. p.18 of Anglesey mentions a coverstone 12½ feet long.

177. BODEWYRD

A standing stone between Plas Bodewyrd and Gwedrog (SH 406903). It is marked as 𝔐aenhir on the one inch Ordnance Survey map of 1841 and as 𝔖tanding 𝔖tone on recent ones. R.C.A.M. p.19 of Anglesey says that it is 13 feet high. *More Mysterious Wales,* by Chris Barber (David and Charles, Newton Abbot, 1986), p.2, has a good photograph and says that the stone is called Carreg Lefn (The Smooth Stone) or Maen Press (The Brass Stone) and there are stories of hidden treasure nearby.

178. CAERHUN
Barclodiad-y-Gawres or The Giantess's Apronful, a Dolmen usually called a Carn in the valley of Afon Tafalog at 1,300 feet (SH 71647165). Carn is marked on most Ordnance Survey maps. R.C.A.M. No. 167 of Caernarfon mentions a cist 8 feet long at the north end of the carn. *Mysterious Wales,* by Chris Barber (David and Charles, Newton Abbot, 1982), p.64, mentions a legend that the stones came from the Island of Mona (Anglesey).

Bwlch y Ddeufaen Stone, Gwynedd.   *Chris Barber*

179. CAERHUN
A standing stone in the pass known as Bwlch y Ddeufaen at 1,350 feet (SH 7152 7177). A.C. (1846), p.73, with illustration. R.C.A.M. No. 173 of Caernarfon.

180. CAERHUN

The Giant's Stick, Arthur's Spear, Picell Arthur or Fron-y-cawr are the various names of a standing stone on the south edge of a Roman road at 1,100 feet (SH 7386 7167). R.C.A.M. No. 176 of Caernarfon. *Mysterious Wales*, by Chris Barber (David and Charles, Newton Abbot, 1982), p.30, describes it as a long needle-shaped stone 7 feet 3 inches high. A giant is supposed to have thrown his stick from Tal y Fan at his dog and it stuck in the ground to form this standing stone.

181. CAERHUN

Cerrig Pryfaid Stone Circle, near Bwlch y Ddwyfan (SH 72437133). A.C. (1846), p.73, mentions Cerrig y Pryfed, The Stone of the Flies. R.C.A.M. No. 177 of Caernarfon says that this stone circle is 75 feet in diameter with fourteen stones.

Maen-y-Bard Dolmen, Gwynedd.   *Chris Barber*

182. CAERHUN

Maen y Bard Dolmen, otherwise referred to as The Bard's Stone, Cwrt-y-Filiast, The Greyhound Kennel, Llech yr Ast or Cwrt-y-Bugail. It stands on the north side of the road to Caernarfon at an altitude of just over 1,000 feet (SH 7406 7179). On the one inch Ordnance Survey map of 1947 it is marked as 𝕮𝖗𝖔𝖒𝖑𝖊𝖈𝖍 and as 𝕭𝖚𝖗𝖎𝖆𝖑 𝕮𝖍𝖆𝖒𝖇𝖊𝖗 on later maps. A.C. (1904), p.198; (1912), p.40. R.C.A.M. No. 178 of Caernarfon.

183. CAERHUN

Porth-llwyd Dolmen on the floor of the Conwy Valley at 25 feet above sea level (SH 7703 6776). It is marked as 𝕮𝖗𝖔𝖒𝖑𝖊𝖈𝖍 on the one inch Ordnance Survey map of 1841 but nothing is shown on later maps. R.C.A.M. No. 180 of Caernarfon states that the capstone was 9 feet 6 inches long and that one of the three uprights was displaced by a flood in 1925.

Clynog Dolmen, Gwynedd (1900).   *John E. Griffith*

184. CLYNNOG

Bachwen Clynnog Dolmen, near Bachwen (SH 4076 4947). It is marked as 𝕮𝖗𝖔𝖒𝖑𝖊𝖈𝖍 on Ordnance Survey map in 1840 and as 𝕭𝖚𝖗𝖎𝖆𝖑 𝕮𝖍𝖆𝖒𝖇𝖊𝖗 on recent editions. A.C. (1848), p.270; (1849), p.1; (1855), p.179; (1867), p.152; (1877), p.333; (1888), p.58; (1895), p.145; (1902), p.155; (1903), p.260; (1904), p.198; (1926), p.429. R.C.A.M. No. 861 of Caernarfon says that the capstone is 9 feet long and the greater part of the upper surface is covered with artificial cup-shaped hollows, approximately 110 in number arranged in no apparent order.

185. CLYNNOG

Maen Dylan, a standing stone at Cefn Graennog (SH 4552 4917). It is marked as 𝕸𝖆𝖊𝖓 𝕳𝖎𝖗 on the 1840 Ordnance Survey map and as 𝕾𝖙𝖆𝖓𝖉𝖎𝖓𝖌 𝕾𝖙𝖔𝖓𝖊 on some later editions. A.C. (1849), p.126. R.C.A.M. No. 855 of Caernarfon says that it is 10 feet high.

186. CLYNNOG

Penarth Dolmen in a field called Caer Goetan between a road and the mouth of the Afon Desach (SH 4300 5107). It is marked as 𝕮𝖗𝖔𝖒𝖑𝖊𝖈𝖍 on the one inch Ordnance Survey map of 1840 and as 𝕭𝖚𝖗𝖎𝖆𝖑 𝕮𝖍𝖆𝖒𝖇𝖊𝖗 on the 1952 map. ...C. (1848), p.270; (1849), pp.1 and 126; (1855), p.179; (1867), p.152; (1877), p.333; (1895), pp.58 and 145; (1902), p.155; (1903), p.260; (1904), p.198. R.C.A.M. No. 862 of Caernarfon with plan.

187. DOLBENAMEN

A standing stone at Fach goch (SH 5684 4115). It is marked as 𝕾𝖙𝖆𝖓𝖉𝖎𝖓𝖌 𝕾𝖙𝖔𝖓𝖊 on the Ordnance Survey map of 1952. R.C.A.M. No. 1024 of Caernarfon states that it is 7 feet 6 inches high, rising to a point.

188. DWYGYFYLCHI

Druids' Circle or Meini Hirion near Cefn Coch and sometimes referred to as Stone Circle at Aber (SH 7219 7463). Most Ordnance Survey maps show it as 𝕾𝖙𝖔𝖓𝖊 𝕮𝖎𝖗𝖈𝖑𝖊. A.C. (1846), p.71; (1848), p.288; (1865), p.137; (1868), p.177; (1882), p.323. R.C.A.M. No. 280 of Caernarfon mentions three circles. Some reports mention

139

twelve stones up to 8 feet high. One of these is called The Deity Stone and another is known as The Stone of Sacrifice.

Meini Hirion, Gwynedd.   *Chris Barber*

189. DWYGYFYLCHI
Meini Hirion, a stone circle near Cefn Coch, sometimes called The Druid's Circle (SH 7228 7466). It is marked as 𝕸aenau 𝕳irion on the 1841 one inch Ordnance Survey maps and as 𝕾tone 𝕮ircle on the 1953 edition. Often it gets confused with the previously mentioned site (206) which is nearby and is called The Druids' Circle in some reports. A.C. (1861), p.151. R.C.A.M. No. 277 of Caernarfon mentions ten stones in a circle 72 feet in diameter.

190. GYFFIN
Maen Campiau, a standing stone near a carnedd and a small stone circle (SH 7478 7496). It is marked as 𝕸aenhir on the 1947 Ordnance Survey map and as 𝕾tanding 𝕾tone on the 1953 edition. A.C. (1912), p.59. R.C.A.M. No. 303 of Caernarfon refers to it as Maen-y-Campiau or the Stone of Games.

191. GYFFIN
A stone circle near Maen-y-Campiau (SH 7472 7528). A.C. (1912), p.55. R.C.A.M. No. 304 of Caernarfon mentions six stones in a circle 40 feet in diameter.

192. HOLYHEAD
A dolmen near Trearddur on the east side of the road going towards Tregof (SH 264802). R.C.A.M. p.23 of Anglesey says that it is on the summit of a low rocky outcrop. It had one upright stone and a recumbent stone 7 feet by 4½ feet by 1 foot thick.

193. HOLYHEAD RURAL
A standing stone on the east side of the road leading to Trearddur Bay (SH 251808). It is marked as 𝕸aen 𝕳ir on the 1839 Ordnance Survey map and as 𝕾tanding 𝕾tone on later editions. A.C. (1867), p.234; (1870), p.362. R.C.A.M. No. 12 of Anglesey, p.23, calls it Coetan Arthur and says that it is 8½ feet high.

194. HOLYHEAD RURAL

A group of standing stones on the summit of Holyhead Mountain (SH 218827). They are marked on the 1839 Ordnance Survey map as 𝔐eini 𝔐oelton or 𝔅ald 𝔖tones. A.C. (1855), p.24, calls them Meini Moelion a group of numerous erect rounded stones. R.C.A.M. No. 7 of Anglesey, p.23, mentions five stones.

195. HOLYHEAD RURAL

Trefignath Dolmen, near Tre Arddu and the railway line (SH 263804). The site is marked as 𝔅urial 𝔠hambers on recent Ordnance Survey maps and as 𝔠romlechau on the 1841 map. A.C. (1855), p.25; (1867), p.284; (1870), p.362; (1908), p.6. R.C.A.M. p.22 of Anglesey has two good photographs.

196. HOLYHEAD RURAL

Two standing stones near Plas Meilw and Bod Warren (SH 227809). They are marked as 𝔐eini 𝔥irion on the 1839 Ordnance Survey map and as 𝔖tanding 𝔖tones on recent editions. A.C. (1855), p.24, mentions two stones at Plas Milo. R.C.A.M. p.23 of Anglesey has a good photograph and says that both stones are 10 feet high with the major axis in line to NNE.

Cerrig Arthur, Gwynedd.   *Chris Barber*

197. LLANABER

Cerrig Arthur is the remains of a small embanked stone circle situated near Sylfaen Farm (SH 6316 1888). A.C. (1984) mentions five stones on a flattened circle and one stone of considerable size just within the ring.

198. LLANABER

Hengwm Stone Circle near Pen-y-dinas (SH 6163 2031). It is marked as 𝔠arnedd 𝔥engwm on Ordnance Survey maps and sometimes referred to as a carn circle or a portal dolmen. A.C. (1920), pp.112-4. *History of Merioneth*, by E. G. Bowen and C. A. Gresham (Llandyssul, 1967), Vol. I, p.105, No. 163 and plan and illustration on p.90.

Glasfryn Stone, Gwynedd.   Chris Barber

199. LLANAELHAEARN

Glasfryn Standing Stone, in a field near Llyn Glasfryn, east of the A499 between Llanaelhaearn Village and Four Crosses (SH 403425). *More Mysterious Wales,* by Chris Barber (David and Charles, Newton Abbot, 1986), p.6, has a good photograph and says that the stone is associated with the story of a young lady who long ago used to be the Glasfryn well keeper. One day she was careless and forgot to replace the cover on the well. During the night the water gushed out and formed a deep lake. For her mistake the lady well keeper was turned into stone.

200. LLANARMON

A standing stone in the farmyard at Plasdu (SH 4115 4028). A.C. (1903), p.261, says that it was 10 feet 2 inches in height and 10 feet 3 inches in circumference. R.C.A.M. No. 1098 of Caernarfon mentions that it was recumbent and 11 feet in length.

201. LLANBABO

A standing stone to the west of Bodeiniol Farm and near Meiriogen (SH 368858). It is marked as 𝔖tanding 𝔖tone on the 1953 Ordnance Survey map and later editions. R.C.A.M. No. 3 of Anglesey, p.36, says that it is 8 feet 6 inches high.

anbedr Stones, Gwynedd.   *Chris Barber*

202. LLANBEDR
Standing stones between the main road to Harlech and Afon Atro (SH 5833 2701). There are now only two stones which are about 7 and 10 feet high. They are surrounded by iron railings which also enclose a young oak tree and a mass of brambles. Some reports mention a third stone about 3 feet high which J.G.W. did not see in August, 1967. A.C. (1867), p.154 and (1904), p.49.

203. LLANBEDR
Stone circle between Waun Hir and Tal-y-ffynonau at about 750' altitude (SH 610240). It is marked as Stone Circle on Ordnance Survey map. When J.G.W. visited the site on 21st August, 1976, he observed fourteen stones. They were difficult to find, for none of them were more than 2 feet 6 inches high.

204. LLANBEDROG
Mynydd Tir Cwmmwd Cromlech on the east side of Mynydd Tycwmwd near Tanymynydd (SH 3250 3110). A.C. (1847), p.99; (1872), p.51. R.C.A.M. No. 1580 of Caernarfon.

205. LLANBEDR-Y-CENIN
A standing stone in the churchyard (SH 585269). It is about 3 feet high with a single spiral neatly incised. A.C. (1904), p.149.

206. LLANDANWG
Arthur's Quoit, the remains of a dolmen between Harlech Castle and the beach, on the side of a road (SH 576317). *The Cambrian Traveller's Guide and Pocket Companion* (1808) provides details mentioning a large flat stone that was supported by three others near Harlech Castle.

207. LLANDDWYE-IS-Y-CRAIG
The remains of a dolmen called Cors y Gedol or Coetan Arthur, on the banks of Afon Ysgethin at Pont Fadog (SH 6033 2283). On Ordnance Survey maps it is marked as Burial Chamber. A.C. (1869), p.134; (1920), p.132. The drawing in William

Stukeley's *Itinerarium* (plate 94) shows that the huge capstone which measures about 12 feet by 10 feet was thrown down to its present position before the end of the 18th century. It is said to have been hurled to this location by Arthur from the summit of Moelfre Hill.

Bryn Celli Ddu Dolmen, Gwynedd.   *Chris Barber*

208. LLANDDANIEL FAB

Bryn Celli Ddu Dolmen near Pant-y-Crug (SH 508702). It is one of the best-known dolmens in Wales and is marked on recent Ordnance Survey maps as 𝔅𝔯𝔶𝔫 𝔠𝔢𝔩𝔩𝔦 𝔡𝔡𝔲 𝔠𝔥𝔞𝔪𝔟𝔢𝔯𝔢𝔡 𝔠𝔞𝔦𝔯𝔫. A.C. (1847), p.1; (1854), p.205; (1860), p.364; (1869), p.140; (1895), p.157; (1908), p.8; (1931), pp.216-58; (1969), pp.17-48; (1985), p.269. R.C.A.M. p.44 of Anglesey with plan and photographs. *Bryn Celli Ddu, Anglesey,* by Frances Lynch (a leaflet produced by the Ministry of Public Buildings and Works on behalf of the Welsh Office, 1970), has some useful data, plan and photographs and part of it is in Welsh. There are over fifty other references to this dolmen.

209. LLANDDEINIOLEN

A stone circle near Pen Dinas and Ffynnon Cegin Arthur (Arthur's Kitchen Well) (SH 5470 6490). It is marked as 𝔖𝔱𝔬𝔫𝔢 𝔠𝔦𝔯𝔠𝔩𝔢 on one inch Ordnance Survey map of 1953. R.C.A.M. No. 1193 of Caernarfon calls it Cairn, Glyn Arthur and says that it is an oval of twenty stones.

210. LLANDDONA

A standing stone about 300 yards east of Cremlyn Dolmen near Brynglas (SH 572776). It is marked on the 1946 Ordnance Survey map as 𝔐𝔢𝔦𝔫𝔥𝔦𝔯 and 𝔖𝔱𝔞𝔫𝔡𝔦𝔫𝔤 𝔖𝔱𝔬𝔫𝔢 on later editions. R.C.A.M. No. 4 of Anglesey, p.45, says that it is 9½ feet high and is of green mica schist.

211. LLANDDONA

A standing stone 260 yards SSE of Cremlyn Dolmen, near Cremlyn (SH 572774). On the 1953 and 1962 Ordnance Survey maps, it is shown as one of two 𝔖𝔱𝔞𝔫𝔡𝔦𝔫𝔤 𝔖𝔱𝔬𝔫𝔢𝔰. R.C.A.M. No. 5 of Anglesey, p.45, says that it stands 7½ feet high.

The 'patterned stone' outside Bryn Celli Ddu Dolmen.   *Chris Barber*

212. LLANDDYFNAN
Arthur's Quoit, a dolmen near the road at Glyn (SH 5150 8174). It is marked as 𝕮𝖗𝖔𝖒𝖑𝖊𝖈𝖍 on the 1947 Ordnance Survey map and as 𝕭𝖚𝖗𝖎𝖆𝖑 𝕮𝖍𝖆𝖒𝖇𝖊𝖗 on later editions. A.C. (1908), p.7; (1966), p.24. R.C.A.M. No. 8 of Anglesey, p.48.

213. LLANDDYFNAN
Standing stone near The Rectory leaning at an angle of 45° towards the north (SH 502787). It is marked as 𝕸𝖆𝖊𝖓 𝕳𝖎𝖗 on Ordnance Survey maps from 1841 to 1947 and then afterwards shown as 𝕾𝖙𝖆𝖓𝖉𝖎𝖓𝖌 𝕾𝖙𝖔𝖓𝖊. R.C.A.M. No. 12 of Anglesey, p.49.

214. LLENDEGAI
Yr Hen Allor Dolmen at Sling on land belonging to Ffynon Bach Farm (SH 6055 6686). On the 1962 Ordnance Survey map it is marked as 𝕭𝖚𝖗𝖎𝖆𝖑 𝕮𝖍𝖆𝖒𝖇𝖊𝖗. A.C. (1867), p.62; (1869), p.127; (1904), p.198. R.C.A.M. No. 259 of Caernarfon.

215. LLANDEGFAN
A standing stone south-west of the church on a bank between Redair groeshon and Plas Cadnant (SH 557737). R.C.A.M. No. 3 of Anglesey, p.50, says that it is 9½ feet high. *A Shell Guide of North Wales*, by Elizabeth Beazley and Lionel Brett (Faber and Faber, London, 1971), p.80, has a good photograph.

216. LLANDEUSANT
Bedd Bronwen Dolmen, sometimes called Bedd Branwen or Bod-Deiniol, in a field west of the farmhouse of Bod-Deiniol (SH 361850). On Ordnance Survey maps from 1953 it is shown as 𝕭𝖊𝖉𝖉 𝕭𝖗𝖆𝖓𝖜𝖊𝖓. A.C. (1908), p.9; (1971), p.11. *Mysterious Wales,* by Chris Barber (David and Charles, Newton Abbot, 1982), p.33, under Branwen's Grave, Treffynon has a photograph.

Llety'r Filiast Dolmen, Gwynedd (1900).   *John E. Griffith*

217. LLANDUDNO
Llety'r Filiast Dolmen at Maes y Farell, halfway up Great Orme's Head (SH 7721 8295). A.C. (1904), p.198; (1912), p.146. R.C.A.M. No. 378 of Caernarfon has a plan and illustration. *The Archaeology of the Great Orme's Head, North Wales,* by J. Smith Jnr. (B. Woodcock, Llandudno, 1875), p.16, calls it a

cromlech in which the bones of the mythical hag Keridwen (the reputed mother of the bard Taliesin) are supposed to be interred.

Maen Sigl, Gwynedd.   *Chris Barber*

218. LLANDUDNO

Maen Sigl, a rocking stone at Pen-y-ddinas on Orme's Head (SH 775830). It is also known as Cryd Tudno or Tudno's Cradle. R.C.A.M. No. 367 of Caernarfon. Unfortunately it was thrown off its rocking position before 1860.

219. LLANDWROG

Maen Llwyd, a standing stone in Glynllifon Park on the east side of the main road (SH 4449 5415). It is marked as 𝕸𝖆𝖊𝖓 𝕷𝖑𝖜𝖞𝖉 on the Ordnance Survey map of 1962. A.C. (1875), p.303 and 381; (1932), p.199. R.C.A.M. No. 1237 of Caernarfon says that it is 9 feet 6 inches high.

220. LLANDYFRYDOG

Carreg Leidr, a standing stone in a field near the church (SH 447844). On the Ordnance Survey map of 1841 it is marked as 𝕮𝖆𝖗𝖊𝖌 𝖞 𝕷𝖑𝖊𝖎𝖉𝖗 (Rock of the Robber) and as 𝕮𝖆𝖗𝖗𝖊𝖌 𝖑𝖊𝖎𝖉𝖗 on the 1953 map and later. A.C. (1867), p.346, says that it is 5 feet high. It looks like a hump-backed man and a story is told about a man who stole the church bible and was turned into stone while carrying it away.

221. LLANDYFRYDOG

Maen Chwyf, the remains of a dolmen at Bryndyfrydog near the crossroads (SH 432857). On all Ordnance Survey maps it is marked as 𝕸𝖆𝖊𝖓 𝕮𝖍𝖜𝖞𝖋. A.C. (1855), p.23, calls it Maen Chwyt. R.C.A.M. No. 5 of Anglesey, p.52. *The Lost Land of Arthur*, by J. Curning Walter (1909), p.48, says that it is in the wooded grounds of Llwydiarth and is a rocking stone called Arthur's Quoit.

222. LLANEDWEN

Plas Newydd Dolmen in Plas Newydd Park is one of the best-known in Wales and is remarkable for the size of its chamber and coverstone (SH 520697). It is marked as 𝕮𝖗𝖔𝖒𝖑𝖊𝖈𝖍 on the Ordnance Survey map of 1841 and as 𝕭𝖚𝖗𝖎𝖆𝖑 𝕮𝖍𝖆𝖒𝖇𝖊𝖗 on 1947 and later maps. A.C. (1860), p.367; (1870), pp.51-6; (1880), pp.81-96; (1872), p.106; (1908), p.8; (1862) has a frontispiece illustration; (1983), p.1.XX, has a copy of an

Plas Newydd Dolmen, Gwynedd (1900).   *John E. Griffith*

old print; (1985), p.269. R.C.A.M. No. 8 of Anglesey, p.56, has a full description, plan and photographs. Amongst the many references to this dolmen, the earliest with an illustration is *Druidical Antiquities*, published by S. Hooper on 16th April, 1784, which shows two capstones with the larger one resting on five upright stones.

Bryn-yr-Hen-Bobl Dolmen, Gwynedd (1900).   *John E. Griffith*

223. LLANEDWEN
Bryn-yr-Hen-Bobl Dolmen in Plas Newydd Park. The name means "The Hill of the Old People" (SH 519690). It is marked as 𝔅𝔲𝔯𝔦𝔞𝔩 ℭ𝔥𝔞𝔪𝔟𝔢𝔯 on the one inch Ordnance Survey map of 1947, 𝔏𝔬𝔫𝔤 𝔅𝔞𝔯𝔯𝔬𝔴 on the 1953 map and as ℭ𝔥𝔞𝔪𝔟𝔢𝔯𝔢𝔡 ℭ𝔞𝔦𝔯𝔫 on later maps. A.C. (1870), p.50; (1880), p.81; (1908), p8; (1935), p.253. R.C.A.M. No. 9 of Anglesey, p.57, has a plan and photograph.

224. LLANEGRYN
Bryn Seward Standing Stone on the side of a track between Friog and Cyfanned (SH 6260 1175). 𝔥𝔦𝔰𝔱𝔬𝔯𝔶 𝔬𝔣 𝔐𝔢𝔯𝔦𝔬𝔫𝔢𝔱𝔥, by E. C. Bowen and C. A. Gresham (Llandyssul, 1967), Vol. I, p.65, No. 80, says that it is a pointed slab 7 feet 6 inches high.

225. LLANENDDWYN
Bron-y-Foel Dolmen near Caer Ffynnon and Bron-y-Foel on Moelfre (SH 611250). Marked as ℭ𝔯𝔬𝔪𝔩𝔢𝔠𝔥 on early Ordnance Survey maps and as 𝔅𝔲𝔯𝔦𝔞𝔩 ℭ𝔥𝔞𝔪𝔟𝔢𝔯 on later editions. A.C. (1869), p.133 and an illustration opposite p.136 under Cadair Arthur. The capstone was 15 feet 8 inches by 6 feet 10 inches according to the *Royal Commission on Ancient Monuments* No. 283.

226. LLANENDDWYN
Dolmen near Bron-y-Foel on the side of the old road from Llanbedr to Bontddu (SH 6078 2462). *Royal Commission on Ancient Monuments* No. 296 says that the capstone measures 13 feet by 8 feet but *History of Merioneth*, by E. G. Bowen and C. A. Gresham (Llandyssul, 1967), Vol. I, p.21, has a plan and states that the capstone is 9 feet long and 7 feet wide.

Two Dolmens at Dyffryn Ardudwy, Gwynedd.   *Chris Barber*

227. LLANENDDWYN
Two dolmens adjoining the school in the village of Duffryn Ardudwy (SH 5887 2284). On early Ordnance Survey maps they are marked as ℭ𝔯𝔬𝔪𝔩𝔢𝔠𝔥 and as 𝔅𝔲𝔯𝔦𝔞𝔩 ℭ𝔥𝔞𝔪𝔟𝔢𝔯 on later ones. A.C. (1868), p.466-9; (1869), p.132, and (1920), p.133 with plan. They are variously referred to as Arthur's Quoit, Carreg Arthur or Coetan Arthur.

228. LLANENGAN
    Cilau Dolmen near Trwyn-Llech-y-doll and Cilau uchaf on the coast
    (SH 2960 2353). On the Ordnance Survey map of 1952 it is marked as 𝔅urial 𝔠hamber.
    A.C. (1923), p.306. R.C.A.M. No. 1601 of Caernarfon says that the capstone is
    12 feet by 9 feet by 3 feet lying collapsed.

229. LLANFAELOG
    Bodfeddan Stone on the side of the main road at Llainwen (SH 356747). It bears
    a Latin inscription and is marked as 𝔍nscribed 𝔖tone on the Ordnance Survey maps
    from 1953. A.C. (1985), p.267, mentions it as a large standing stone which carries
    an early Christian inscription. R.C.A.M. No. 4 of Anglesey, p.65, says that it is 6
    feet high.

230. LLANFAELOG
    Pentre Traeth Dolmen on the banks of the Afon Crugyll (SH 339742). It is marked
    as 𝔅urial 𝔠hamber on the one inch Ordnance Survey maps of 1953 and 1962.
    A.C. (1855), p.25; (1871), p.55; (1908), p.8. R.C.A.M. No. 2 of Anglesey, p.65.

Ty Newydd Dolmen, Gwynedd (1900).   *John E. Griffith*

231. LLANFAELOG
    Ty Newydd Dolmen on the crest of a broad ridge near the road at Ty Newydd
    (SH 344739). It is marked as 𝔅urial 𝔠hamber on the Ordnance Survey maps of 1953,
    1962 and 1981. A.C. (1855), p.25; (1864), p.44; (1908), p.7; (1936), p.93; (1985),
    p.267. R.C.A.M. No. 3 of Anglesey, p.65, has a plan and photograph and says
    that the massive coverstone is 12¾ feet by 5¼ feet, resting on three uprights. When
    excavated, one-hundred-and-ten pieces of broken white quartz were found in a
    deposit of black earth over the entire floor of the chamber.

232. LLANFAETHLU
    A standing stone of chlorite sericite quartz schist on the side of the main road near
    Fadog-fach (SH 318863). Recent Ordnance Survey maps show 𝔖tanding 𝔖tone but
    the 1841 map marks it as 𝔐aen 𝔥ir. A.C. (1855), p.23, calls it a conspicuous object.
    R.C.A.M. No. 4 of Anglesey says that it is 9¼ feet high, 6 feet broad and 1 foot
    thick, on page 69.

233. LLANFAIR
    A dolmen overlooking the sea between Gwern Einion and Pensarn (SH 5873 2861).

It is marked as 𝔠𝔯𝔬𝔪𝔩𝔢𝔠𝔥 on the one inch Ordnance Survey map of 1840 and as 𝔅𝔲𝔯𝔦𝔞𝔩 𝔠𝔥𝔞𝔪𝔟𝔢𝔯 on later editions. A.C. (1869), p.134 with illustration.

234. **LLANFAIR**
Standing stone called Carreg near crossing track south of Fonlief Hir (SH 5989 3096). Marked as 𝔠𝔞𝔯𝔯𝔢𝔤 on Ordnance Survey maps. *History of Merioneth*, by E. G. Bowen and C. A. Gresham (Llandyssul, 1967), Vol. I, p.64, No. 62, says that it is a tapering column 6 feet high.

235. **LLANFAIR**
Standing stone on the side of a track near Fonlief Hir (SH 6015 3130). It is marked as 𝔖𝔱𝔞𝔫𝔡𝔦𝔫𝔤 𝔖𝔱𝔬𝔫𝔢 on Ordnance Survey maps. *History of Merioneth* (Llandyssul, 1967), Vol. I, p.64., No. 63, has an illustration and states that this tall thin grey stone is 8 feet 6 inches high.

236. **LLANFAIR**
Standing stone set in a field called Cae Meini Hirion Bach between Pen-yr-allt and Hengaeau near Bryn Hyfryd (SH 5844 2902). R.C.A.M. No. 322. *History of Merioneth*, by E. G. Bowen and C. A. Gresham (Llandyssul, 1967), Vol. I, p.64, No. 60, states that it is 10 feet high.

237. **LLANFAIR-IS-GAER**
Arthur's Cromlech or Coetan Arthur near Llanfair Hall, 50 yards east of Maen y Bard and sometimes referred to as Roe Wen East Dolmen (SH 5154 6604). On the 1922 Ordnance Survey map it is marked as 𝔠𝔯𝔬𝔪𝔩𝔢𝔠𝔥 and as 𝔅𝔲𝔯𝔦𝔞𝔩 𝔠𝔥𝔞𝔪𝔟𝔢𝔯 on 1953 and 1962 maps. A.C. (1888), p.58, mentions an old saying that anyone who sleeps under Coetan Arthur through the night of St. John's Festival would rise in the morning as strong as a giant or as weak as a dwarf. A.C. (1904), p.198; (1912), pp.40-1; (1923), p.127. R.C.A.M. No. 1252 of Carmarthen mentions that the capstone is 12 feet by 8 feet by 3 feet 6 inches.

238. **LLANFAIR-IS-GAER**
Maen-y-bard Dolmen near Arthur's Cromlech, close to Llanfair Hall (SH 513660). A.C. (1904), p.198; (1912), pp.40-41. R.C.A.M. No. 283 of Caernarfon says that it is known as Cwt-y-Bugail, Llech-yr-Ast or Cwt-y-Filiast. The capstone rests on four upright stones and measures 9 feet by 8 feet.

239. **LLANFAIR-MATHAFARN-EITHAF**
Benllech Dolmen near the coast by Bryn-y-felin (SH 5190 8275). A.C. (1855), p.25; (1965), pp.12-21, gives details of excavations in 1965 with plans and photographs.

240. **LLANFAIR-MATHAFARN-EITHAF**
Pont-y-Saer Dolmen, between Llyn Cadarn and the coast (SH 5101 8245). It is marked as 𝔠𝔯𝔬𝔪𝔩𝔢𝔠𝔥 on Ordnance Survey maps up to 1947 and then as 𝔅𝔲𝔯𝔦𝔞𝔩 𝔠𝔥𝔞𝔪𝔟𝔢𝔯. A.C. (1855), p.25; (1868), p.89; (1875), p.34; (1908), p.7; (1933), p.185; (1936), p.24. R.C.A.M. No. 2 of Anglesey, p.69.

241. **LLANFAIR PWLLGWYNGYLL**
Ty Mawr Dolmen, near the road at Four Crosses (SH 540721). On the Ordnance Survey map of 1947 it is marked as 𝔠𝔯𝔬𝔪𝔩𝔢𝔠𝔥 and as 𝔅𝔲𝔯𝔦𝔞𝔩 𝔠𝔥𝔞𝔪𝔟𝔢𝔯 on later editions. A.C. (1873), p.23; (1985), p.268. R.C.A.M. No. 2 of Anglesey, p.73, says that the capstone is 11 feet by 8 feet and formerly rested on three uprights.

242. **LLANFECHELL**
A dolmen at Foel Fawr and Gors (SH 361919). On the 1941 Ordnance Survey map it is marked as 𝔠𝔯𝔬𝔪𝔩𝔢𝔠𝔥 while the 1953 and later editions show it as 𝔅𝔲𝔯𝔦𝔞𝔩 𝔠𝔥𝔞𝔪𝔟𝔢𝔯. A.C. (1855), p.24; (1870), p.366. R.C.A.M. No. 5 of Anglesey on p.78.

243. **LLANFECHELL**
A standing stone between the village and Carrog, some 450 yards north of the church (SH 370916). On modern Ordnance Survey maps it is marked as 𝔖𝔱𝔞𝔫𝔡𝔦𝔫𝔤 𝔖𝔱𝔬𝔫𝔢. R.C.A.M. No. 6 of Anglesey, p.78, says that it is a flat slab of schist 8½ feet high.

244. LLANFECHELL

Maen Arthur or Arthur's Stone between Maes Mawr and Coeden (SH 368903). It is marked as 𝔐𝔞𝔢𝔫 𝔄𝔯𝔱𝔥𝔲𝔯 on Ordnance Survey maps from 1841 to the present edition. A.C. (1855), p.23. R.C.A.M. of Anglesey does not mention it, although the stone is shown on the map.

Meini Hirion, Gwynedd.   *Chris Barber*

245. LLANFECHELL

Meini Hirion, a triangular setting of three upright stones on a farm called Cromlech between the village and Foel Fawr (SH 364917). These appear to be marked as 𝔐𝔢𝔦𝔫𝔦 𝔥𝔦𝔯𝔦𝔬𝔫 on all the Ordnance Survey maps. A.C. (1855), p.23; (1861), p.59; (1985), p.264. R.C.A.M. No. 4 of Anglesey, p.78, has two photographs and says that the stones are 6½ feet high.

246. LLANFIHANGEL-TRE'R-BEIRDD

Maen Addwyn on the side of the road leading from Plas Llanfihangel, north of Capel Coch (SH 461833). It is marked as 𝔐𝔢𝔦𝔫𝔦 𝔄𝔡𝔡𝔴𝔶𝔫 on the 1841 Ordnance Survey map but as 𝔐𝔞𝔢𝔫 𝔄𝔡𝔡𝔴𝔶𝔫 on 1953 and later maps. A.C. (1855), p.23; (1867), p.345. R.C.A.M. No. 2 of Anglesey, p.85, says that it is 10½ feet high.

248. LLANGIAN

Yr Allor Dolmen near a small farm called Henefaul at the foot of Foel Gron Hill (SH 3033 3085). A.C. (1872), p.51; (1923), p.306. R.C.A.M. No. 1635 of Caernarfon mentions that the capstone is 12 feet long by 12 feet broad.

249. LLANGIAN

Standing Stone near Pandy on the level brow of the east side of the Horon Valley (SH 2878 3230). R.C.A.M. No. 1634 of Caernarfon states that it is 7 feet high and roughly quadrilateral at the base. It tapers to a ridge at the top, the lower 5 feet having been partly dressed to make a regular pillar, probably in recent years.

Henblas Dolmen, Gwynedd (1900).   *John E. Griffith*

250. LLANGRISTIOLUS

Henblas Dolmen, south-east of Henblas House (SH 422725). It is marked as 𝔠𝔯𝔬𝔪𝔩𝔢𝔠𝔥 on the one inch Ordnance Survey map of 1841. A.C. (1855), p.25, calls it the most gigantic cromlech in Great Britain. A.C. (1866), p.466. R.C.A.M. No. 3 of Anglesey, p.96.

Barclodiad y Gawres Dolmen, Gwynedd.   *Chris Barber*

251. LLANGWYFAN

Barclodiad y Gawres (The Giantess's Apronful), a dolmen on a coastal headland known as Mynydd Cnwc near Pen-y-Cnwc (SH 328707). It is marked as 𝔅𝔞𝔯𝔠𝔩𝔬𝔡𝔦𝔞𝔡 𝔶 𝔊𝔞𝔴𝔯𝔢𝔰 on Ordnance Survey maps from 1841, but the most recent editions show it as a 𝔠𝔥𝔞𝔪𝔟𝔢𝔯𝔢𝔡 𝔠𝔞𝔦𝔯𝔫. A.C. (1855), p.25; (1869), p.403; (1870), p.369; (1871), pp.310-311; (1908), p.7; (1967), pp.1-22; (1985), p.266. R.C.A.M. p.97 No. 3 of Anglesey has a plan and photograph. There is an old tradition that the mound was formed by a giantess dropping an apronful of stones that she was carrying for some building project. Below Barclodiad y Gawres is the rock of Arthur's Cave, where legend has it that Arthur sheltered during a war with the Irish.

252. LLANGWNADL

A standing stone on the crown of a slight hill on the farm of Penybont (SH 2084 3252). On the Ordnance Survey maps of 1840 it is marked as 𝕸aenhir and as 𝕾tanding 𝕾tone on the 1952 map. A.C. (1903). p.261, says that it is 9 feet high. R.C.A.M. No. 1640 of Caernarfon.

253. LLANGYBI

A standing stone north-west of Trallwyn on level ground (SH 39754168). It is marked as 𝕾tanding 𝕾tone on the 1952 Ordnance Survey map and as 𝕸aen 𝕳ir on earlier maps. R.C.A.M. No. 1264 of Caernarfon mentions that it is 8 feet high and the top has been split diagonally into a pointed form.

Bodwyr Dolmen, Gwynedd.   *Chris Barber*

254. LLANIDAN

Bodowyr Dolmen at the top of a slight ridge near Bodowyr Farm (SH 462682). On the 1841 Ordnance Survey map it is marked as 𝕮romlech, then as 𝕭urial 𝕮hamber on 1953 and later maps. A.C. (1860), p.367; (1869), p.263; (1878), p.24; (1908), p.8. R.C.A.M. No. 9 of Anglesey, p.103, has a photograph and plan. The cover stone is 8 feet by 6 feet.

255. LLANIDAN

A dolmen near Perthi-duon Farm, between the village of Bryn Siency and Ty Coch (SH 480668). The 1841 Ordnance Survey map shows it as 𝕮romlech and maps from 1953 onwards show 𝕭urial 𝕮hamber. A.C. (1846), p.467, refers to Perthi Cromlech near Trefarthin being 9 feet long and 7 feet broad. There is a tradition that a giant was buried near this cromlech with his head turned towards the east. A.C. (1869), p.264; (1908), p.8. R.C.A.M. No. 10 of Anglesey, p.103.

256. LLANIDAN
A stone circle near Castell Bryn Gwyn (SH 462670). It is marked as 𝕾𝖙𝖔𝖓𝖊 𝕮𝖎𝖗𝖈𝖑𝖊 on the 1953 and 1962 Ordnance Survey maps and as 𝕾𝖙𝖆𝖓𝖉𝖎𝖓𝖌 𝕾𝖙𝖔𝖓𝖊𝖘 on 1981 maps. A.C. (1871), p.34, under Tre'r Dryw bach. R.C.A.M. No. 11 of Anglesey, p.103, mentions two large erect stones remaining, one 18 feet high, 10 feet wide and 2 feet thick, and suggests that originally there was a circle of eight or nine stones. *Gibson's Camden* (1772), Vol. I, p.61, states that there were 12 stones in the circle.

257. LLANRHWYDRYS
A standing stone on the side of the road near Pen-yr-orsedd (SH 333904). This is now in part of Llanfechell Parish and the stone was marked as 𝕸𝖆𝖊𝖓 𝕳𝖎𝖗 on the one inch Ordnance Survey maps of 1841, but on the 1953 and later editions it is shown as 𝕾𝖙𝖆𝖓𝖉𝖎𝖓𝖌 𝕾𝖙𝖔𝖓𝖊. R.C.A.M. No. 3 of Anglesey, p.109, has a good photograph and says that the stone is 12¼ feet high.

258. LLANRHWYDRYS
A standing stone on the side of the road leading to Cemlyn Bay near Pen-yr-orsedd (SH 334906). On Ordnance Survey maps from 1953 it is marked as 𝕾𝖙𝖆𝖓𝖉𝖎𝖓𝖌 𝕾𝖙𝖔𝖓𝖊. A.C. (1955), p.23, refers to two stones 8 feet high. R.C.A.M. No. 4 of Anglesey, p.109, has a photograph.

259. LLANSADWRN
Cremlyn Dolmen near Hafoty Covert and Cremlyn (SH 568776). The Ordnance Survey map of 1947 shows 𝕮𝖗𝖔𝖒𝖑𝖊𝖈𝖍 and later editions indicate 𝕭𝖚𝖗𝖎𝖆𝖑 𝕮𝖍𝖆𝖒𝖇𝖊𝖗. A.C. (1908), p.7. R.C.A.M. No. 3 of Anglesey, p.45.

260. LLANSADWRN
A dolmen near Hendrefor on a small natural rise in a field adjoining Trevor or Trevawr (SH 551773). It is shown as 𝕮𝖗𝖔𝖒𝖑𝖊𝖈𝖍 on the Ordnance Survey maps of 1947 and earlier but as 𝕭𝖚𝖗𝖎𝖆𝖑 𝕮𝖍𝖆𝖒𝖇𝖊𝖗 on later maps. A.C. (1908), p.8; (1985), p.262. R.C.A.M. No. 6 of Anglesey, p.113.

261. LLANTRISANT
Maen-y-gored, a standing stone on the banks of the River Alaw near Tregwelhyth (SH 341832). The 1841 one inch Ordnance Survey maps show it as 𝕸𝖆𝖊𝖓-𝖞-𝖌𝖔𝖗𝖊𝖉 and on 1953 and later maps is shown as 𝕾𝖙𝖆𝖓𝖉𝖎𝖓𝖌 𝕾𝖙𝖔𝖓𝖊. A.C. (1855), p.24. R.C.A.M. No. 3 of Anglesey, p.114, says that it is 8½ feet high but it has been broken into three pieces and is held together with metal straps.

262. LLANYSTUMDWY
Coetan Arthur Dolmen near Ystumcegid Isaf on a low hill (SH 49794132). It is marked as 𝕮𝖗𝖔𝖒𝖑𝖊𝖈𝖍 on Ordnance Survey maps of 1947 and before, and as 𝕭𝖚𝖗𝖎𝖆𝖑 𝕮𝖍𝖆𝖒𝖇𝖊𝖗 on later editions. A.C. (1855), p.179; (1869), p.136; (1872), p.136; (1903), p.260; (1904), p.148 with photograph. R.C.A.M. No. 1378 of Caernarfon has a plan. It is also called Ytumcegid Cromlech and Arthur's Quoit. There is a legend that it had been thrown there by Arthur from a hill near Beddgelert.

263. LLANYSTUMDWY
Cefn Isaf Dolmen, on level ground at Rhoslan (SH 4834 4088). It has a very large domed capstone which is mushroom-shaped and supported by four upright stones. It is marked as 𝕮𝖗𝖔𝖒𝖑𝖊𝖈𝖍 on the one inch Ordnance Survey map of 1947 and as 𝕭𝖚𝖗𝖎𝖆𝖑 𝕮𝖍𝖆𝖒𝖇𝖊𝖗 on later editions. A.C. (1849), p.2; (1855), p.150; (1869), p.137; (1904), p.148. R.C.A.M. No. 1377 of Caernarfon has a plan and a photograph and says that local memory in 1924 recorded the existence of a surrounding stone circle.

264. LLANYSTUMDWY
A standing stone north of Bettws-fawr on the summit of a low hill (SH 4646 4059). It is marked as 𝕳𝖎𝖗𝖋𝖆𝖊𝖓 on the Ordnance Survey maps of 1840 and 1952. R.C.A.M. No. 1374 of Caernarfon says that it is a pillar of grey granite 8 feet 6 inches high.

265. LLECHCYNFARWY
Maen llech Gwern Farwydd (The Slate Stone in Grove of Alders and Beech Trees)

in a field adjoining the church (SH 382812). It is marked as 𝕸𝖆𝖊𝖓 𝕳𝖎𝖗 on the one inch Ordnance Survey map of 1841. A.C. (1855), p.24, says that it was broken up for mending a wall. *The Scientific Journey Through England and Wales and Scotland,* by Thomas Walford (John Booth, London, 1818), under Llech-Cynfarwy, mentions it as a stone of memorial 9 feet high.

266. LLECHWEDD
Maen Penddu, a standing stone in the line of an old enclosure bank (SH 7391 7358). It is marked as 𝕸𝖆𝖊𝖓 𝕻𝖊𝖓𝖉𝖉𝖚 on Ordnance Survey maps of 1947 and 1953. A.C. (1912), p.59. R.C.A.M. No. 594 of Caernarfon. It is also known as Maen y Campau.

Maen Twrog, Gwynedd.   *Chris Barber*

267. MAENTWROG
A standing stone known as Maen Twrog stands against the west wall of the parish church (SH 664406). R.C.A.M. No. 469 of Merioneth. Twrog is supposed to have thrown this stone from the top of Moelwyn, a mountain to the north of here. On landing in the valley, the stone crashed a pagan altar and the imprint of St. Twrog's hand is claimed to be still visible on the surface of this megalith.

Coetan Arthur, Gwynedd (1900).   *John E. Griffith*

268. PENLLECH

Coetan Arthur, a dolmen between Mynydd Cefn Amwlch and Cefn Amwlch (SH 22973456). It is marked as 𝕮𝖗𝖔𝖒𝖑𝖊𝖈𝖍 on the 1840 one inch Ordnance Survey map and as 𝕭𝖚𝖗𝖎𝖆𝖑 𝕮𝖍𝖆𝖒𝖇𝖊𝖗 on the 1952 edition. A.C. (1847), p.97, calls it Mynydd Cefn Amwlch Cromlech, Coitan Arthur and Arthur's Quoit from a tradition that Arthur Gawr (Arthur the Giant) cast it off from Carn Madryn, a mountain a few miles off, and that his wife brought the other three stones in her apron and placed them as supporters or props to the Coitan. A.C. (1855), p.179; (1926), p.442. R.C.A.M. No. 1689 of Caernarfon has a plan and an illustration, plate 1.

269. PENRHOS LLIGWY

Lligwy Dolmen on the side of the road leading to Chapel Lligwy, 1¼ miles east of the Parish Church (SH 5015 8610). It is marked as 𝕭𝖚𝖗𝖎𝖆𝖑 𝕮𝖍𝖆𝖒𝖇𝖊𝖗 on 1953 and later Ordnance Survey maps. A.C. (1855), p.25; (1908), p.7; (1909), pp.217-231; (1933), p.68; (1966), pp.22-23; (1867), p.135, has an illustration and plan. R.C.A.M. No. 5 of Anglesey, p.135, says that the capstone weighs 25 tons and is 18 feet 3 inches by 15 feet 9 inches and 3 feet 6 inches. It is also called Arthur's Quoit or Coetan Arthur. *Mona, Enchanted Island,* by Geoffrey Eley (The Priory Press Ltd., Royston, Hertfordshire, 1968), p.126, gives details of an important symbolic story relating to dolmens. A fisherman is given a golden ball by a witch after he had fallen asleep under the dolmen. *A Shell Guide, North Wales,* by "Elizabeth Beazley and Lionel Brett (Faber and Faber, London, 1971), p.96, describes it as "A tremendous monument, reduced to the ridiculous by public park type railings, like a whale in a shrimping net".

270. RHIW

Tan-y-Muriau Dolmen on the slopes of Mynydd Rhiw overlooking Porth Neigul (SH 288287). It is marked as 𝕭𝖚𝖗𝖎𝖆𝖑 𝕮𝖍𝖆𝖒𝖇𝖊𝖗 on the 1952 Ordnance Survey map. A.C. (1903), p.260; (1917), pp.135-8. R.C.A.M. No. 1755 of Caernarfon has a plan and illustration.

Yr Allor Dolmen, Gwynedd (1900).   *John E. Griffith*

271. RHOSCOLYN
Yr Allor (The Altar) Dolmen near the road between Bron ddel and Pwllpilla (SH 269767). The one inch Ordnance Survey maps for 1841, 1953 and 1962 have it marked as Cromlech but the 1981 map has Gromlech. A.C. (1855), p.25. *Portfolio of Photographs of the Cromlechs of Anglesey and Caernarvonshire*, by John E. Griffith (Bangor, c.1900), has a photograph of only one solitary upright stone 5 feet 6 inches high close to the farmhouse of Cromlech.

272. TRAWSFYNNYDD
Llech Idris, a standing stone between Rhiw Goch and Afon Gain (SH 7311 3108). Marked as Llech Idris on recent Ordnance Survey maps and shown on side of road near Pig Idris. R.C.A.M. No. 565 of Merioneth. The giant Idris Gawr is reputed to have thrown this 10-feet-high stone from the summit of Cader Idris.

273. TRAWSFYNNYDD
Maen Llwyd, a standing stone near Tydin Sais and Brynre (SH 7070 3297). Marked as Maen Llwyd on recent Ordnance Survey maps. R.C.A.M. No. 566 of Merioneth.

274. TREFDRAETH
A standing stone called Tyddyn Bach near the Afon Cefn and on the west side of the Malldraeth marsh (SH 409693). A.C. (1855), p.24. R.C.A.M. No. 5 of Anglesey, p.148, says that it is 8½ feet high. Anglesey Antiquarian Society and Field Club Transactions (1938) has a photograph opposite p.28 and says that Tyddyn Bach is of Felspathic Quartzite.

275. TREFLLYS
A dolmen called Cist Gerrig which now looks like an armchair (SH 5433 3840). It is marked as Cist Cerrig on the 1962 Ordnance Survey map. A.C. (1938), p.141. R.C.A.M. No. 1418 of Caernarfon has a plan and photograph.

276. TREFLLYS
A standing stone on the side of road junction at Pentrey Felin (SH 5266 2968). A.C. (1917), p.400. R.C.A.M. No. 1417 of Caernarfon mentions that it stands 10 feet above the pavement and bears the date 1712 with a cross.

277. YNYSCYNHAERN

The remains of a stone circle, north of Cwm mawr on ground gently falling to the east (SH 5535 4145). A.C. (1849), p.3. R.C.A.M. No. 1455 of Caernarfon mentions six stones out of thirty-eight upright stones marking the remains of a circle described in 1772.

Llech Idris, Gwynedd.   *Chris Barber*

MID GLAMORGAN

278. COITY
   Coed Parc Garw Dolmen in a boundary hedge near Heol Spencer and road at Bryncetwin (SS 926819). It is marked as 𝕮𝖗𝖔𝖒𝖑𝖊𝖈𝖍 on Ordnance Survey maps of 1947 and later. R.C.A.M. No. 39 of Glamorgan.

279. GELLIGAER
   Fochriw Standing Stone on Cefn-y-Brithdir between Tir-Phil and Fochrhiw (SO 126040). This may be the remains of a small dolmen as 𝕮𝖎𝖘𝖙𝖋𝖆𝖊𝖓 is shown here on the one inch Ordnance Survey map of 1833. A.C. (1875), pp.183 and 370; (1901), p.57; (1939), p.34.

Cefn Gelligaer Stone, Mid Glamorgan.   *Chris Barber*

280. GELLIGAER
   Cefn Gelligaer Stone, near the road to Caerphilly and Marchant-y-Wayn (SO 104034). On the Ordnance Survey maps of 1947 and 1956 it is marked as 𝕾𝖙𝖆𝖓𝖉𝖎𝖓𝖌 𝕾𝖙𝖔𝖓𝖊. A.C. (1875), p.370. *More Mysterious Wales,* by Chris Barber (David and Charles, Newton Abbot, 1986), p.93, has a good photograph and says that it is sloping at a crazy angle and is 8 feet 6 inches high. There was an inscription on its eastern face which was defaced before 1859. Treasure is said to be buried beneath the stone.

281. GELLIGAER
Tegernacus Standing Stone, which has been moved to the National Museum of Wales at Cardiff. It originally stood near the chapel at Brithdir (SO 137026). A.C. (1939), p.35, has a good photograph of the standing stone in its original position and records that the site is now marked by a concrete pillar. The original was 9 feet high. *Glamorgan,* by A. Morris (Newport, Mon., 1907), p.467, calls it Maen Teyrnog and has an illustration. This may be Maen Teyrnas, meaning Stone of the Kingdom.

Pumpeius Stone, now in Margam Museum.

282. KENFIG
Bedd Morgan Morganwg, a standing stone between Kenfig and Margam (SS 828818). It is marked on the one inch Ordnance Survey map of 1923 as 𝔓umpeius 𝔖tone (𝔍nscribed). A.C. (1846), p.182; (1939), p.38. *Lapidarium Walliae, The Early Inscribed and Sculptured Stones of Wales,* by J. P. Westwood (Oxford, 1876), p.19, calls it Bedd Morgan Morganwg the sepulchere of Prince Morgan and has an illustration showing the Latin and Ogham inscriptions.

283. LALESTON
Two standing stones in a field north of Laleston village called Cae'r-hen-Eglwys (SS 879809). They were still in position when visited in July, 1983. *Annals of South Glamorgan,* by Marianne Robertson Spencer (W. Spurrell and Son, Carmarthen,

1913, and reprinted in 1970), mentions two tall menhirs about 20 feet apart and nearly 6 feet in height, known locally as Yr hen Eglwys (The Old Church), and has a photograph.

284. LLANTRISANT

Standing stone at Miskin in the bottom of a shallow valley (ST 0585 8075). A.C. (1977), p.17, gives a full account of the excavation of this hitherto unnoticed standing stone of pennant sandstone, which was 34ft. high, and has a few good photographs. It was excavated during the construction of the M4 motorway, which now passes over the site of this standing stone.

285. PENTYRCH

Cae-yr-Arfau, Cae yrfa or Cae Arfon, a dolmen on the side of the railway line between Cae-yr-Arfau and Pen-y-garn near Llantrisant (ST 080821). Cae-yr-arfau is marked on Ordnance Survey maps of 1947 and Burial Chamber on 1982 maps. A.C. (1875), pp.180-182, says that the capstone is 10 feet long. A.C. (1913), p.111; (1915), p.420. R.C.A.M. No. 41 of Glamorgan.

Carreg Siglo, Mid Glamorgan.   *Chris Barber*

286. PONTYPRIDD

Carreg Siglo or Shaking Rock on mountainside at Pentre Bach (ST 082902). Ordnance Survey maps from 1947 have Carreg Siglo marked. *Glamorgan*, by A. Morris (Newport, Mon., 1907), p.445, refers to it as the most celebrated stone in the county, weighing fifteen tons and was 10 feet 6 inches by 10 feet and 5 feet in height. It was also called Maenchwyf. *More Mysterious Wales*, by Chris Barber (David and Charles, Newton Abbot, 1986), p.207, has a good photograph. According to the Archdruid Iolo Morganwg this was the site of the original Gorsedd, or assembly of the Welsh Bards. *Megalithomania*, by John Mitchell (Thames and Hudson, 1982), p.161, has a photograph of the Pontypridd Rocking Stone taken in 1910 showing it being used for a political meeting. It appears that for some strange reason this rocking stone gets no mention in any archaeological book.

POWYS

287. ABBEY CWMHIR

Standing stone on Cambo Hill with two carns nearby (SO 048697). It is marked as 𝕾tanding 𝕾tone on the one inch Ordnance Survey map of 1947. R.C.A.M. No. 8 of Radnor calls it a low and somewhat pointed boulder of 2½ feet high.

288. ABERHAFSEP

Llwyn-y-Torw Stone Circle on a level terrace of land to the west of a small lake (SO 0257 9726). A.C. (1982), p.136, has a description and plan. It is a true circle 60ft. in diameter and thirty-nine stones can be traced. There may have been as many as ninety stones originally. The height of the stones varies from 9ft. to 1ft. 6in.

Battle Stone, Powys.   *John G. Williams*

289. BATTLE

A large grey standing stone at the bottom of a steep slope from Battle Church near a road and old railway line from Brecon (SO 006306). It is about 12 feet high and has a low mound about 2½ feet high running north from the north side of the stone. It is marked as 𝕸aen 𝕳ir on Ordnance Survey maps of 1831, 1920, 1925 and 1947 but, on the 1950 and 1967 maps, its position is shown as 𝕿umulus. *A Topographical Dictionary of Wales,* by Samuel Lewis (London, 1844), p.72, is the only book to mention this stone, which still stands prominently in the rural landscape.

290. BEGUILDY
A standing stone in the centre of a field called Maes y Garreg on Pontycaragh Farm (SO 200791). It resembles a battered human face and is 5 feet high. It is marked as Standing Stone on Ordnance Survey map of 1947. R.C.A.M. No. 80 of Radnor. One local story is that the Devil threw the stone from his chair at Craig y Don near Knighton, Radnor, aiming it at Beguildy Church, but it fell short by half-a-mile and the stone is still supposed to bear Satan's fingerprints.

291. BERRIEW
Maen Beuno on the banks of the River Severn near Duffryn (SJ 210011). An inscribed standing stone 6 feet high which leans over at an angle. It is shown as Maen Beuno on the Ordnance Survey maps of 1836 and 1953. A.C. (1857), p.299, has an illustration. R.C.A.M. of Montgomery, p.4.

292. BETTWS DISSERTH
A stone circle on Gelli Hill about 1 mile north-east of Upper Gilwern Farm (SO 095583). It is marked as Carn on the one inch Ordnance Survey map of 1947. R.C.A.M. No. 41B of Radnor, p.13, describes it with plan. There are twelve stones in the circle, none of which are more than 2 feet high.

293. BRYNGWYN
A Christianised standing stone which formerly stood just outside the south-east corner of the church. In recent years it was moved inside the church (SO 187496). A.C. (1876), p.215; A.C. (1893), p.243. R.C.A.M. p20 of Radnor refers to a drawing made in about 1698 in Edward Llwyd's *Parochiala* Pt. I, p.35. It is of a reddish sandstone of the type not found in this locality.

294. BRYNGWYN
A small stone circle near the source of a little stream called the Glasnant on the boundary of the parishes of Bryngwyn and Glascwm (SO 168521). R.C.A.M. No. 65 of Radnor with plan on p.19. The circle was of at least twelve stones with a diameter of 29 yards. Only six stones now remain.

295. CHURCHSTOKE
Stone circle at The Whetstones at the foot of the north slope of Corndon Hill and on the south side of the road leading to Cliffdale (SO 306975). R.C.A.M. No. 116 of Radnor. *Salopia Antiqua* (1841), p.33, has a description of this stone circle before it was destroyed. The highest stone appears to have been about 4 feet high and there were originally between four and nine stones in the circle.

296. CLYRO
Crossfoot Standing Stone in a field adjoining the road from Clyro to Newchurch near Crossfoot (SO 319458). It is marked as Stone on modern Ordnance Survey maps. R.C.A.M. No. 13 of Radnor describes it as 6 feet high but it is in fact less than 5 feet in height.

297. CRAY
Standing stone above the reservoir road and old railway track on the side of Nant Gihirych (SN 886203). It is marked as Stone on the one inch Ordnance Survey map of 1925 and was seen in position before 1960 by J.G.W. Since that time, it seems to have fallen.

298. CRICKHOWELL
Gwernvale Dolmen on the side of the A40 near the left-hand side of the entrance to Gwernvale Manor Hotel (SO 211192). It is marked as Cromlech on the Ordnance Survey maps of 1947 and earlier and as Burial Chamber on the 1967 map and later editions. A.C. (1862), p.233; (1936), p.271. It was excavated by Richard Fenton on 26th May, 1804 and after the main road was diverted in 1977 it was again excavated and full details appear in *Gwernvale and Penywyrlod*, by W. J. Britnell and H. N. Savory (Cardiff, 1984). *More Mysterious Wales,* by Chris Barber (David and Charles, Newton Abbot, 1986), p.30, has a modern photograph of it after the road diversion.

299. CRICKHOWELL

A standing stone near Gwern-y-Butler by the Llanbedr Road. It used to be known as the Turpillian Stone and stood on the boundaries of the parishes of Crickhowell, Llanbedr and Llangenny, but it was removed some time before 1961 (SO 227194). It is marked as Stone on the one inch Ordnance Survey map of 1831. A.C. (1847), p.25; (1849), p.324; (1862), p.234.

Great Oak Standing Stone, Powys.   *John G. Williams*

300. CRICKHOWELL

Llangenny Lane Standing Stone or Great Oak Road Standing Stone in some tall fir trees in a field on the east side of Great Oak Road (SO 223185). It is marked as Stone on the Ordnance Survey maps of 1831 and 1947. This is a large stone over 6 feet high which does not appear to have been mentioned in any archaeological work. *The Magic of Obelisks,* by Peter Tomkins (Harper and Row, New York, 1981), p.374, has two illustrations of John G. Williams dowsing at this standing stone.

301. CWMDU

Gliffaes Standing Stone on a farm called Llwyn-y-Fedwen near Gliffaes Hotel (SO 157204). It is marked as Maenhir on the Ordnance Survey maps of 1831, 1947 and 1951, and as *Standing Stone* on the 1967 edition. It is about 12 feet high by 4 feet square and has large horizontal cracks and a blackened patch near its base as if the stone had been melted and cooled off in situ. A.C. (1849), p.323. *South Wales Argus* (Newport, 12th July, 1968), p.8, *Sketchbook No. 756,* written and illustrated by Fred J. Hando, has an illustration and says that it is 14 feet high.

302. CWMDU

The Fish Stone in Penmyarth Park on the banks of the River Usk between Penmyarth and Llangynidir Bridge. It is about 18 feet high and is the tallest standing stone in Wales (SO 183199). It is marked as Standing Stone on the one inch Ordnance Survey map of 1967 and shown on a plan of a lease dated March, 1825, from William Augustus Gott to Thomas Johnson. A.C. (1849), p.309, says that it is of old red sandstone and it is believed to have originated from a quarry on the other side of the River Usk. *South Wales Argus* (Newport, 12th July, 1968), p.8, *Sketchbook No. 756,* written and illustrated by Fred J. Hando, refers to it as this unique Fish Stone like a leaping fish and has an illustration. *Mysterious Wales,* by Chris Barber (David and Charles, Newton Abbot, 1982), p.5, has a photograph and says that on Midsummer Eve it is reputed to jump into the river and go for a swim.

303. CWMDU
Tretower Standing Stone in a field adjoining and west of the A479 Crickhowell to Talgarth Road and standing in a hawthorn hedge (SO 181219). It is marked as *Maenhir* on the Ordnance Survey maps of 1831, 1947 and 1951, and as *Standing Stone* on the 1967 map. This stone is about 8 feet high and has long grooves and deep holes on its west side.

304. DAROWEN
Maen Llwyd Standing Stone in a field called Meini Llwydion near the roadside at Tal-y-wern (SH 828005). On the 1952 Ordnance Survey map it is shown as *Maen Llwyd* and on the 1974 edition it is marked as *Standing Stone.* A.C. (1856), p.194, calls it Cerrig y Noddfa. R.C.A.M. No. 31 of Montgomery says that it is of mountain grit 6 feet high.

305. DAROWEN
The Sanctuary Stone on Cefn Coch near Commins Coch (SH 836032). It is marked as *Maen Llwyd* on the 1952 Ordnance Survey map and as *Standing Stone* on the 1974 edition. R.C.A.M. No. 31 of Montgomery says that it is 3 feet 9 inches high.

306. EVENJOBB
A standing stone between Rough Close and Hindwell Farm in an open field (SO 262613). It is marked as *Standing Stone* on the one inch Ordnance Survey maps of 1911, 1920 and 1947. R.C.A.M. No. 172 of Radnor seems to refer to this standing stone as Oarstone or Hoarstone.

307. FENNIFACH
A large standing stone on the side of an old railway line near Cradoc Station (SO 017302). It was over 6 feet high and badly overgrown when seen in July, 1985. On the Ordnance Survey maps of 1920, 1925, 1947 and 1951 it is marked as *Maen Hir* and as *Standing Stone* on the 1967 edition.

308. FENNIFACH
Maen y Morwynion, The Maiden's Stone, used to stand under a hedgerow near the old Cradoc Railway Station. It is now in Brecon Museum and the carving on it was supposed to represent a Roman soldier and his wife. It is likely that this was a prehistoric standing stone used by the Romans (SO 005300). *Maen-y-morwynion* is marked on Ordnance Survey maps of 1831, 1925, 1947 and 1952. A.C. (1847), p.235; (1849), p.311; (1853), p.311; (1858), p.309; (1872), p.385; (1878), p.236.

309. GLASCWM
Graig Fawr Stone Circle between the Builth to Kington Road and the River Edw on the south side of the farm called Graig Fawr (SO 144579). It is marked as *Stone Circle* on Ordnance Survey maps of 1911, 1920 and 1947. A.C. (1860), p.21, says that the circle has 37 stones. R.C.A.M. No. 189 of Radnor.

310. KERRY
A stone circle on Kerry Hill near the main road with tumuli nearby (SO 158860). It is marked as *Stone Circle* on the Ordnance Survey map of 1947. There are eight stones in the circle with one in the centre and the stones are up to 2 feet 6 inches in height. One pair of stones on the east side has a pattern of small circular hollows which seem to include the circle of six dots. This is a very ancient symbol which can also be seen on a large stone to the east of Arthur's Stone, Cefn Bryn, Reynoldston, West Glamorgan. R.C.A.M. No. 282 of Montgomery has a full description and plan.

Maen-y-Morwynion, Powys, in its original position.

311. **KINNERTON**

Two standing stones in a field near the church (SO 246627). Both stones are 2 feet 6 inches high and they are about 10 yards apart. They are shown as 𝔖𝔱𝔞𝔫𝔡𝔦𝔫𝔤 𝔖𝔱𝔬𝔫𝔢 on the Ordnance Survey maps of 1911, 1920 and 1947. R.C.A.M. No. 209 of Radnor refers to them being south of Kinnerton Court. *Ancient Mysteries of Britain,* by Janet and Colin Bord (Grafton Books, London, 1986), p.58, has a photograph.

312. **LLANAFON FAWR**

A standing stone between Y Garth and Garnoeth with carns nearby at 1,000 feet altitude (SN 948558). It is marked as 𝔖𝔱𝔬𝔫𝔢 on the 1833 Ordnance Survey map and as 𝔖𝔱𝔞𝔫𝔡𝔦𝔫𝔤 𝔖𝔱𝔬𝔫𝔢 on the editions of 1911, 1920 and 1947. When seen and photographed by J.G.W. in June, 1966, it was a large upright stone over 6 feet high of a greyish colour and standing in marshy ground near a farm called Fronwen.

313. **LLANAFON FAWR**

A standing stone on the right-hand side of the road going towards Cilmary on the side of the River Chwefru (SN 975552). It is marked as 𝔖𝔱𝔬𝔫𝔢 on the Ordnance Survey map of 1833 and shown as 𝔖𝔱𝔞𝔫𝔡𝔦𝔫𝔤 𝔖𝔱𝔬𝔫𝔢 on the maps of 1911, 1920 and 1947. A local farmer in June, 1966, told J.G.W. that it was called St. Arfan's Stone and that it had some connection with St. Arvan. *A History of the County of Brecknock,* by Theophilus Jones (Glanusk Edition, 1910), Vol. II, p.226, refers to a maenhir about 6 feet high on Whefri side as still continuing to preserve the memory of Bishop Afan, Ifan or Jeuan. Other writers say that it marks the spot where St. Arvan, a Welsh saint or bishop, was murdered.

314. **LLANBADARN FYNYDD**

Banc Du Stone Circle, north-west of Banc Carn (SO 041793). It is also known as 𝔉𝔬𝔴𝔩𝔢𝔯'𝔰 𝔄𝔯𝔪𝔠𝔥𝔞𝔦𝔯, which is marked on Ordnance Survey maps from 1950. He was at one time the squire of Cwmhir so this is a comparatively modern name for an ancient site. R.C.A.M. No. 240 of Radnor. The circle is 60 feet in diameter with five remaining stones, the tallest of which is 3 feet high and is known as Fowler's Horse Block. Originally there were nineteen stones.

315. **LLANBRYNMAIR**

A stone circle called Lled Croen yr ych (The Width of an Ox's Hide) on the level summit of the hill called Newydd Fynyddog (SH 904005). 𝔏𝔩𝔢𝔡-𝔆𝔯𝔬𝔢𝔫-𝔶𝔯-𝔶𝔠𝔥 is marked on the Ordnance Survey maps of 1953. A.C. (1866), p.540, mentions five stones in the circle with a diameter of 81 feet. The stones are about 2 feet high. R.C.A.M. No. 308 of Montgomery has a description and plan. *More Mysterious Wales,* by Chris Barber (David and Charles, Newton Abbot, 1986), p.17, says that according to legend two long-horned oxen were separated by the valley of the Twymyn. They stood on top of their respective hills and bellowed until they died of grief because they could not come together. The one which died on Newydd Fynyddog was skinned and his skin was marked by the circle of stones spread over the place of internment.

316. **LLANDDETTY**

Gilestone, a very large maenhir at Talybont on Usk in a field between the farmhouse called Gilestone and the River Usk (SO 116237). It is marked as 𝔐𝔞𝔢𝔫 𝔥𝔦𝔯 on the Ordnance Survey maps of 1947 and 1951 and as 𝔖𝔱𝔞𝔫𝔡𝔦𝔫𝔤 𝔖𝔱𝔬𝔫𝔢 on the 1967 and later editions. It is about 9 feet high, 5 feet long and 3 feet wide.

317. **LLANDRINDOD WELLS**

Dragon Stone or Carreg gwibe on Carregwiber Bank about 2 miles south-east of the town near a stream (SO 081594). It is marked as 𝔆𝔞𝔯𝔯𝔢𝔤 𝔤𝔴𝔦𝔟𝔢𝔯 on the Ordnance Survey map of 1833 and as 𝔆𝔞𝔯𝔯𝔢𝔤𝔴𝔦𝔟𝔢𝔯 on 1947 and 1951 maps. R.C.A.M. of Radnor mentions it. This stone stands about 2½ feet out of the ground and is 4 feet long and 2 feet wide and is near a roadway leading to a farm. It is a slatey-blue stone with seams of white quartz a few inches thick and should be called the Serpent Stone according to a local farmer interviewed by J.G.W. in March, 1963.

Llanbrynmair Stone Circle, Powys.   *Chris Barber*

Gilestone, Powys.   *John G. Williams*

169

318. LLANDRINDOD WELLS

Known as The Temple, the site and remains of a stone circle in a small triangular ornamental garden near the centre of the town and Trinity Church (SO 058612). R.C.A.M. No. 111 of Radnor. *Illustrated Guide to Llandrindod Wells,* by W. J. Bufton (London, 1906, Revised Edition), has a street map which shows The Temple (stone circle) with nine stones, which is mentioned on p.22 where it states that two of the stones are beyond doubt true relics of Druidism, the others having been removed for building purposes.

319. LLANGADFAN

Dol Garreg Stone on the banks of the Afon Banw near Maes Llymystyn (SH 974119). It is marked as Standing Stone on the Ordnance Survey map of 1953. A.C (1856), p.193. R.C.A.M. p.98 of Montgomery. The stone is 43 inches high and is known locally as Maen Cadfan.

Golden Grove Stone, Powys.   *Chris Barber*

320. LLANGENNY

Golden Grove Standing Stone in the field near the buildings of Golden Grove between Druid's Altar and the Dragon's Head Inn, above the River Grwyne on sloping ground (SO 240178). This stone is about 4½ feet high and of a greyish limestone which is squarely shaped. It is quite distinctive when seen and the adjoining place names are suggestive of an ancient association.

321. LLANGENNY

The Growing Stone, a tall maen hir at the entrance to Cwrt y Gollen military camp on the left side of the A40 from Crickhowell to Abergavenny (SO 232169). It is marked as Maenhir on the Ordnance Survey maps of 1831 and 1947 and as Standing Stone on the 1967 edition. *The Illustrated History and Biography of Brecknockshire,* by Edwin Poole (Brecon, 1886), p.324, says that it is composed of old red sandstone and is 13 to 14 feet high. It stands behind railings under some large oak trees opposite a small military museum and is inconspicuous although it is the second largest and tallest standing stone in the old county of Brecon.

Carreg Wen Llech, Powys.   *Chris Barber*

322. LLANGYNIDIR

Carreg Waen Llech, a tall porous grey standing stone in marshy ground on Llangynidir Mountain about 50 yards from the road. There are excellent views from here of the Black Mountains across the valley of the River Usk (SO 164175). On the Ordnance Survey map of 1831 it is marked as 𝔖tone. The 1947 and 1951 maps show it as 𝕮areg 𝔚aen 𝕷lech and it is marked as 𝕮arreg 𝔚aun 𝕷lech on the 1967 edition. Although it is prominent and stands over 6 feet high, it does not seem to have been recorded in any book. An unusual feature is that it has peculiar lines of holes running down its west and east sides while the other two sides are smooth.

323. LLANHAMLACH

Maen Iltyd, a dolmen in a field across the road from Maneast Court (SO 098264). This is marked in a variety of ways on the Ordnance Survey maps. In 1831 it was shown as 𝕸aen 𝕴llid, in 1947 as 𝕿y 𝕴lltyd, in 1951 as 𝕿y 𝕰lltyd, in 1952 as 𝕿y 𝕴lltyd 𝕷ong 𝕭arrow and in 1967 as 𝕿y 𝕴lltud 𝕷ong 𝕮airn. A.C. (1849), p.317; (1852), p.273; (1856), p.106; (1862), p.233; (1867), p.347 with illustration and plan; (1903), p.173 mentions that the chamber was said to be used as a hermit's cell; (1936), p.280; (1981), pp.131-9, has plans, photographs and references and deals with the stone carvings. Early writers sometimes refer to it as the hermitage of St. Illtyd and in *Curiosities of Great Britain, England and Wales,* by Thomas Dugdale (London, 1835), p.1,072, it describes the dolmen as a cistfaen or stone chest with some antique characters believed to be the workmanship of the recluse. *More Mysterious Wales,* by Chris Barber (David and Charles, Newton Abbot, 1986), p.32, has a photograph and mentions that more than sixty inscribed crosses and other symbols are visible on the slabs, but they are carved at a much later date than the original erection of the dolmen.

324. LLANHAMLACH

A standing stone on the right side of the A40 from Abergavenny to Brecon in the hedge opposite Llanhamlach Church (SO 089267). It is marked as 𝕸aen 𝕳ir on the Ordnance Survey maps of 1947 and 1951 and as 𝔖tanding 𝔖tone on 1967 maps. Although there have been extensive road improvements in this area since 1960, the standing stone has been protected by iron railings. It is a greyish stone about 4 feet 6 inches tall and 2 feet square. Here in 1959 some strange photographs were obtained suggesting a concentration of ultra-violet light near the standing stone. *The Illustrated History and Biography of Brecknockshire,* by Edwin Poole (Brecon, 1886), p.145, mentions it as traditionally being the spot from which St. Peter preached, hence the name of the mansion opposite which is called Peterstone Court.

325. LLANIDLOES WITHOUT

Careg Wen or Garreg Wen (The White Rock) on the north-east slopes of Plynlimon Mountain near Blaen Hafron (SN 886829). These are two white stones also known as Y Fuwch Wen A'rllo or "The White Cow and Calf", standing close to one another near the source of the River Severn. The tallest stone is 6 feet high and the other one is 4 feet high. They are marked as 𝕮areg 𝔚en on the Ordnance Survey map of 1952. A.C. (1856), p.193, mentions Carregwen, an erect stone. R.C.A.M. of Montgomery, p.115.

326. LLANIGON

A dolmen at Penyrworlod in a field near a farm called Pantyvithel (SO 225398). It is marked as 𝕷ong 𝕮arn on the Ordnance Survey maps of 1952 and 1967. A.C. (1921), p.296; (1936), p.275. *Gwernvale and Penwyrlod,* by W. J. Britnell and H. N. Savory (Cardiff, 1984).

327. LLANRHAIADR YN MOCHNANT

A stone circle with avenue called Rhos-y-Beddau (SJ 064301). R.C.A.M. of Montgomery, p.124, has a description and plan. *Montgomery Collections* (1871), p.241, mentions a circle of thirteen stones about 2 feet high with a diameter of 41 feet.

328. LLANSANTFFRAID CWMEUDDWR

Beddau Foleu Stone Circle, 1 mile south-east of the east end of Pen-y-garreg Reservoir and 600 yards north of Carreg Bica (SN 923660). It is marked as 𝔅eddau 𝔉olau on the Ordnance Survey maps of 1920, 1947, 1953 and 1967. R.C.A.M. No. 408 of Radnor says that there were six stones standing with five fallen, all about 3 feet high. Nearby to the south-east is a standing stone called Dol Folau Stone, which is 2 feet 6 inches high.

329. LLANSANTFFRAID CWMEUDDWR

Four Stones on Rhos-y-Gelynnen above Caban Coch Reservoir (SN 906631). They are marked as 𝔖tanding 𝔖tones on the Ordnance Survey maps of 1920 and 1947 and as 𝔖tone 𝔕ow on the 1953 edition. R.C.A.M. No. 402 of Radnor says that there were four standing and one prostrate and has a photograph.

330. LLANSANTFFRAID CWMEUDDWR

Y Maen Serth, a standing stone on the ridge above Nant Gwynllyn and about ½ mile east of Clap yr Arian (SN 944697). It is marked as 𝔐aen 𝔖erth on the Ordnance Survey maps of 1833, 1947 and 1953. R.C.A.M. No. 403 of Radnor has a photograph which shows it leaning at an angle. It is 7 feet 2 inches high and there is a cross cut on the upper side facing south-east. *Radnorshire,* by W. H. House (E. J. Thurston, Hereford, 1949), p.318, says that it marks the spot where Einon Clud was murdered by Roger Mortimer in 1176 and it is still known locally as the Prince's Grave.

331. LLANSTEPHAN

A large standing stone at the top of a steep field near Rhydnest (SO 127412). It is marked as 𝔖tanding 𝔖tone on the Ordnance Survey maps of 1911, 1920, 1947, 1951 and 1967. R.C.A.M. No. 444 of Radnor says that it is 7 feet 11 inches high and tapers to a width of 2 feet at the top. There seem to be a few unrecorded carvings near the top of the stone.

332. LLANFIHANGEL BRYNPABUAN

Saith Maen or Seven Stones on Rhos Saith Maen with a number of carns nearby (SN 949602). On the Ordnance Survey map of 1833 the site is marked as 𝔖aith 𝔐aen and shown as a line of seven stones running east and west of the side of a track. It is also marked as 𝔖aith 𝔐aen on the Ordnance Survey maps of 1920, 1947 and

1953. *Map of South Wales Showing the Distribution of Long Barrows and Megaliths* (published by the Ordnance Survey, Southampton, 1936), lists these stones as No. 8.

333. LLANFIHANGEL NANT BRAN
Maen Richard Standing Stone on the side of a track on top of the mountain near Cefn Bola Maen (SN 967347). Maen Richard is marked on Ordnance Survey maps of 1831, 1920, 1947, 1952, 1953 and 1967. It is about 4 feet 6 inches high and had a small hollow on one side when seen by J.G.W. in 1958.

334. LLANFIHANGEL NANT BRAN
A stone circle on a mountain top near Nant Bran and Mardy (SN 920383). On the one inch Ordnance Survey map of 1967 it is marked as *Stone Circle* and on the 1:25,000 scale map of 1953 it is shown as a circle of five stones with a Bench Mark on the south stone. This is in the middle of an army artillery range, which makes inspection difficult and somewhat risky. *Map of South Wales Showing the Distribution of Long Barrows and Megaliths* (published by the Ordnance Survey, Southampton, 1936), p.16, states that the circle has a diameter of 60 feet with twelve irregularly placed stones varying from 1 to 2 feet in height and lists it as No. 13. *More Mysterious Wales*, by Chris Barber (David and Charles, Newton Abbot, 1986), p.18, calls it Ynyshir Circle, Mynydd Epynt and states that originally there would have been 27 stones in position with a wide gap on the south-west side.

335. LLANFIHANGEL NANT MELAN
Four Stones in a line pointing to a nearby mound above Beili Bedw Mawn pool (SO 157569). The one inch Ordnance Survey map of 1833 shows them as *Four Stones* but only the mound seems to be shown on later maps. R.C.A.M. No. 355 of Radnor calls it a Stone Avenue with tumulus and gives details. When J.G.W. visited the site in 1958, he noted that each of the four stones were of different kinds of material and the one reclining was a black shiny rock.

336. LLANFIHANGEL NANT MELAN
A standing stone near the River Edw and Cwm Mardy (SO 143587). On the Ordnance Survey map of 1833 it is marked as *Maen* and the 1911, 1920 and 1947 maps show it as *Standing Stone*. R.C.A.M. No. 188 of Radnor states that it is 4 feet 6 inches high. J.G.W. photographed it in position in 1960.

Llanwrthwl Stone, Powys.   *Chris Barber*

337. LLANWRTHWL
A standing stone in the churchyard close to the south porch (SN 975637). *Lapidarium Walliae: The Early Inscribed and Sculptured Stones of Wales*, by

J. P. Westwood (Oxford, 1876-9), p.78, states that it is 6 feet high but the upper part appeared to have been broken and it was supposed by some to be of Druidical origin. *More Mysterious Wales,* by Chris Barber (David and Charles, Newton Abbot, 1986), p.152, has a photograph and says that it may safely be assumed that the stone was there long before the church was erected.

338. LLANWRTYD WELLS
A standing stone in a field adjoining the main road opposite The Woollen Factory (SN 885475). It is marked as 𝖘𝖙𝖔𝖓𝖊 on the 1833 Ordnance Survey map and as 𝖘𝖙𝖆𝖓𝖉𝖎𝖓𝖌 𝖘𝖙𝖔𝖓𝖊 on the 1920, 1953 and 1967 maps. When J.G.W. came here and photographed it in 1966, he noted that it was an upright stone of greyish-white colour about 7 feet high. A lady with local knowledge told him that there was a legend that the stone goes down to the nearby stream at night to have a drink.

Llyswen Stone, Powys.   John G. Williams

339. LLYSWEN
A large standing stone in the middle of a field near Llangoed Castle and adjoining the River Wye (SO 124398). It is marked as 𝖘𝖙𝖆𝖓𝖉𝖎𝖓𝖌 𝖘𝖙𝖔𝖓𝖊 on the Ordnance Survey maps of 1947, 1951 and 1967. Woolhope Field Club Transactions (1936-8), p.LIV, under Llangoed. It is a greyish stone 7 feet high sloping towards the west and has lines of small hollows down the one face which could be carved symbols.

340. MACHYNLLETH
Maen Llwyd, a standing stone in a field on the side of the road going to Penegroes (SH 759008). It is shown as 𝖒𝖆𝖊𝖓 𝖑𝖑𝖜𝖞𝖉 on the one inch Ordnance Survey map of 1952. R.C.A.M. Montgomery, p.144, says that it is in a field called Maen llwyd and stands 5½ feet high.

341. MACHYNLLETH
A standing stone near Pwl glas and the banks of the Afon Dyfi (SH 787027). It is shown as 𝖒𝖆𝖊𝖓 𝖑𝖑𝖜𝖞𝖉 on the Ordnance Survey maps of 1837 and 1952. A.C. (1856), p.193. R.C.A.M. of Montgomery, p31, seems to refer to this stone as Garreg Llwyd, which is said to be 7½ feet high.

342. PENDERYN

A rocking stone on the bank of the Afon Pryddin above Glyn Neath and near Ton-y-gilfach (SN 897093). It is marked as 𝕽𝖔𝖈𝖐𝖎𝖓𝖌 𝕾𝖙𝖔𝖓𝖊 on the one inch Ordnance Survey maps of 1923 and 1947. A.C. (1850), p.222, calls it Scwd Wladis Rocking Stone and refers to a report that a number of "navvies" who were employed on the Vale of Neath Railway wantonly overturned it by means of levers and it weighed about 20 tons. *The History of the Vale of Neath,* by D. Rhys Phillips (Swansea, 1925), p.16, calls it Pyrddin Rocking Stone and mentions that the famous Bard, Iolo Morganwg, had heard it termed Maen Gwlych or Maen Goluch, meaning a Stone of Worship in the Face of the Sun. *Mysterious Wales,* by Chris Barber (David and Charles, Newton Abbot, 1982), p.57, says that people had even claimed to crack nuts beneath it.

Bedd Gwl Illtyd, Powys.   *Chris Barber*

343. PENPONT

Bedd Gwyl Illtyd or The Grave of St. Illtyd's Eve, a dolmen at Glyn (SN 975264). It is marked as 𝕭𝖊𝖉𝖉 𝖌𝖜𝖞𝖑 𝕴𝖑𝖑𝖙𝖞𝖉 on the Ordnance Survey maps of 1920, 1925 and 1947, and as 𝕭𝖊𝖉𝖉 𝕴𝖑𝖑𝖙𝖞𝖉 on the 1953 and 1967 editions. A.C. (1981), p.137, mentions two standing stones. *The Brecon and Radnor Express* (Brecon, 16th January, 1969), p.8, says that it is the place where tradition says that St. Illtud lies buried. The spot is marked by two long stones, now fallen and lying with a saucer-like depression and difficult to see because fern and bracken had overgrown the site.

344. ST. HARMONS

Maen Llwyd on the side of the hill above Pant-y-dwr (SN 975745). It is marked as 𝕸𝖆𝖊𝖓 𝕷𝖑𝖜𝖞𝖉 on the Ordnance Survey maps of 1947 and 1952. Unfortunately it was destroyed some time before 1959.

345. ST. HARMONS

A standing stone alongside the Afon Dulas at Gwenfron near Craig-cefn-Llech (SN 951770). It is marked as 𝕾𝖙𝖆𝖓𝖉𝖎𝖓𝖌 𝕾𝖙𝖔𝖓𝖊 on the Ordnance Survey maps of 1947 and 1952. R.C.A.M. No. 586 of Radnor refers to one of two monoliths near Gwenfron Fawr. The fallen one is 7 feet long and 3 feet broad and the one standing is 6 feet high and 5 feet broad. There is a good photograph opposite p.101. When

J.G.W. came here in 1959 he only found one stone, which was about 5 feet high and had a hole on the bottom of the west side.

346. ST. HARMONS

A standing stone in the middle of a field near Henriw and the Afon Dulas and Sychnant (SN 963777). It is marked as 𝕾𝖙𝖆𝖓𝖉𝖎𝖓𝖌 𝕾𝖙𝖔𝖓𝖊 on the Ordnance Survey maps of 1947 and 1952. R.C.A.M. No. 603 of Radnor has a good photograph of a standing stone stated to be 8 feet 2 inches high. It mentions a row of inscribed stones nearby which had an average height of 7 feet and had been destroyed. One stone about 6 feet high was seen by J.G.W. in 1959 and this had some slight indications of carved figures on the north side with a triangle pointing downwards in the centre.

Maen Llia, Powys.   *Chris Barber*

347. SENNY

Maen Llia, a large standing stone above the Afon Lia (SN 924193). It is marked as 𝕸𝖆𝖊𝖓 𝕷𝖑𝖎𝖆 on the Ordnance Survey maps of 1831, 1920, 1925, 1947, 1952, 1953 and 1967. A.C. (1853), p.139; (1858), p.407. *The History of the Vale of Neath*, by D. Rhys Phillips (Swansea, 1925), p.29, states that Maen Llia is 11 feet 2 inches high and 8 feet 4 inches in breadth. On p.743 it says that legend avers that Maen Llia loves fresh water and goes to drink in the River Nedd whenever it hears the crowing of a cock.

348. TALGARTH

Croes Llechan or Slate Croes, the site of a dolmen on the right-hand side of the road from Talgarth to Three Cocks and Hay-on-Wye (SO 167364). It is marked as **Croes-llechau** on the one inch Ordnance Survey map of 1831. Some time before 1950 it was destroyed. A.C. (1856), p.102; (1903), p.29. *A Topographical and Historical Description of South Wales,* by Rev. J. Rees (Sherwood, Neely and Jones, London, 1815), p.138, calls it a very remarkable cromlech. It was not particularly distinguished by its size but from the circumstances of a hawthorn having sprung up at one end of it, so near as to grow against the covering stone and gradually, by its increasing bulk, rose the capstone some inches above its original seat.

Maen Llwd, Powys.   *Chris Barber*

349. TALGARTH

Maen Llwyd, a large standing stone on the upper south slope of Pen Gader on Gader Fawr (SO 226277). It is marked as **Maen Llwyd** on the one inch Ordnance Survey maps of 1831, 1947, 1952 and 1967. In height it is about 7 feet and there are some large circular hollows on the sides of the stone. *Mysterious Wales,* by Chris Barber (David and Charles, Newton Abbot, 1982), p.15, has a photograph and says that this standing stone is at a higher altitude than any other in Wales.

350. TALGARTH
Pen Gader Stone Circle on Pen Gader or Gader Arthur (Arthur's Chair), the second highest peak in the Black Mountains at 2,624 feet above sea level (SO 230287). Some stones about 2 feet high were seen inside a small rough enclosure on the mountain top in 1958. *A Topographical and Historical Description of South Wales,* by Rev. T. Rees (Sherwood, Neely and Jones, London, 1815), p.138, refers to stone circles placed so as to form, if a line were drawn from each and from them to a large stone, an irregular triangle. They are of small loose stones, the whole about 20 yards in circumference; at the apex is the large stone 7 feet high.

Ty Isaf Dolmen remains, Powys.   *Chris Barber*

351. TALGARTH
Ty Isaf ruined dolmen near the top of the Rhiangoll Valley across the road from Cwm Forest (SO 183290). 𝕮𝖗𝖔𝖒𝖑𝖊𝖈𝖍 is marked on the Ordnance Survey map of 1831, 𝕷𝖔𝖓𝖌 𝕭𝖆𝖗𝖗𝖔𝖜 on 1951 and 𝕷𝖔𝖓𝖌 𝕮𝖆𝖎𝖗𝖓 on 1967 maps. A.C. (1936), p.278, with photograph. *The Archaeology of the Welsh Marches,* by S. C. Stanford (Collins, London, 1980), p.46, with plan.

352. TRIANGLAS
Forest Fawr Standing Stone below the slopes of Moel Feity near the River Tawe (SN 855215). It is marked as 𝕾𝖙𝖆𝖓𝖉𝖎𝖓𝖌 𝕾𝖙𝖔𝖓𝖊 on the Ordnance Survey maps of 1920, 1925, 1947, 1952 and 1953. This is a large grey stone about 7 feet high which is just north of Maen Mawr Stone Circle. *A Guide to Prehistoric and Roman Monuments in England and Wales,* by Jacquetta Hawkes (London, 1958), p.204, has mentioin of it.

353. TRIANGLAS
Maen Mawr and stone circle in Fforest Fawr at the head of River Tawe valley below Llyn-y-Fan Fawer in marshy ground (SN 852207). It is marked as 𝕸𝖆𝖊𝖓 𝕸𝖆𝖜𝖗 𝕾𝖙𝖔𝖓𝖊 𝕮𝖎𝖗𝖈𝖑𝖊 on the Ordnance Survey maps of 1920, 1925, 1947, 1952 and 1953. *Map of South Wales Showing the Distribution of Long Barrows and Megaliths* (published by the Ordnance Survey, Southampton, 1936), p.17, calls it Cerrig Duon (Black Stones) Circle, with a diameter of 60 feet and twenty-one stones up to 1 foot 9 inches tall still remaining. The Maen Mawr, an oblong block of sandstone 6 feet high, stands 30 feet outside the circle to the north.

Standing stone near Usk Reservoir, Powys.   *Chris Barber*

354. TRIANGLAS

A standing stone above the west bank of Usk Reservoir between Bryn-maen-du and Gwern-wyddog (SN 834284). The Ordnance Survey maps of 1920, 1925, 1947, 1951 and 1953 have 𝔖𝔱𝔞𝔫𝔡𝔦𝔫𝔤 𝔖𝔱𝔬𝔫𝔢 marked. It is a large greyish stone about 7 feet high which appears to have been originally of a dark reddish colour. It stands in a boggy field and was photographed by J.G.W. in June, 1966 and by C.B. in 1988.

355. TRIANGLAS

Stone circles near the border of the old counties of Brecon and Carmarthen on the slopes of the mountain between Foel Darw and Bryn Mawr (SN 820258). 𝔖𝔱𝔬𝔫𝔢 ℭ𝔦𝔯𝔠𝔩𝔢𝔰 is marked on the Ordnance Survey maps of 1920, 1925, 1947, 1952 and 1953. *Mysterious Wales*, by Chris Barber (David and Charles, Newton Abbot, 1982), p.22, mentions that the circle is 215 feet in circumference and marked by seven stones that are still standing.

356. TRECASTLE

Stone circles on Mynydd Bach adjoining a Roman encampment known as Y Pigwn (The Pole of the Earth), a name originally connected with the stone circles (SN 833311). They are marked on the one inch Ordnance Survey maps of 1920, 1925, 1947 and 1952 as 𝔖𝔱𝔬𝔫𝔢 ℭ𝔦𝔯𝔠𝔩𝔢𝔰. A.C. (1854), p.125. *Maps of South Wales Showing the Distribution of Long Barrows and Megaliths* (published by The Ordnance Survey, Southampton, 1936) lists two circles as Nos. 14 and 15, and states that the larger circle to the north-east has a diameter of 75 feet with twenty-two stones averaging 1 foot in height. The second circle has a diameter of 25 feet with larger stones, of which four remained.

179

357. TREFEGLWYS

A standing stone that was about 6½ feet high and stood on Ffinant Farm (SN 975911). It is marked as an 𝕮𝖗𝖊𝖈𝖙 𝕾𝖙𝖔𝖓𝖊 on the one inch Ordnance Survey map of 1836 and as 𝕾𝖙𝖆𝖓𝖉𝖎𝖓𝖌 𝕾𝖙𝖔𝖓𝖊 on the 1961 Ordnance Survey maps, although it had been destroyed by 1959 and a few large lumps of stone were seen in the stream below the road bridge which were part of this standing stone according to local information given at that time. A.C. (1858), p.193. R.C.A.M. of Montgomery, p.172, says that the field in which it stood is called Cae y Garreg.

The Four Stones, Walton, Powys.   *John G. Williams*

358. WALTON

Four stones near field gate on side of road leading from Walton to Presteign (SO 246608). They are marked as 𝕱𝖔𝖚𝖗 𝕾𝖙𝖔𝖓𝖊𝖘 on the one inch Ordnance Survey maps of 1911, 1920, 1947 and the first one of 1833. A.C. (1863), p.366; (1874), p.215; (1911), p.105, states that there are some deep circular hollows on the top of the largest stone. The four very large stones are from 4 feet to 6 feet high in the form of a rough square, the stones being about 6 feet apart. *Word Lore, The Folk Magazine*, edited by Douglas Macmillan (Folk Press Ltd., London, 1927), Vol. II, p.166, refers to the local legend that the four stones go down to Hindwell Pool when they hear the bells of Old Radnor Church ring. Hindwell Pool is about 800 yards to the east. *Circle of Stones*, by Don Robins (Souvenir Press, London, 1985), plate 17 has a coloured photograph.

359. WALTON

A standing stone in a field about 300 yards east north-east of the Four Stones near Hindwell Farm (SN 249608). It is marked as 𝕾𝖙𝖆𝖓𝖉𝖎𝖓𝖌 𝕾𝖙𝖔𝖓𝖊 on the one inch Ordnance Survey maps of 1911, 1920 and 1947. R.C.A.M. No. 615A of Radnor says that it is a somewhat shapeless monument about 4 feet high and its surface is marked with deep fissures. When visited by J.G.W. in September, 1977, he noted that it was a rounded grey stone about 2 feet 6 inches above the ground.

360. YSTRADFELLTE

Maen Madoc, a large tall standing stone at Plas-y-gors (SN 918157). It is marked as 𝕸𝖆𝖊𝖓 𝕸𝖆𝖉𝖔𝖈 on the Ordnance Survey maps of 1831, 1920, 1925, 1947, 1952, 1953 and 1967. Standing 11 feet high, it is an inscribed stone with crude capitals, some reversed, which read downwards. The stone was moved and reset a few yards away by the Ministry of Works in 1940. A.C. (1858), p.406; (1901), p.68; (1939), p.30. *Wales a History,* by Wynford Vaughan Thomas (Michael Joseph, London, 1985), p.343, has a recent photograph of Maen Madoc which it calls a Roman milestone.

Saeth Maen, Powys.   *Chris Barber*

361. YSTRADGYNLAIS

Saith Maen or Seven Stones on the slopes of Cribarth (the Crest of the Bear) above Craig-y-Nos Castle (SN 833155). 𝕾𝖆𝖊𝖙𝖍𝖒𝖆𝖊𝖓 is marked on Ordnance Survey maps of 1831 and 𝕾𝖆𝖎𝖙𝖍 𝕸𝖆𝖊𝖓 on 1920, 1925, 1947, 1952 and 1953 maps. It consists of a line of seven stones about 10 yards long running east to west and five stones are still standing between 2 feet 6 inches and 5 feet in height. They are greyish-white in colour with flecks of quartz visible. This line of stones points to the stone circle of Maen Mawr or Cerrig Duon in the west and to Seven Stones across the valley to the east. *Mysterious Wales,* by Chris Barber (David and Charles, Newton Abbot, 1982), p.12, has a photograph and a description.

362. YSTRADGYNLAIS

Seven Stones or Saith Maen on the slopes of Y Wern at 1,400 feet on the opposite side of the valley to the other group or line of stones called Saith Maen (SN 862146). The one inch Ordnance Survey map of 1831 shows a line of six stones running north and south and marked as 𝕾𝖆𝖎𝖙𝖍𝖒𝖆𝖊𝖓. These are marked as 𝕾𝖆𝖎𝖙𝖍 𝕸𝖆𝖊𝖓 on the Ordnance Survey maps of 1920, 1925, 1947, 1952 and 1953. It is odd that this line of stones does not seem to be mentioned in any published work, although it has been shown on Ordnance Survey maps since 1831.

363. LLANTWIT MAJOR

Two remarkable standing stones which used to stand on the north side of the churchyard (SS 966687). *The Book of South Wales,* by Chas F. Cliffe (1847), p.102, describes one as a curiously carved pyramidal stone 7 feet high and reputed to be part of a heathen altar. *Llantwit Major — Its History and Antiquities,* by Marie Trevelyan (John E. Southall, Newport, Mon., 1910), p.78, has an illustration of this stone pillar and refers to it as a remarkable stone of the greatest of interest to antiquarians, which formerly stood against the exterior of the north wall of the western church but was inside the edifice.

364. MARCROSS

The remains of a cromlech called The Old Church near the village of Marcross (SS 923694). A.C. (1856), p.106; (1894), p.337; (1895), p.323. R.C.A.M. No. 38 of Glamorgan refers to Long Cairn, Cae'r Eglwys near the Nash Lighthouse called the Old Church.

365. ST. LYTHANS

A cromlech at Duffryn in a field near a road junction (ST 100723). It is shown as Cromlech on the one inch Ordnance Survey map of 1833 and as Long Barrow on the

1947 and 1956 maps. A.C. (1862), p.98; (1870), pp.70-72; (1874), p.70; (1875), pp.171-4; (1888), p.421; (1915), p.257. R.C.A.M. No. 42 of Glamorgan has a plan. *A Topographical and Historical Description of South Wales*, by Rev. T. Rees (Sherwood, Neely and Jones, London, 1815), calls it Llech-y-Filiast and states that it has been conjected that it was derived from the circumstance of the early Christians envincing their contempt for these vestiges of pagan worship by converting them into kennels for their dogs and to other mean uses. *Annals of South Glamorgan*, by Marianne Robertson Spencer (W. Spurrell and Son, Carmarthen, circa 1914), p.173, has a photograph and says that there is a hole through the end stone through which it was suggested that the spirit of the departed was supposed to take flight when his remains had been deposited in their last earthly home. *Mysterious Wales*, by Chris Barber (David and Charles, Newton Abbot, 1982), p.27, mentions that on Midsummer Eve the capstone is supposed to spin around three times and, if you make a wish there on Hallowe'en, it will come true. The field in which this cromlech with its capstone of 14 feet by 10 feet stands is known as the "Accursed Field" and it is claimed that nothing will grow in it.

Tinkiswood Dolmen, South Glamorgan.   Chris Barber

366. ST. NICHOLAS

Tinkinswood Dolmen or Long Barrow in a field at Tinkinswood (ST 082733). It is marked as 𝕮𝖗𝖔𝖒𝖑𝖊𝖈𝖍 on the one inch Ordnance Survey maps of 1833 and as 𝕷𝖔𝖓𝖌 𝕭𝖆𝖗𝖗𝖔𝖜 on maps of 1947 and 1956. This dolmen is sometimes confused by writers with the dolmen at Duffryn in the adjoining parish of St. Lythans. The capstone itself is 22 feet by 3 feet and weighs over 40 tons. A.C. (1856), p7; (1862), pp.98 and 102; (1869), p.187; (1874), p.71; (1875), p.171; (1888), p.373; (1915), pp.253-320; (1913), p.100; (1916), pp.239-294; (1933), p.39. R.C.A.M. No. 40 of Glamorgan with plan. It is called Castell Corrig or Castell Careg, Llech-y-Filiast, Llech-y-Filast, Maes-y-Filiast or Gwal-y-Filiast. *Prehistoric and Roman Remains*, by R. E. M. Wheeler (1925), p.70, mentions the old belief that anyone who slept within the dolmen on a spirit night would suffer one of the following calamities — he would either die, go raving mad or become a poet. *Folk Lore and Folk Stories of South Wales*, by Marie Trevelyan (1905), p.126, relates several stories about the dolmen. *Mysterious Wales*, by Chris Barber (David and Charles, Newton Abbot, 1982), p.29, has a photograph and mentions various legends including one which says that around the cromlech are stones said to be women who had danced on a Sunday and were turned into stone.

367. BRITON FERRY

Carreg Hir, a standing stone which has been moved about 20 yards from its original position and now stands in the playground of Cwrt Sart School on the east side of the main road opposite Giant's Grave (SN 744953). R.C.A.M. No. 554 of Glamorgan says that it is set up in a concrete plinth and is 7½ft. above the plinth. *Wales An Archaeological Guide,* by Christopher Houlder (Faber and Faber, London, 1974) p.158, mentions that it is just visible from the gate in Old Road when the school is closed, but gives the wrong Ordnance Survey reference.

368. CLYDACH

Carreg Bica or Maen Bredwan on Mynydd Drumau ¾-mile east south-east of Tirmynydd Farm (SS 725995). It is marked and shown as an Erect Stone on the one inch Ordnance Survey maps of 1830 and as Carreg Bica on the 1982 Ordnance Survey map. R.C.A.M. No. 553 of Glamorgan says that it is a monolith of local sandstone 13ft. high. *Glamorgan, Its History and Topography,* by C. J. O. Evans (Cardiff, 1943), p.355, calls it the Maen Bradwen, which is known locally as Carreg Bica, the pointed stone. It is said to bathe in the Neath river once a year on Easter morning. In a charter of King John to William de Breos in 1203, it is mentioned as "meynhirion", a Gower boundary.

369. KNELSTON

Knelston Hall Stone, immediately north of the ruined parish church (SS 469891). It is marked as Standing Stone on Ordnance Survey maps of 1981. *Transactions of the Swansea Scientific Society* (1910-11), p.117; *Prehistoric Gower,* by J. G. Rutter (Swansea, 1949), p.47.

370. KNELSTON

Standing stones near a footpath in a field which heads towards Burry (SS 463902). They are marked as Meini Hirion on the 1946 Ordnance Survey maps and as Standing Stones on the 1956 edition. The tallest stone is about 6 feet high and had a groove running down one side when seen by J.G.W. in 1956. R.C.A.M. No. 543 of Glamorgan. *Prehistoric Gower,* by J. G. Rutter (Swansea, 1949), p.47.

371. KNELSTON

A standing stone on the side of a footpath leading Higher Mill (SS 465901). It is marked as Standing Stone on Ordnance Survey maps of 1956 and 1981. R.C.A.M. No. 546 of Glamorgan mentions a stone recumbent and 9ft. long.

372. LLANGYFELACH

Carn Llechart Dolmen, near Llecharth Farm on Rhyd-y-Clydach (SN 698063). Carn Llecharth is marked on the one inch Ordnance Survey map of 1830 and Carn Llechart is marked on the 1923 and 1947 maps. A.C. (1847), p.375; (1920), p.368. R.C.A.M. No. 31 of Glamorgan has a plan. *A Critical History of the Celtic Religion, containing an Account of the Druids,* by John Toland (London, 1747), p.128, mentions it as a Druid's altar. *Glamorgan,* by A. Morris (Newport, Mon., 1907), p.466, describes it as a large stone circle with twenty-four stones.

373. LLANRHIDIAN LOWER

The Greyhound Inn Stone immediately north of the Greyhound Inn at Oldwalls (SS 487920). It is marked as Standing Stone on the Ordnance Survey map of 1981. This is a large white stone about 5 feet high in a hedge about 50 yards from the Greyhound Inn on the opposite side of the road. R.C.A.M. No. 550 of Glamorgan calls it a triangular block of quartz conglomerate 4ft. 6in. high. *Prehistoric Gower,* by J. G. Rutter (Swansea, 1949), p.47.

374. LLANRHIDIAN LOWER

Mansel Jack or Samson's Jack, a standing stone near a windmill (SS 477922). This stone has been moved from its original position to the village green. Its original position is marked as Samson's Jack Standing Stone on the Ordnance Survey maps of 1966 and 1981 and it is shown as Standing Stone on 1956 maps. R.C.A.M. No 548 of Glamorgan says that it was then incorporated in a field bank and was a quartz

Mansel Jack and Pitton Cross Stones, West Glamorgan.   *Chris Barber*

conglomerate 9ft. high rising to a blunt point. *Prehistoric Gower,* by J. G. Rutter (Swansea, 1949), p.47, No. 5.

375. LLANRHIDIAN LOWER
Pitton Cross Standing Stone on the side of a trackway west of Oldwalls (SS 484919). It is shown as 𝔖𝔱𝔞𝔫𝔡𝔦𝔫𝔤 𝔖𝔱𝔬𝔫𝔢 on the larger scale Ordnance Survey maps of 1956 and 1961. R.C.A.M. No. 549 of Glamorgan says that it is a quartz conglomerate which is ivy-clad and 2.2 metres high. *Prehistoric Gower,* by J. G. Rutter (Swansea, 1949), p.47, No. 6.

376. PENMAEN
Giants' Graves or Parc-le-Breos Tomb or Chambered Long Carn in Parc Cwm north-west of Parkmill (SS 5372 8933). 𝔓𝔞𝔯𝔠-𝔩𝔢-𝔅𝔯𝔢𝔬𝔰 is marked on Ordnance Survey maps of 1947 and 1981. A.C. (1871), pp.168-172; (1887), p.198; (1937), p.159 and pp.175-6. R.C.A.M. No. 36 of Glamorgan has a frontispiece photograph taken from the air. *Mysterious Wales,* by Chris Barber (David and Charles, Newton Abbot, 1982), p.40, under Giants' Graves, Cwm, says that it was opened in 1869.

377. REYNOLDSTON
Arthur's Stone, the very large and most noted dolmen in Wales, on top of Cefn Bryn about 300 yards north of the main road (SS 491905). It is marked as 𝔄𝔯𝔱𝔥𝔲𝔯'𝔰 𝔖𝔱𝔬𝔫𝔢 on the first Ordnance Survey map of 1830 and later editions. A.C. (1849), p.300; (1850), p.102; (1866), p.337; (1869), p.187; (1870), pp.23-33; (1886), p.337; (1920), pp.330-3; (1937), p.45, with illustration and plans; p.117 and pp.159-161. R.C.A.M. Vol. I No. 33 of Glamorgan has a photograph and plan dated 1974. It states that the Welsh name is first mentioned in a Triad of the 10th century. There are over 70 literary references to Arthur's Stone and it is better documented than any other prehistoric stone monument in Wales.

378. RHOSSILI
Sweye's Houses, two dolmens on the east flank of Rhossili Down (SS 421898). 𝔖𝔴𝔢𝔶𝔫𝔢'𝔰 𝔥𝔬𝔲𝔰𝔢𝔰 is marked on the Ordnance Survey maps of 1946 and 1948 and 𝔖𝔴𝔢𝔶𝔫𝔢'𝔰 𝔥𝔬𝔴𝔢𝔰, 𝔅𝔲𝔯𝔦𝔞𝔩 ℭ𝔥𝔞𝔪𝔟𝔢𝔯𝔰 on maps of 1966 and 1981. A.C. (1870), pp.39 and 181; (1937), pp.159-61. R.C.A.M. No. 32 of Glamorgan has a plan.

379. SWANSEA
Bon-y-Maen, a standing stone at Bon-y-Maen (SS 678953). 𝔅𝔬𝔫-𝔪𝔞𝔢𝔫 is marked on the one inch Ordnance Survey map of 1947. R.C.A.M. No. 551 of Glamorgan calls it a sandstone monolith 6ft. high. *Prehistoric Gower,* by J. G. Rutter (Swansea, 1949), p.47, No. 9. *An Antiquarian Survey of Gower,* by W. L. Morgan (1899), pp.67-8, mentions it as a block of pennant sandstone standing erect in the hedge of a garden opposite Bon-y-Maen Inn.

EXAMPLES OF SCEMB LINES

No. 1 centred around Harold Stone at The Home Farm, Bosherton, Dyfed.

Line A No. 1. Line commences at Hanging Stone Dolmen between the crossroads at Sardis and Thurston in the Parish of Burton in the County of Dyfed (SM 972083), which is marked as 𝔅urial 𝔠hamber on 1983 Ordnance Survey map scale 1:50,000 and goes south through

No. 2. An earthwork at Hundleton, Dyfed, on the side of the main road near Bowett (SM 969008), which is marked 𝔈arthwork on the above-mentioned map and continues south through

No. 3. A probable standing stone site at Yerbeston, which is on the road leading north from the church at St. Petrox in the Parish of Stackpole Elidyr, Dyfed (SR 968981). Yerbeston is marked on the above-mentioned map. This line continues south and ends at

No. 4. Harold Stone at The Home Farm, Bosherton in the Parish of Stackpole, Elidyr, Dyfed (SR 968958), which is marked 𝔥arold 𝔰tone on the above-mentioned map. This is nearly 10 miles south of Hanging Stone Dolmen at Burton and this parish name may be a corruption of Burstone or Bearstone, which might have been the name of the dolmen.

Line B No. 1. Tumulus on Mount Sion Down on the Artillery Range at Warren, Dyfed (SR 916951), is the starting point and the line goes ENE through

No. 2. Harold Stone which is (A No. 4) above

No. 3. through to ancient fort on Greenala Point (SS 008965)

No. 4. on through to end at King's Quoit Dolmen on cliffs near Manorbier Castle, Dyfed (SS 060972).

Line C No. 1. Starts at Devil's Quoit Standing Stone on Stackpole Warren in the Parish of Stackpole Elidyr, Dyfed (SR 980950), and goes NW

No. 2. through Harold Stone which is (A No. 4) above and ends at

No. 3. Devil's Quoit Dolmen near the road above Broomhill Burrows at Angle Dyfed (SM 887008).

Line D No. 1. Commences at the site of a standing stone where Lady Cawddor's Stone Seat has been since 1881 above Fish Ponds on Stackpole Warren in the Parish of Stackpole Elidyr, Dyfed (SR 978947), and goes NW through

No. 2. Harold Stone which is (A No. 4) above

No. 3. on The Devil's Quoit Standing Stone at Sampson Farm, St. Petrocs, Dyfed (SR 965963), and ends at a

No. 4. tumulus near Walloston Green at Hundleston, Dyfed (SM 926003).

Line E No. 1. Starts at the standing stone site which is (D No. 1) above and goes NW

No. 2. through a large round earthwork on the Artillery Range near Pricaston Warren at Castlemartin, Dyfed (SR 907964), and continues to an

No. 3. ancient fort at Warren, Dyfed (SR 903966), and ends at a

No. 4. tumulus on the side of a track above Linney Burrows, Warren, Dyfed (SR 889969).

Line F No. 1. Begins at the tumulus above Linney Burrows which is (E No. 4) above and goes ENE through a

No. 2. tumulus near Browslate at Warren, Dyfed (SR 906972) and ends at a

No. 3. probable standing stone site at Yerbeston, Stackpole, Elidyr, Dyfed, which is (A No. 3) above.

The so-called Solar Angle of 23½° can be found between the lines E and F detailed above.

There are numerous other SCEMB lines and Solar Angles connecting the above-mentioned sites.

Examples of SCEMB lines centred around a standing stone at Llanfechell, Anglesey.

Line A No. 1. Starts at the 8½-feet-high standing stone near Carrog and N of the church at Llanfechell, Anglesey (SH 370916) and goes SE through

No. 2. Maen Chwyf, which is traditionally a rocking stone sometimes called Arthur's Quoit at Llandyfrydog, Anglesey (SH 432857), on through to

No. 3. Carreg Leidr, a 5-feet-high maenhir on a knoll near the church at Llandyfrydog, Anglesey (SH 447844) and ends at a

No. 4. large round earthwork on the S side of the main road between Rhos Owen and Treffos at Llansadwrn, Anglesey (SH 540757).

Line B No. 1. Begins at a tall maenhir, 9½ feet high near Werthyr at Amlwch, Anglesey (SH 418928) and goes SSW through the standing stone near Carrog.

No. 2. Llanfechell, Anglesey, which is (A No. 1) above, on to another tall

No. 3. standing stone which is 12 feet high and is near Pen-yr-Orsedd, Llanhwydrys, Anglesey (SH 333904), where this line ends.

Line C No. 1. Standing stone at Llanfechell as (A No. 1) above almost due south to

No. 2. Maen Arthur or Arthur's Stone near Maes Mawr at Llanfechell, Anglesey (SH 368903) and through to end at

No. 3. Bedd Branwen, a dolmen near Treffynnon, Llandeusant, Anglesey (SH 361850).

Line D No. 1. Maen Chwyf or Arthur's Quoit at Llandyfrydog which is (A No. 2) above, SW through

No. 2. Presaddfed Dolmens at south end of Llyn Llywenan at Bodedern, Anglesey (SH 345810) to end at an

No. 3. ancient settlement site or camp near Tai Croesion, Llechylched, Anglesey (SH 324758).

Line E No. 1. Carreg Leidr at Llandyfrydog (SH 447844) which is (A No. 3) above, goes SE to

No. 2. Arthur's Quoit, a dolmen near Glyn at Llanddyfrian, Anglesey (SH 515817), and ends at a

No. 3. standing stone site which was shown as an 𝕰𝖗𝖊𝖈𝖙 𝖘𝖙𝖔𝖓𝖊 on the east slopes of Mynydd Crwgarth on the one inch O.S. map of 1841, near The Wern, Llanddona, Anglesey (SH 570795).

Line E is crossed at an angle of 23½° by another SCEMB line which starts from Cremlyn Dolmen at Llansadwrn, Anglesey (SH 568776), to small stone circles at Pant-y-Saer, Benllech, Anglesey (SH 514825), then to Hill Fort, a large round ancient camp at Llanallgo, Anglesey (SH 495846) and ends at another small stone circle at Plas Bodafan Llaneugrad (SH 489853), which is not shown on modern Ordnance Survey maps but is recorded in *Royal Commission of Ancient Monuments, Anglesey*, on p.63 as No. 5.

"The earth's surface is traversed by lines and 'ganglia' of spiritual forces, following the solar windings, such as you see in the windings of a coil in scientific engines. These lines and focal points have an attractive power over man; they draw him into their focus".

Frederick Bligh Bland, 1919
(N.B. written 6 years before Alfred Watkins wrote "The Old Straight Track")

GLOSSARY

Alignment	A series of menhirs which have been arranged in straight lines.
Blind Spring	Dowser's term for spring where water does not appear on the surface of the ground.
Burial Barrow	A structure of large stones believed to have been used as a burial place. Sometimes confused with a dolmen.
Camp	Large enclosed areas of pre-Roman date that may have been fortified.
Carn	A large ancient mound of rocks and earth.
Corridor Tomb	A chamber entered by a gallery or a corridor.
Cromlech	This is another name for a dolmen. It is a number of stones arranged to enclose a space which may be circular, elliptical or even rectangular in shape. In France the word is also sometimes used for a stone circle.
Cup and Ring Marks	Artificial depressions in stones in circular or conical forms of unknown date and use.
Dolmen	Three or four standing stones supporting a large capstone. Dolmens are generally regarded as burial chambers and indeed skeletons have often been found inside them. But it is likely that the bodies were inserted at a much later date than when the dolmens were originally constructed.
Earthworks	Huge man-made mounds of ancient date, sometimes called camps.
Logan Stones	Large stones which are critically balanced and may be rocked when a slight pressure is applied at a certain point. Consequently they are also known as Rocking Stones. The largest one in the world is at Tandil in the Argentine and weighs over 700 tons. Despite its enormous weight, it is so delicately poised that it rocks in the wind.
Megalith	This term comes from the Greek — mega (big) and lithos (stone). A megalithic monument is a prehistoric construction made of large stones.
Menhir	A Breton word for a standing stone. It is a tall rough pillar of stone with its base set into the earth. Men means stone and hir means long.
Standing Stone	A single large stone standing in the ground.
Stone Circle	A large circle (sometimes egg-shaped) of ancient erect stones.
SCEMB Lines	Alignments of three or more prehistoric sites which include only standing stones, stone circles, carns, earthworks, mounds or tumuli and burial barrows.
Solar Angles	Angles of 23½°, which is the angle of the earth's declination to the sun, or multiples thereof.
Tumulus	A large round earthen mound.

SUGGESTED BOOKS FOR FURTHER READING

Barber, Chris. *Mysterious Wales* (David and Charles, Newton Abbot, 1982; Paladin paperback, 1983).

Barber, Chris. *More Mysterious Wales* (David and Charles, Newton Abbot, 1986; Paladin paperback, 1987).

Bord, Janet and Colin. *Mysterious Britain* (Garnstone Press, 1972; Paladin paperback, 1974).

Bord, Janet and Colin. *The Secret Country* (Elek Books, London, 1976; Paladin paperback, 1978).

Bord, Janet and Colin. *A Guide to Ancient Sites in Britain* (Latimer New Dimensions, 1978; Paladin/Granada Publishing, 1979).

Graves, Tom. *Needles of Stone* (Turnastone Press, 1978; Panther/Granada Publishing, 1980).

Grinsell, Leslie V. *Folklore of Prehistoric Sites in Britain* (David and Charles, 1976).

Hawkes, Jacquetta. *A Guide to Prehistoric and Roman Monuments in England and Wales* London, 1951).

Houlder, Christopher. *Wales, An Archaeological Guide* (Faber and Faber, London, 1974).

Mitchell, John. *The Earth Spirit: Its Ways, Shrines and Mysteries* (Thames and Hudson, 1975).

Mitchell, John. *Megalithomania: Artists, Antiquarians and Archaeologists at the Old Stone Monuments* (Thames and Hudson, 1977).

Mitchell, John. *View Over Atlantis* (Thames and Hudson, 1983).

Robins, Don. *Circles of Stone* (Souvenir Press, 1985).

Screeton, Paul. *Quicksilver Heritage: The Mystic Leys: Their Legacy of Ancient Wisdom* (Thornsons Publishers, 1974).

Thom, Alexander. *Megalithic Sites in Britain* (Oxford University Press, 1967).

Underwood, Guy. *The Pattern of the Past* (Sphere Books, London, 1972).

Watkins, Alfred. *The Old Straight Track* (Methuen and Co., London, 1925; Garnstone Press, 1975).

OTHER TITLES BY CHRIS BARBER

Walks in the Brecon Beacons.

Exploring the Waterfall Country.

Ghosts of Wales.

Exploring the Brecon Beacons National Park.

Exploring Gwent.

Mysterious Wales.

More Mysterious Wales.

Cordell Country.

The Romance of the Welsh Mountains.

Hando's Gwent.

LIST OF ARTICLES WRITTEN BY JOHN G. WILLIAMS

Abergavenny Historical Notes (Abergavenny 1964).

Notables of Abergavenny and Area published in the Abergavenny Chronicle in fifty different weekly editions in 1982.

Prehistoric Standing Stones of Herefordshire. The Woolhope Field Club Transactions for 1966 (p.255).

Standing Stones and Secret Systems. Journal of the British Society of Dowsers. No. 184, June 1979 (p.34); also in Journal No. 143 (p.81).

The Sacred and Secret Pi Design. Research into Lost Knowledge Organisation Newsletter No. 30 Spring-Summer 1987.

King Arthur and the Grail. Research into Lost Knowledge Organisation Newsletter No. 32, Spring-Summer 1987.

Stonehenge, Scemb Lines and Solar Angles. Stonehenge Viewpoint No. 70, March/April 1986, Santa Barbara, California, U.S.A.

Scemb Lines and Solar Angles. Stonehenge Viewpoint, November/December 1984.

INDEX OF SITES

The references are to page numbers and page numbers in bold *italics* indicate illustrations.